Who's Who
of
THE YORKSHIRE
COUNTY CRICKET CLUB

Compiled by Paul Dyson
Foreword by Martyn Moxon

GREAT NORTHERN

Great Northern Books Limited
PO Box 1380, Bradford, BD5 5FB
www.greatnorthernbooks.co.uk

ISBN: 978-1-912101-53-5

Design and layout: David Burrill

CIP Data
A catalogue for this book is available from the British Library

To Denise, who has happily lived in a cricketing environment for 47 years but has only a little more appreciation of the game than she did on April 1st, 1971.

In memory of Tony Woodhouse and Roy Wilkinson; all those who research into The Yorkshire County Cricket Club will always be in their debt.

ALSO BY THE AUTHOR

The Counties and Test Cricket (1989)

The Benson & Hedges Cup Record Book (1997)

A Century of Headingley Tests (1999)

100 Greats – Yorkshire County Cricket Club
(2001 – co-authored with Mick Pope)

Yorkshire's 30 Championships (2002)

50 Classic Matches – Yorkshire County Cricket Club
(2007 – co-authored with Mick Pope)

Headingley 125 (2016)

FOREWORD

by Martyn Moxon

It was during my time as captain of The Yorkshire CCC when, in 1992, the Club welcomed official overseas cricketers for the very first time in its history. As most people are aware, the first beneficiary of this change in policy was the young Sachin Tendulkar who went on to become one of the greatest batsmen the game has ever seen.

One of the things which struck me about Sachin was his knowledge of Yorkshire and its cricketing heritage; he knew more about our traditions even than some of our own players. It also struck me at the time, and has often done so since, that the successes which we have had over the years have tended to have been taken for granted and it took a 19-year-old to reinforce how highly regarded Yorkshire is in the world of cricket. Only New South Wales in Australia, Barbados in the West Indies and Bombay in India have dominated their domestic first-class tournaments in a similar way to that which Yorkshire has done in the County Championship – still the competition most English players strive to win above all others.

Of course, I learnt a great deal about the county's cricketing history from my father, as many Yorkshire boys do; the great players – Hirst, Rhodes, Sutcliffe, Hutton – the periods of almost continuous success – 1900-02, 1922-25, the 1930s, the 1960s – but, more importantly, how to play the game, not just from a technical point of view, but how to possess an approach which combined the Yorkshire way of striving to win at the same time as playing the game fairly and in the right spirit.

I was very fortunate to be able to captain our great club – what an honour! Although my six years at the helm did not, sadly, produce any trophies, I would like to think that when members and supporters look back on the early-1990s they can empathise with the progress which was made during that period of re-building. I would like to think that we continued to play the game in the Yorkshire way as well as developing young players and laying down some foundations for the future.

I am now fortunate again to hold another high profile post within the Yorkshire set-up. My return to the county for the 2007 season coincided with a new management team at the helm and it was not many years before a couple of near-misses were eventually superseded by the exciting County Championship wins of 2014 and 2015.

Yorkshire has a great tradition of the game being coached to a very high level. As I have already mentioned, it often starts with a parent; the process usually continues at a nearby club (how lucky we are that there are so many in Yorkshire) and then may advance to area age-group teams before, for a select few, experience in representing the county. All along this route boys and girls are given a top-quality education in how to bat, bowl, field and keep wicket so that if they are ever good enough to come to our Academy, as a first stage in our professional set-up, they will have been thoroughly grounded in the arts of the game.

My predecessors with the county such as George Hirst, Arthur Mitchell and Doug Padgett, had the title of County Coach. My remit, as Director of Cricket, is much wider but it is most rewarding to be able to follow on in their footsteps and be able to help all first-team players with the finer points of their game. In addition, however, the wider view of my post gives me a perspective on the overall scene and it is very gratifying to be able to witness at first hand the kind of progression I have outlined, not to mention the responsibilities which the overseeing of it all brings.

Enough of me, I am pleased to be able to write the foreword to this latest volume which adds to our understanding of all of those who have played cricket for Yorkshire's first eleven. It is an incredibly detailed publication and one that I'm sure anyone with an interest in Yorkshire cricket will find fascinating and informative.

Martyn Moxon
The Yorkshire CCC
March 2018

INTRODUCTION

The inspiration for this volume came as a result of a conversation a few years ago with my esteemed colleague Mick Pope who thought it a good idea to compile an updated version of Tony Woodhouse's *A Who's Who of Yorkshire County Cricket Club*. This was published in 1992 and as its predecessor, Peter Thomas' *Yorkshire Cricketers*, dated from 19 years before that, Mick's assessment of the situation was spot on. As both Messrs Thomas and Woodhouse undertook considerable scholarly research in putting their respective books together it would have been most remiss of me not to allow the modern reader to benefit from this and so I have unashamedly utilised their work to a considerable degree. It would be quite wrong of me to disagree with their viewpoints, particularly when viewed from a contemporary angle, so much of what they have written is repeated herein although written in my own prose. In addition, Tony's *The History of Yorkshire County Cricket Club* (1989) is the definitive story of the Club's first 125 years and his writings remain pre-eminent amongst the county's researchers over the last 50 years, or so.

In the intervening 27 years since 1991, the last season which Tony's book includes, some 145 more cricketers have made their debuts for Yorkshire's first eleven and, therefore, must be included in this latest work of reference in the series. For this book to remain within the budget of the average cricket fan, therefore, the word-count on each player has had to be reduced from that of the previous similarly-titled books. Those who are interested in details on players from the more distant past are recommended to have all three volumes in their possession so as to have the maximum amount of information on each cricketer in the relatively minimum amount of space.

The main body of the text includes all those who have played first eleven cricket for Yorkshire CCC, even those who represented the Club in only a shortened form of the professional game. Not included in this section, however, are the 59 players who represented 'Yorkshire' only in the period from 1833 to 1862, i.e. prior to the formation of the County Club. They have their places in Appendix 1.

Unfortunately, the many sources which I have used disagree, occasionally, on certain matters of fact especially concerning details of a player's birth or death. Although most of these instances relate to players from the 19th century a more recent example is the Australian Greg Blewett who had one season with Yorkshire in 1999. Four sources state that he was born on October 29th, but three state the 28th! Every effort has been made, by a small team of colleagues, to establish the correct version of events in each of these cases which number about 80 in total. To a very great degree this has been achieved and it is very strongly believed that each player's heading-lines are now definitive. The overwhelming majority of the work in this direction has been undertaken by Mick Pope; his delving into records of various types has often produced the correct details but in 27 cases we have had to purchase certificates in order to produce the definitive dates. Unfortunately, it is not known for some players what their playing style was; the reference '?HB' is most frustrating to have to insert. Anyone who can supply correct information on any of these matters – especially regarding JH Wood - is most welcome to contact me c/o Archives Committee, Yorkshire CCC, Headingley Cricket Ground, Leeds, LS6 3BU.

There are also several issues concerning the figures as given in Appendix 3. The term 'first-class' was first used in 1864 but not officially defined until 1947 and, even then, it was not applied retrospectively. The Association of Cricket Statisticians and Historians has published a list of matches which it regards as 'important' prior to 1864 as well as defining the status of some games of dubious authenticity from 1864 to 1946. Unfortunately, the official records of Yorkshire CCC, with regard to the position of five matches, do not agree with this compilation. As this book relates directly to the Club's records of its players I have taken its own stance. This means that for those 32 players who played in those matches, which date from 1878 to 1893, their career records as shown in Appendix 3 are at variance with those on cricketarchive.com.

Sadly there are also other instances where career records differ from those in Yorkshire CCC's Yearbook to those in other sources. In every case, except where I have been able to prove that the Yearbook is in error, I have used the figures from the Yearbook. The late Roy Wilkinson spent a considerable time poring over the county's official scorebooks in order to compile fully accurate career records. It would be most remiss of me to ignore his painstaking research.

The year(s) following the word 'Career' near the start of each player's profile refer(s) only to his time in the Yorkshire first eleven, in any of the three formats. Following this the word 'Amateur' may appear. This applies to those who played before 1963 when cricketers were all Gentlemen (amateurs) or Players (professionals). For those who received their Yorkshire cap, an honour instituted in 1884, this is next noted and, including the cap number, is a detail never previously published. Similarly, players who received a benefit or other financial reward granted by the Club, an honour first given in 1891, have next the relevant year stated as well as the type of award. I have not included the amounts of these as they have become meaningless with the passage of time as well as more difficult to authenticate. The most up-to-date list may be found in the Yorkshire Year Book for 2006. In the main body of the text for each player I have, unless exceptional circumstances merit it, eschewed the use of averages. These, for both batting and bowling, have varied considerably in standard and their use can be most misleading when quoted out of the context of the period in which each cricketer played.

The word-count for each player relates approximately to the number of games in which he appeared for Yorkshire. Little is known about some players and this is reflected in their entry. Others played little for Yorkshire but had more distinguished careers elsewhere and this is given due prominence. Similarly, for those whose county career was entirely with Yorkshire but who spent a great deal of time in the international game that aspect of their career is appropriately highlighted. I have not set out with a particular list of details which should be included about each player, rather I have chosen to include what is interesting and important about each one so that their profile is a reflection of their career and their own place in Yorkshire's and cricket's history. In general I have not mentioned in the text the statistical information which is included about each player in Appendix 3. The choice of which players merit having their profile accompanied by a picture also, in general, reflects their contribution to Yorkshire cricket. However, there are exceptions to this and some subjectivity has entered into this selection, there being players pictured who made their names more with other teams than with Yorkshire, or in other aspects of the game.

I hope that readers find this a useful work of reference; I also hope some of them will feel motivated towards trying to find out more about certain cricketers and thus enhance our knowledge of them. This may be via the clubs for which they played, schools they attended or localities in which they were born or died. I also wish good luck to whomsoever is inspired to compile this book's update sometime around 2040!

Paul Dyson
Knaresborough, March 2018

NOTE: All facts and figures are correct as on October 31st 2017.

GLOSSARY

Included in the brief tabular section of each player's profile is an initialled indication of his playing styles. RHB and LHB indicate whether the player bats right-handed or left-handed and wicket-keepers are shown by WK. For bowlers the descriptions are not so simple and the following abbreviations have been used:

LB	Leg-breaks	SLC	Left-arm chinamen
LBG	Leg breaks and googlies	RF	Right-arm fast
LF	Left-arm fast	RFM	Right-arm fast-medium
LFM	Left-arm fast-medium	RM	Right-arm medium pace
LMS	Left-arm medium-slow	RMF	Right-arm medium-fast
LRF	Left-arm round-arm fast	RL	Right-arm lobs
LRMF	Left-arm round-arm medium-fast	RRF	Right-arm round-arm fast
LRS	Left-arm round-arm slow	RRM	Right-arm round-arm medium pace
LSM	Left-arm slow-medium	RRMF	Right-arm round-arm medium-fast
OB	Off-breaks	RS	Right-arm slow
SLA	Left-arm orthodox spinner	RU	Right-arm underarm

Other initials and terms used in the main body of the text may not be familiar to all readers and some explanations follow.

BBL – Big Bash League: an Australian Tweny20 competition
ESCA – English Schools' Cricket Association
IPL – Indian Premier League: a Twenty20 competition
MCC – Marylebone Cricket Club
ODI – one-day international: matches involving Test-playing countries and others with 'ODI status'
T20I – an international match of 20 overs per side
YCB – Yorkshire Cricket Board
YSCA – Yorkshire Schools' Cricket Association

At the time of writing it cannot be certain how many other terms used in the book will be known and understood in the years to come, the fluctuating cricketing scene being more unpredictable than at any time in the game's history. Some of these are:

Test cricket – matches between countries, or groups of countries, originally of three days' duration, five-day matches later becoming standard.
First-class cricket – matches of three-five days in length, i.e. including Test matches. This was the only form of the game played professionally until 1963.
County Championship/Championship – a competition held between the first-class counties; its games were, initially, of three days' duration but four-day matches were gradually introduced in the latter part of the twentieth century and became standard before the teams were divided into two Divisions, with promotion and relegation, in 2000.
List A cricket (limited-overs matches) – games of between 40 and 65 overs per side. These began in 1963, 50-overs eventually becoming the standard length.
Twenty20 cricket – matches played over 20 overs per team. These began in 2003.
White-ball cricket – matches designed to be played in one day or part of one day, i.e. List A and Twenty20 games. A white-ball and coloured clothing were used to off-set the disadvantage of playing under floodlights, which many matches were.

Therefore the players profiled in this book whose careers were wholly prior to 1963 only played in first-class cricket. Those whose careers were partly, or wholly, between 1963 and 2002 played in two formats and those whose careers were partly, or wholly in the period since 2003 could play in three formats.

Academy – the Yorkshire Academy for young cricketers which provided a team in league cricket.

Gentlemen – a team made up entirely of cricketers who played as amateurs until the status was abolished after the 1962 season.

Players – a team which existed until 1962 and which was made up entirely of cricketers who played as professionals.

It is assumed that the reader knows which counties were first-class and which played in the Minor Counties Competition. Durham played in the latter until 1992 and then in the County Championship and the one-day competitions.

References to Sheffield United and other clubs which bear the same name for different sports always imply the cricket club unless specified.

Ackroyd, Alfred

Born: 29/08/1858, Birkenshaw,
Bradford
Died: 03/10/1927, Eccles, Lancashire
RHB, RMF/RF. Career: 1879.
Amateur

Having been in the first eleven at Uppingham School for three years, Alfred Ackroyd made his first-class debut at the age of 19. His one game for Yorkshire, at Lord's against Middlesex, was his second and final first-class match and this may have been something to do with criticism of his bowling action.

Allen, Spencer

Born: 20/12/1893, Halifax
Died: 09/10/1978, Bradford
LHB, SLA. Career: 1924. Amateur

A successful career with Leeds preceded Spencer Allen's debut for Yorkshire at the age of 30 but that match at Lord's against Middlesex was the only one in which he played. A teacher at Leeds Modern School, he was a professional with Queensbury.

Allen, William Reginald

Born: 14/04/1893, Sharlston,
Wakefield
Died: 14/10/1950, Normanton
RHB, WK. Career: 1921-25

An injury to Arthur Dolphin gave Reg Allen his chance and he kept wicket in 20 matches in 1921 taking 32 catches and making 19 stumpings. Dolphin returned in 1922 and Allen played in only ten more games, spread over three seasons. In 1925 he made the only half-century of his career – a score of 95 not out against Hampshire at Hull which was the highest innings of the match.

A long career with Castleford

included him leading the club to the Yorkshire Council Championship in 1935.

Ambler, Joseph

Born: 12/02/1860, Lascelles Hall,
Huddersfield
Died: 10/02/1899, Lascelles Hall,
Huddersfield
RHB, RFM. Career: 1886

Four games for Somerset in 1883, while he was professional with Yatton near Bridgewater, and four for Yorkshire three years later were the sum total of Joe Ambler's first-class career. Very tall, he was a genuine all-rounder in club cricket, being an important player for Lascelles Hall.

Anderson, George

Born: 20/01/1826, Aiskew, Bedale
Died: 27/11/1902, Aiskew, Bedale
RHB. Career: 1863-69

In a first-class career which started in 1850 and spanned 20 seasons, George Anderson played for several different teams. These included the

North, All-England XI, and 'Yorkshire' in its pre-official years. Tall and powerfully built, he played freely off the front foot and was very strong on the leg side.

The only Yorkshireman on the 1863/64 tour of Australia and New Zealand, he made the highest score of his career in the following summer – an innings of 99 not out against Nottinghamshire when he rescued his side from 72 for six at Trent Bridge but ran out of partners. He topped Yorkshire's batting averages in each of the Club's first two seasons and scored 2,535 runs in his full first-class career.

Anderson, Paul Napier

Born: 28/04/1966, Driffield
RHB, RMF/M. Career: 1988

A first-class match against the Sri Lankans was Paul Anderson's only game in senior cricket. Injury-prone, he played for Driffield and Bowling Old Lane and later emigrated to New Zealand where he umpired in club and women's cricket.

Anson, Claude Esmond

Born: 14/10/1889, Bradford
Died: 26/03/1969, Cawood
RHB, RM. Career: 1924. Amateur

A product of Pocklington School, Claude Anson played in just one county match - against Derbyshire at Chesterfield - but also captained Yorkshire against Scotland in a non-first-class match. His club cricket was for York, Cawood, whom he captained, and the Yorkshire Gentlemen.

Appleton, Charles

Born: 15/05/1844, Kirk Ella, Hull
Died: 26/02/1925, Standish, Wigan, Lancashire
RHB, WK. Career: 1865. Amateur

Charles Appleton played for Rossall School first eleven and then in matches involving local teams and the touring All-England XI while still a teenager. An occasional wicket-keeper, this influenced his selection for Yorkshire when the regular 'keeper, Ned Stephenson, went on strike with four other players. He later lived in London and played club cricket in that area including a spell as captain of Richmond, Surrey.

Appleyard, Robert

Born: 27/06/1924, Wibsey, Bradford
Died: 17/03/2015, Harrogate
RHB, RFM/RM/OB.
Career: 1950-58.
Cap No 94, 1951. Testimonial: 1959

After experiencing family tragedies as a boy, Bob Appleyard was dogged throughout his short playing career by illness and injury but he was one of the most skilful bowlers in Yorkshire's history. Tall, he could bowl at pace with the new ball and later turn to spin when the pitch deteriorated. He was virtually unplayable on a sticky wicket and produced such variety of pace and length on good pitches that no batsman could ever feel completely secure.

At the age of 14 Appleyard took five for five in the YSCA Cup Final and was soon playing club cricket for Manningham Mills and Bowling Old Lane. Service with the Royal Navy delayed his introduction to first-class cricket until the age of 26 but he made up for lost time by taking exactly 200 wickets in his first full season in 1951 – the only player ever to do so – his career-best analysis of eight for 76 coming in the final game of the season against MCC at Scarborough. Sadly an attack of

tuberculosis restricted his appearances to one game in 1952 and none in 1953 but he came back so well that he was selected to play for England.

Appleyard took 31 wickets in nine Tests and topped the averages in both Australia and New Zealand on the 1954/55 tour. Only two more full seasons were possible after this due to a shoulder injury and, at the age of 34, his contract was not renewed. Later he was on the Yorkshire committee and put a great deal of energy into the establishment of the Yorkshire Academy and the re-development of Bradford Park Avenue as well as serving as Yorkshire's President in 2006-08.

Armitage, Charles Ingram

Born: 28/04/1849, Birkby Grange, Huddersfield
Died: 24/04/1917, Honley, Huddersfield
RHB, LFM. Career: 1873-78.
Amateur

The sum total of Charles Armitage's first-class career was two

county games in 1873 and a match against the Australian tourists five years later. His club cricket was for Huddersfield, Lascelles Hall, Scarborough and Yorkshire Gentlemen.

Armitage, Thomas

Born: 25/04/1848, Walkley, Sheffield
Died: 21/09/1922, Pullman, Chicago, USA
RHB, RRM/RL. Career: 1872-78

An effective all-rounder, Tom Armitage toured Australia in 1877/78 and appeared in what became known as the first two Test matches. Each of his best performances for Yorkshire came at Bramall Lane, Sheffield in 1876: an innings of 95 against Middlesex and figures of seven for 26 against Surrey (13-46 in the match).

A portly figure, Armitage's solid batting was complemented by his cunning lob bowling which had a high arc. He played as professional for Longsight and Keighley before his county career and later emigrated to America to coach but became groundsman at Pullman CC in 1902.

Ash, David Leslie

Born: 18/02/1944, Bingley
RHB, SLA. Career: 1965

David Ash attended Fulneck School and batted well for Yorkshire second eleven but his senior experience was very short. He had a long career elsewhere, playing for Cumberland for 16 seasons from 1968 and was professional at two clubs – Penrith, for whom he took over 500 wickets, and Keighley with whom he topped the Bradford League bowling averages when aged 45.

Ashman, John Robert

Born: 20/05/1926, Rotherham
LHB, SLA. Career: 1951

A club career with Bowling Old Lane and Sheffield United preceded John Ashman's county cricket. This consisted of one match for Yorkshire and two seasons (1953-54) with Worcestershire for whom he took 57 wickets in 33 matches.

Ashraf, Moin Aqueeb

Born: 05/01/1992, Bradford
RHB, RFM. Career: 2010-13

Figures of five for 32 in Moin Ashraf's second Championship match – against Kent at Headingley – showed promise. He made a very valuable contribution, as a 'death' bowler, to Yorkshire's successful 2012 season in the Twenty20 competition with 15 wickets in 12 matches including a best performance of four for 18 at Derby. He was released in 2015 but in 2016 he appeared for Northamptonshire in T20 matches and was with Leeds/Bradford MCCU in 2016-17.

Aspinall, Ronald

Born: 26/10/1918, Almondbury, Huddersfield
Died: 16/08/1999, Almondbury, Huddersfield
RHB, RMF. Career: 1946-50.
Cap No 88, 1948

Despite having to wait to play for Yorkshire until he was aged 27 Ron Aspinall made up for lost time by achieving match figures of 14-65 at Northampton in his first full season, this including a career-best eight for 42. Injury-prone, his most successful season was 1948, a year after he had taken 90 wickets for the second eleven – a total which remains the team's third-best. He coached at St Peter's School, York, spent seven seasons with Durham and 22 years as a first-class umpire.

Aspinall, Walter

Born: 24/03/1858, Elland
Died: 27/01/1910, North Quay, Brisbane, Australia
RHB, WK. Career: 1880

Walter Aspinall kept wicket for Yorkshire in two games at the end of George Pinder's final season but was not retained. Most of his club cricket was with Halifax and he also played for Elland. He emigrated to Australia in the 1880s and his death appears to have been caused by him committing suicide by drowning.

Asquith, Frederick Thomas

Born: 05/02/1870, Kirkstall, Leeds
Died: 11/01/1916, Hull
?HB, WK. Career: 1903

Fred Asquith played in only one first-class match - in 1903 against Gloucestershire at Bramall Lane, Sheffield as a replacement for 'keeper David Hunter. He played for Sheepscar Leather Works Club and later kept wicket for Hull Town for many years.

Athey, Charles William Jeffrey

Born: 27/09/1957, Middlesbrough
RHB, RM, WK. Career: 1976-83.
Cap No 120, 1980

Bill Athey showed outstanding promise at Acklam Hall High School and with Middlesbrough, Saltburn and Bowling Old Lane. An attractive opening and early-middle order batsman with a classical technique he became a regular in the Yorkshire side in 1978. Two years later he passed 1000 runs for the first time and made his Test debut in the Centenary match against Australia at Lord's.

Disillusioned with the in-fighting which dominated the county at this time he left Yorkshire and moved to Gloucestershire with whom he spent nine seasons including one as captain in 1989. The highlight of Athey's career was probably the 1986/87 tour of Australia when he opened the batting in all five Tests, the Ashes being retained, and all 14 ODIs in two victorious tournaments. In 1992 he moved to Sussex before becoming coach for Worcestershire for three years from 1998. After playing for Suffolk and Paignton he later became coach at Dulwich College.

Yorkshire had four different captains in the eight years Athey spent with the county and, sadly, he never really fulfilled his potential on home territory. Nevertheless he played in 23 Tests, 31 ODIs, including six in the 1987 World Cup, and eventually scored over 25,000 runs in first-class cricket and more than 13,000 in limited-overs matches.

Atkinson, George Robert

Born: 21/09/1830, Ripon
Died: 03/05/1906, West Bowling, Bradford
RHB, RRMF/RM. Career: 1863-70

George Atkinson played for Leeds and Birkenhead Park as a professional and first represented 'Yorkshire' two years before the Club was formed. He bowled with a deceptive action, approaching the wicket with both arms swinging like a windmill, but was very accurate.

Atkinson's other first-class teams included the North and the United England XI. In 62 first-class matches he took 165 wickets and later coached at Marlborough College and Rossall School and umpired in the County Championship for two seasons from 1893.

Atkinson, Henry Tom

Born: 01/02/1881, Sculcoates, Hull
Died: 23/12/1959, Driffield
RHB, RMF. Career: 1907

Making a pair and taking neither a wicket nor a catch against Worcestershire at Bradford summed up Harry Atkinson's experience of first-class cricket. His club cricket was for Driffield, for whom he opened the batting. He served as a county councillor and on his death certificate his second forename is Tran.

Azeem Rafiq

Born: 27/02/1991, Karachi, Pakistan
RHB, OB. Career: 2008-
Cap No 179, 2016

At the age of 21 Azeem Rafiq became the youngest player to lead Yorkshire in a competitive match since 1923. This was in Yorkshire's successful T20 season in 2012 when he led the side in six of its nine group games to five wins and a no result.

Azeem's first season in the Championship, aged 18, included 100 at Worcester and his five for 50 at Chelmsford in 2012 showed further all-round promise. He played for Derbyshire while on loan in 2011 and club cricket later for Sheffield & Phoenix and Sheffield Collegiate.

Azeem was released in 2014 but then re-signed two years later and continued to play with some success especially in white-ball cricket. In 2017 he was easily Yorkshire's leading wicket-taker in the Royal London Cup and his T20 success included five for 19 against Northamptonshire at Headingley.

Azeem Rafiq bowling against Somerset at Taunton in 2017.

Backhouse, Edgar Norman

Born: 13/05/1901, Sheriff Hutton, York
Died: 01/11/1936, High Wycombe, Buckinghamshire
RHB, LMS/M. Career: 1931

Called up from the Lord's ground staff when Edgar Oldroyd had been taken ill, Edgar Backhouse played at The Oval against The Rest when Yorkshire was the Champion County. He played for Staffordshire in the Minor Counties Championship from 1934 and was its professional when he was killed in a road accident.

Badger, Henry Dixon

Born: 07/03/1900, Clifton Green, York
Died: 10/08/1975, Barnard Castle, Durham
RHB, RF. Career: 1921-22. Amateur

Henry Badger was in the first eleven at Shrewsbury School for three years and played for Oxford University in three first-class matches in 1921 but did not obtain a Blue.

Bainbridge, Alfred Brian

Born: 15/10/1932, Middlesbrough
RHB, OB. Career: 1961-63

As a quality off-spinning understudy to Ray Illingworth, Brian Bainbridge played just five games in three seasons but twice took five wickets in an innings, the best being six for 58 against Essex at Harrogate in his debut season. He played for Middlesbrough and Saltburn and coached the U-17 Joe Lumb XI in the 1980s.

Baines, Francis Edmund

Born: 18/06/1864, Ecclesall, Sheffield
Died: 17/11/1948, Worksop, Nottinghamshire
RMF. Career: 1888

A Roses match at Bramall Lane in which he made a duck and did not bowl represented the experience Frank Baines had in first-class cricket. He also played for Sheffield Bankers.

Bairstow, Arthur

Born: 14/08/1868, Great Horton, Bradford
Died: 07/12/1945, Bucklow Hill, Cheshire
RHB, WK. Career: 1896-1900.
Cap No 29

Of the several wicket-keepers who played for Yorkshire as deputy to David Hunter, 'Sandy' Bairstow was regarded as the best. He played for the North in the 1897 Scarborough Festival and his final first-class match was for an England XI against the Australians at Bradford in 1902. He was one of the least experienced Yorkshire cricketers to ever be awarded a county cap. Most of his time in club cricket was spent with South Kirkby.

Bairstow, David Leslie

Born: 01/09/1951, Bradford
Died: 05/01/1998, Marton-cum-Grafton, Boroughbridge
RHB, RM, WK. Career: 1970-1990.
Cap No 115, 1973. Benefit: 1982.
Testimonial: 1990

"He wasn't a great batsman and he wasn't a great wicket-keeper but he was a great cricketer." So spoke Phil Carrick at the funeral of David Bairstow who had tragically committed suicide at the age of only 46.

Bairstow famously first played for Yorkshire at the age of 18 when still at school. He sat one of his A Level examinations at 7.00am so that he could be at Park Avenue, Bradford – which was fortunately not too far from Hanson Grammar School - to play against Gloucestershire. Twenty years later his career concluded with him being the only Yorkshire player to score over 10,000 runs and effect over 1,000 dismissals in first-class cricket. He is second on the list for most dismissals in limited-overs matches for the county.

Bairstow started as a bowler with Laisterdyke, where his father kept wicket, at the age of nine and moved to Undercliffe five years later, returning there after his county

career. On his debut for Yorkshire he immediately impressed with his ability and enthusiasm and soon became a fixture in the side. Brisk and efficient behind the stumps he took some brilliant catches off the faster bowlers when at full stretch.

International honours came his way in 1979 when he made his Test debut and one of the highlights of his career was to play in the Centenary Test against Australia at Lord's a year later. However competition from Alan Knott and Bob Taylor, principally, meant that he played in

only four Tests although a longer run in the England team brought him 21 caps in ODIs.

Bairstow's never-say-die attitude was encapsulated in a Benson & Hedges Cup game in 1981 when he struck nine sixes and three fours in an innings of 103 not out at Derby. His tenth-wicket stand of 80 with Mark Johnson brought a highly improbable victory and the same county suffered a year later at Scarborough when Bairstow took 11 dismissals (including seven in an innings) to break both Yorkshire records for first-class cricket.

Rewarded with the captaincy of his county in 1984 he led Yorkshire for three seasons with his usual pride and ebullience but a weak side could not deliver success. However, as one of Yorkshire's most popular players, he will always be remembered for the way he played the game – resolutely and with unending vigour.

Bairstow, Jonathan Marc
Born: 26/09/1989, Bradford
RHB, RM, WK. Career: 2009–
Cap No 169, 2011

Such was the promise of Jonny Bairstow that he played for the Academy for nine seasons and concluded his school career at St Peter's, York by being the first winner of the Wisden Schools Cricketer of the Year. His Yorkshire debut came while on a brief course of study at Leeds Metropolitan University and his international debut came two years later followed by his first Test in 2012.

It took time for Bairstow to establish himself at the highest level but being given the gloves on a regular basis led to his first century in his 22nd Test. Although his 'keeping originally came in for criticism it improved considerably and his aggressive batting has a ruthless quality about it, his ability to take county attacks apart serving Yorkshire well. This was very evident in 2015 when he averaged 92.33 (scoring 1,108 runs) in the County Championship – a figure beaten for Yorkshire by only two other players. He also shares two record-wicket partnerships for the county: for the fourth and seventh wickets with Joe Root and Tim Bresnan, respectively.

It also took time for Bairstow to gain a regular place in England's white-ball teams but he eventually succeeded as an opener in 50-overs cricket, a role in which he had done well for Yorkshire. One of the highlights of him having a regular place in the Test team was in 2016 when he broke the world record for most Test runs in a calendar year by a wicket-keeper. In 2017 he passed the 100 dismissals-mark in Test cricket – the first Yorkshire player to do so.

Jonny Bairstow celebrates reaching 200 at Trent Bridge in 2011.

Baker, George Robert
Born: 18/04/1862, Malton
Died: 06/02/1938, Wing,
Buckinghamshire
RHB, RF. Career: 1884

A stylish and attacking batsman as well as a brilliant fielder, George Baker had brief careers with clubs in the Malton and Leeds areas, as well as Yorkshire, but on moving to Bury he played for Lancashire for 13 seasons. In over 200 games for the Red Rose county he scored more than 7,000 runs and was even awarded a benefit match against Yorkshire.

In retirement he coached for 12 years at Harrow School and was groundsman on the Rothschild family's private ground in Leighton Buzzard.

Baker, Robert
Born: 03/07/1849, Hunmanby, Filey
Died: 21/06/1896, Scarborough
RHB, RRF/FM. Career: 1874-75.
Amateur

As secretary of Scarborough CC, for the last 26 years of his life, Bob Baker was a good club all-rounder. He was instrumental in administering the development of the North Marine Road ground in the early 1870s as well as the early years of the Festival. His career with Yorkshire was very brief.

Baker, Thomas Michael
Born: 06/07/1981, Dewsbury
RHB, RFM. Career: 2001

Four List A games for Yorkshire and one Championship match for Northamptonshire in 2005 represent Tom Baker's inter-county career. He was a member of Yorkshire's Academy and toured South Africa with the full county squad in 2001.

Balderstone, John Christopher
Born: 16/11/1940, Longwood,
Huddersfield
Died: 06/03/2000, Carlisle, Cumbria
RHB, SLA. Career: 1961-69

Probably the only sportsman to play professionally at two sports on the same day, Chris Balderstone left Leicestershire at Chesterfield at close of play in September 1975 with his score on 51 not out. He played for Doncaster Rovers v Brentford in the evening then took his score to 116 on the following day and figures of three for 28 helped his second county win the Championship.

Club cricket at Paddock and Baildon, as professional with the latter, preceded a disappointing Yorkshire career. An attractive early-order batsman and useful spin bowler in helpful conditions, he took on a new lease of life with Leicestershire. He won the match award in the Benson & Hedges Cup final against Yorkshire in 1972, played in two Tests in 1976 and continued in first-class cricket until the age of 45 by which time he had scored over 19,000 runs.

Balderstone then took up umpiring and stood for 12 seasons in first-class cricket before suddenly being claimed by cancer. Huddersfield Town was his first football club but he played for Carlisle United for ten seasons including one in the First Division.

Ballance, Gary Simon
Born: 22/11/1989, Harare, Zimbabwe
LHB, LB. Career: 2008-
Cap No 172, 2012

Gary Ballance came to Yorkshire via his uncle, former Zimbabwe captain Dave Houghton, encouraging him to take up a scholarship at Harrow, before playing for Derbyshire. On joining Yorkshire he gradually developed into a middle-order batsman proficient in all three

Gary Ballance batting against Sussex at Hove in 2015.

formats. In the six games in the Champions League of late-2012 he was easily his county's highest scorer and in List A cricket averaged over 50. In 2013 he was the County Championship First Division's leading run-scorer and made his Test debut in Australia in the following winter.

In early-2015 Ballance scored his 1,000th Test run in only his 17th innings – the third fastest for England. However, with a prominently back-foot technique Ballance was later tested and dropped twice but his appointment as Yorkshire captain for 2017 did much to compensate for this. His appetite for scoring runs at county level remained undimmed and he was comfortably Yorkshire's leading batsman in the Championship in 2017.

Barber, Alan Theodore

Born: 17/06/1905, Ecclesall, Sheffield
Died: 10/03/1985, Ludgrove,
Wokingham, Berkshire
RHB. Career: 1929-30. Amateur.
Cap No 66, 1930

Alan Barber played first-class cricket for Oxford University for three seasons from 1927, captaining the team in his final year. He was also

captain at soccer and gained a golf Blue. He took over the Yorkshire captaincy in his second season and led the county to third position in the Championship. With the side mainly young and in transition, he was an inspiring leader.

Barber retired from cricket at the age of 25, having scored over 2,000 first-class runs, to take up teaching at Ludgrove (prep) School and was headmaster there for 36 years.

Barber, Wilfred

Born: 18/04/1901, Cleckheaton
Died: 10/09/1968, Bradford
RHB, RFM. Career: 1926-47.
Cap No 63, 1929. Testimonial: 1946

One of the stalwarts of the highly-successful Yorkshire teams of the 1930s, Wilf Barber was an opening batsman with Gomersal but when he eventually gained a regular place in the county side it was in the middle order. Batting tenaciously but in an attractive style, he scored over 1,000 runs in every season from 1932 to 1939 except one. His best season was in 1935 when he scored over 2,000 runs and made his highest score of 255 against Surrey at Sheffield. His form resulted in selection for two Test matches against South Africa and he spent the following winter in Australia and New Zealand with a non-Test playing MCC party.

Barber added to his value to the side by being a brilliant outfielder and following retirement he coached for the North Riding Education Authority combining this with being professional with Lidget Green and then King Cross. His final post was as coach at Ashville College, Harrogate, a position he fulfilled for four years in the early-1960s. He remains in Yorkshire's records as the joint-holder, with Maurice Leyland, of the best second wicket partnership in first-class cricket.

Barraclough, Eric Scott

Born: 30/03/1923, Great Horton, Bradford
Died: 21/05/1999, Bradford
RHB, RFM. Career: 1949-50

Just one of Eric Barraclough's two first-class matches was in the County Championship. He played for Undercliffe and in 15 seasons as a professional with Bradford scored over 8,000 runs.

Bates, Willie

Born: 19/11/1855, Lascelles Hall, Huddersfield
Died: 08/01/1900, Lepton, Huddersfield
RHB, OB. Career: 1877-87

At Melbourne in January 1883 Willie Bates, better known as Billy, took the first hat-trick by an England bowler. His analysis of seven for 28 was followed by another seven wickets in the second innings and a knock of 55 meant that he became the first player from any country to score a half-century and take ten wickets in a

Test. For his efforts he was presented with a mounted emu's egg.

A genuine all-rounder, Bates became professional with Rochdale at the age of 17. When given his opportunity with Yorkshire he seized it with both hands and took over 80 wickets in each of his first five full seasons. On five occasions he passed 1000 runs in a season and almost completed the double in 1881.

A hard-hitting and fast-scoring batsman, Bates complemented this skill with accurate and well-flighted spin-bowling. He was particularly popular in Australia, which he toured five times, and where he played all of his 15 Tests in which he scored 656 runs and took 50 wickets. His overall first-class totals were 10,249 runs and 874 wickets.

Tragically, Bates was hit in the eye by a stray ball when involved in net practice on his final tour. Although he regained some partial sight, it was the end of his first-class career. Spells as professional with Haslingden and Leek plus some coaching in South Africa provided some compensation but subsequent depression resulted in a suicide attempt. His final end came after the funeral of John Thewlis where he contracted a cold which developed into pneumonia.

Bates, William Ederick

Born: 05/03/1884, Kirkheaton,
Huddersfield
Died: 17/01/1957, Belfast, N Ireland
RHB, SLA. Career: 1907-13.
Cap No 44, 1908

Son of Billy and father to Ted who played for, and managed, Southampton FC, the younger Bates never quite managed to establish himself in the Yorkshire side. A solid batsman, and brilliant outfielder, he never scored a century for the county but when playing for Glamorgan for 11 seasons from its inaugural Championship campaign in 1921 he made 10 centuries, including 200 not out against Worcestershire at Kidderminster in 1927, as well as taking over 200 wickets. His final first-class run-tally came to almost 16,000.

The move to Wales came about through becoming professional at Briton Ferry in 1914. He later had a similar engagement with Broughton Hall while playing for Cheshire and coached in Ireland for several years.

Batty, Gareth Jon

Born: 13/10/1977, Bradford
RHB, OB. Career: 1997

Gareth Batty had two years with the Academy but appeared only once for Yorkshire – in a first-class match - before moving to Surrey in 1999. He played for Worcestershire from 2002 to 2009 during which time he appeared in seven Tests and ten ODIs before returning to Surrey whom he captained from 2015, leading it to three consecutive final appearances in the Royal London Cup. He returned briefly to the Test side in late-2016 after a gap of 142 Tests – a world record.

Batty, Jeremy David

Born: 15/05/1971, Bradford
RHB, OB. Career: 1989-94

Elder brother of Gareth, Jeremy Batty began with Bingley and made his debut for Yorkshire aged only 18 as a very promising tall off-spinner. He had three full seasons, his best being in 1991 when he took 41 wickets in first-class matches including a career-best six for 48 against Nottinghamshire at Worksop. A move to Somerset in 1995 for two seasons was followed by five years in the Minor Counties Championship with Cheshire, Shropshire and Buckinghamshire.

Bayes, George William

Born: 27/02/1884, Flamborough,
Bridlington
Died: 06/12/1960, Flamborough,
Bridlington
RHB, RF. Career: 1910-21

George Bayes played in no more than a handful of matches in each of the five seasons in which he was selected to represent Yorkshire. His best performance of five for 83 against Hampshire at Bramall Lane, Sheffield came in his final season. Scarborough, Castleford and Tong Park were the main clubs for which he played.

Beaumont, Harold

Born: 14/10/1916, Thongsbridge,
Holmfirth
Died: 15/11/2003, Huddersfield
RHB, RM. Career: 1946-47

Although Harold Beaumont first played for Yorkshire second eleven in 1938 he had to wait until after the Second World War before making his first team debut. Most of his first-class matches were in the

Championship-winning season of 1946. Having begun in league cricket with Thongsbridge he joined Spen Victoria but also had one season with Crompton as a professional in 1949.

Beaumont, John

Born: 16/09/1854, Armitage Bridge, Huddersfield
Died: 01/05/1920, Lambeth, London
RHB, RF. Career: 1877-78

An accurate and hostile bowler, John Beaumont had a hugely successful career with Surrey for whom he took over 400 wickets in seven seasons. This period started seven years after his few matches for Yorkshire and included an MCC trip to Australia. He also played for Armitage Bridge and Holbeck and was professional for Accrington in 1893.

Bedford, Harry

Born: 17/07/1907, Morley
Died: 05/07/1968, Croydon, Surrey
RHB, LBG. Career: 1928

A promising all-rounder, Harry Bedford was aged only 21 when he had his only season in first-class cricket. Three-quarters of his career wickets came in one of the seven innings in which he bowled when he took six for 91 against Derbyshire at Dewsbury.

Bedford, Walter

Born: 24/02/1879, Royston, Barnsley
Died: 28/07/1939, Balby, Doncaster
RHB, RFM. Career: 1903

A stint as professional with Morley preceded Walter Bedford's very short career in first-class cricket. Thereafter he became professional and groundsman with Doncaster and turned to amateur status so as to become the club's captain.

Bell, John Thomson

Born: 16/06/1895, Batley
Died: 08/08/1974, Guiseley, Leeds
RHB, LBG. Career: 1921-23

A correct and solid opening batsman, John Bell could not secure a regular place in the Yorkshire team but spent eight successful seasons with Glamorgan. He scored over 7,000 runs for the Welsh county including two double-centuries. The higher of these was 225 against Worcestershire at Dudley in 1926 during one of three seasons when he passed the 1,500-run mark.

Bell was one of a number of players released by Glamorgan in 1931 because of financial constraints but he returned to live in Yorkshire and later had four seasons from 1948 as a first-class umpire.

Berry, John

Born: 10/01/1823, Dalton, Huddersfield
Died: 26/02/1895, Haslingden, Lancashire
RHB, RRM. Career: 1863-67

A nephew of George (see Appendix 1) John Berry first played for 'Yorkshire' 14 years before the Club's formation. He played for Dalton for ten years but in 1852 moved to Sheffield to act as servant of MJ Ellison (see Appendix 1) and had several seasons with clubs in that city.

A hard-hitting batsman with a good defence, Berry scored over 1,000 runs in his full first-class career and later moved to Lancashire where he was professional with Accrington.

Berry, Joseph

Born: 29/11/1829, Dalton, Huddersfield
Died: 20/04/1894, Fartown, Huddersfield
RHB, RM. Career: 1864-74

No relation to John Berry, Joseph played in two matches for 'Yorkshire' in 1861 and just three for the official County Club. His club cricket was mainly with Darlington and Lockwood and he later coached at Magdalen College, Oxford University for 11 seasons as well as umpiring in a small number of first-class matches.

Berry, Philip John

Born: 28/12/1966, Saltburn
RHB, OB. Career: 1986-90

Phil Berry was not able to gain a regular place in the Yorkshire side and so left the county and Yeadon, with whom he had been professional for three seasons, after 1991. He then played for Durham in its first three seasons in first-class cricket, after touring with the county squad to Zimbabwe, and had a little more success. An analysis of seven for 113 against Middlesex at Lord's in 1992 was his best performance.

Best, Tino la Bertram

Born: 26/08/1981, Bridgetown, Barbados
RHB, RF. Career: 2010

So poor was the form of Tino Best as Yorkshire's overseas player that he played in only half of the Championship matches for which he was available although he did top the bowling averages in the 40-over competition. Always fast and often hostile, he was too erratic and inconsistent.

Best's career peaked in the 2004 Caribbean season when he took 49 wickets in 11 first-class matches for Barbados and played in all four Tests against England. He totalled 25 Tests and 26 ODIs and also played for Hampshire in 2016.

Betts, George

Born: 19/09/1841, Sheffield
Died: 26/09/1902, Brightside, Sheffield
RHB. Career: 1873-74

A hard-hitting batsman, George Betts scored 44 not out in his debut match but ran out of partners. A pair in his second game signified the end of his first-class career. He played for at least four clubs local to Sheffield, including as professional for Hallam.

Bevan, Michael Gwyl

Born: 08/05/1970, Belconnen, ACT, Australia
LHB, SLC. Career: 1995-96.
Cap No 140, 1995

A very influential overseas player for Yorkshire, Michael Bevan brought a winning mentality to a county which had experienced mediocrity for several years. He helped Yorkshire achieve some successes which it had not experienced for over 20 years.

Although he scored over 19,000 first-class runs at an average approaching 60 it is as a one-day player for which he will be chiefly remembered as his 232 ODIs, but only 18 Tests, for Australia testify. He was one of the first to be called a 'finisher' and would often remain not out having seen his side to victory, this contributing to him having the highest average in the world in List A matches.

Binks, James Graham

Born: 05/10/1935, Hull
RHB, LB, WK. Career: 1955-69.
Cap No 97, 1957. Benefit: 1967

Regarded by many as the best wicket-keeper in England for a good ten years, the mere two Tests played by Jimmy Binks were scant reward for a player who practised his art with minimum fuss and maximum consistency.

After short periods with Hull Town and Leeds he made his debut for Yorkshire at the age of 19 and then played in a staggering 412 consecutive Championship games until his retirement. In his 15 years behind the stumps he missed just one county match – against Oxford University in 1964 and this was only due to him being called up to play for MCC.

It made little difference as to which of Yorkshire's great bowlers he was 'keeping. He had to cope with high pace, fast-medium pace, to which he often stood up to the wicket, or quality off-spin and left-arm spin which could break in either direction. He always seemed to take the ball in a completely unflappable manner. The 1960 season was his best in terms of figures: his 96 catches remain a national record and his 107 victims are still the best for Yorkshire. He is responsible for four of the county's five best seasons by a wicket-keeper – the four consecutive ones of 1960-63. Another tribute to his consistency of excellence when at his peak.

In India in 1963/64 illness had struck several members of the MCC party so Binks was drafted into the side for two Tests in which England's current 'keeper, Jim Parks, also played. Binks kept wicket and Parks played only as a batsman! This shows who was the better 'keeper. So depleted was the England team that Binks even opened the batting, despite being a regular number ten for Yorkshire, in three of his four innings. At Bombay (now Mumbai) he scored 55 and shared a century stand with Brian Bolus - a rare success for Binks although he reached the giddy heights of 95 against Middlesex at Lord's in 1964.

It is hard for anyone to recall ever

seeing Binks drop a catch and such was his skill that his ability to take the ball cleanly resulted in only one injury – a broken finger in 1966, the discomfort of which he played through. He played for Lincolnshire for two seasons in the early-1970s then started working for a USA engineering firm and emigrated to California.

Binns, John

Born: 31/03/1870, Woodhouse Carr, Leeds
Died: 08/12/1934, Leeds
RHB, RMF, WK. Career: 1898

John Binns deputised for David Hunter behind the wicket in just one match and effected three stumpings but took no catches! He was later professional with Armley, Leeds.

Bird, Harold Dennis

Born: 19/04/1933, Barnsley
RHB, RM/OB. Career: 1956-59

It is perfectly possible that cricket has never had a more devoted servant than 'Dickie' Bird, someone who has fulfilled many of the roles which the game has to offer. A first appearance for Barnsley at the age of 16 showed promise but this was only much later fulfilled. A total of 14 games in four seasons with Yorkshire concluded when he was infamously dropped after making what would remain his highest first-class score of 181 not out against Glamorgan at Bradford.

A move to Leicestershire followed but despite playing in as many as 79 matches in five seasons his batting average actually worsened even though he passed 1,000 runs in his first season. Solid and thorough in approach he gained his reward in the unlikely setting of Paignton where five seasons as player-coach produced over 10,000 runs. Gaining qualifications as a coach opened up more opportunities and summers with Plymouth College alternated with appointments in Rhodesia (now Zimbabwe) and Transvaal (now Gauteng).

In 1970 Bird began that part of his career for which he is most famous – as an umpire of the highest quality. Joining the first-class list was followed by him being promoted to stand in Test matches only three years later. Despite his nervous and eccentric disposition he made decisions quickly and accurately and was always able to diffuse on-field tensions with a quiet and humorous phrase. Unusual incidents tended to occur when he was present such as snow stopping play at Buxton in 1975 when Derbyshire were playing Lancashire and in 1988 at Headingley when a blocked drain flooded part of the outfield in a Test match involving West Indies. He stood in three World Cup finals and when he retired from the international stage his 66 Tests were a world record.

Retirement from the first-class list in 1998 brought him the opportunity to watch Yorkshire, still his favoured county, as well as provide more entertainment on the after-dinner circuit. He was rewarded in 2012 for his dedication to the game with the status of his MBE of 1986 being raised to that of OBE. What may well have given him the greatest pleasure, however, was being elected President of Yorkshire CCC for 2014 and 2015 and seeing at first hand, because he never missed a match, his beloved team win two County Championship titles. Hugely popular wherever he went, the county and cricket have never had a better ambassador.

'Dickie' Bird, as Yorkshire CCC president, with the 2014 County Championship trophy.

Birkenshaw, Jack

Born: 13/11/1940, Rothwell, Leeds
LHB, OB. Career: 1958-60

Far more fulfilled with Leicestershire than he had ever been with Yorkshire, Jack Birkenshaw was so appreciated by the midland county that in 1974 he broke its Benefit record having made his Test debut in the previous winter. It was ironic that it was the same Ray Illingworth who usually kept him out of the Yorkshire side who was his county captain when at his peak as a player.

Birkenshaw did not spin the ball greatly but his high action allied with considerable accuracy, deceptive flight and subtle variations enabled him to take 908 first-class wickets in 17 seasons with Leicestershire. His one year with Worcestershire was followed by seven years as a first-class umpire.

It was as a coach, however, that he was most successful, partly with Western Australia but especially in guiding Leicestershire, a team without stars, to two County Championships in his ten-year tenure as Cricket Manager for which he was rewarded with a second benefit and an MBE in 2011.

Birtles, Thomas James Denton

Born: 26/10/1886, Higham, Barnsley
Died: 13/01/1971, Attenborough, Nottinghamshire
RHB, LBG. Career: 1913-24

A century in the Roses match of 1914 at Sheffield was the only time Tommy Birtles passed 50 in first-class cricket. It came during the only season in which he was given a regular place in the side. The intervention of the 1914-18 War halted his progress but he played for Barnsley for 20 years and also coached at Gresham's School, Norfolk. A noted soccer-player, he played on the right-wing for Barnsley, Swansea and Portsmouth.

Blackburn, John Derek Hepburn

Born: 27/10/1924, Headingley, Leeds
Died: 19/02/1987, Steeton, Keighley
RHB. Career: 1956. Amateur

John Blackburn captained Bradford for nine years, leading the club to three Priestley Cup wins, and he later served on the Yorkshire committee having had the shortest-possible county career.

Blackburn, Joseph Scott

Born: 24/09/1852, Holbeck, Leeds
Died: 08/07/1922, New Wortley, Leeds
RHB, RF. Career: 1876-77

A noted fast bowler in league cricket, in which he was involved with at least seven different clubs in the Leeds area, Joe Blackburn had one first-class match – with United North of England XI – in addition to his six for Yorkshire. He played more for Batley than any other team.

Blackburn, William Edward

Born: 24/11/1888, Clitheroe,
Lancashire
Died: 03/06/1941, Heaton, Bolton,
Lancashire
RHB, RF/FM. Career: 1919-20.
Amateur

A Captain in the Army, William Blackburn was a genuine fast bowler who had an excellent record for Yorkshire. His 45 wickets in ten games included a best of five for 17 against Derbyshire at Bradford in 1919 but he played for the county only because the committee thought he had been born at Sawley - near Clitheroe but in the old West Riding. His main clubs were both on Merseyside - Hightown and Liverpool.

Blain, John Angus Rae

Born: 04/01/1979, Edinburgh,
Scotland
RHB, RMF. Career: 2004-10

John Blain made both his first-class and List A debuts for Scotland at the age of 17 and played for Northamptonshire from 1997 before moving to Yorkshire. After three seasons he moved onto the coaching staff but returned to play in just one match in 2010.

He continued to play for Scotland until 2009 in both domestic and international competitions including the World Cup in 2007. Blain usually bowled economically but his lack of speed meant that he did not normally trouble professional batsmen. He later became Cricket Professional at Loretto School in his native city.

Blake, Wilfred

Born: 29/11/1854, Embsay, Skipton
Died: 28/11/1931, Burnley, Lancashire
RHB, RRM. Career: 1880

Known as Fred in his playing days, he had one match with Lancashire in 1877 and just two with Yorkshire three years later. He played for several clubs including Keighley (as professional), Lockwood, Settle and Burnley for whom he played for over 20 seasons and also captained. His mother's name was Blakey and he later added his father's name so that his death certificate shows Wilfred Blake Uttley.

Blakey, Richard John

Born: 15/01/1967, Huddersfield
RHB, WK. Career: 1985-2004.
Cap No 129, 1987. Benefit: 1998

The defining moment in Richard Blakey's career occurred in 1988 when he was asked to take over as wicket-keeper from the injured David Bairstow. Three years later the role became permanent.

Initially a highly-promising batsman, Blakey made his debut aged 18 and two years later he became the county's youngest-ever player to score a double-century. A product of Rastrick Grammar School and Elland, he had a sound defence but batted with an attacking approach and this served him well in limited-overs cricket. He holds the Yorkshire record for most dismissals in this form of the game.

Although he kept wicket efficiently and in a quiet, unobtrusive manner, his batting suffered. Four centuries in 1987 were followed by only nine over the remaining 15 years of his first-class career. It was ironic that his highest innings – 223 not out against Northamptonshire at Headingley – came in his final season but being placed as low as number nine in the order had not helped his cause. When Test cricket came his way in 1992/93

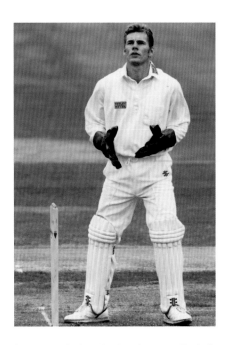

he conceded only five byes in India's combined total of 1,151 but scored a mere seven runs in four innings.

After three years on the coaching staff Blakey concluded his connection with Yorkshire at the end of 2006 and went into business promoting sport.

Blamires, Emanuel

Born: 31/07/1850, Bradford
Died: 22/03/1886, Bradford
LHB, LRF. Career: 1877

Registered at birth as Nimrod Blamires, he was professional with Burnley in 1873 and also played for Dalton, Huddersfield before his one match for Yorkshire. This was followed by 32 games over the next four seasons with Surrey for whom he took 127 wickets. He returned to Yorkshire to act as professional with Manningham.

Blewett, Gregory Scott

Born: 28/10/1971, North Adelaide, South Australia
RHB, RM. Career: 1999.
Cap No 147, 1999

Greg Blewett had already played in 34 Tests and 32 ODIs for Australia when he came to Yorkshire. Unfortunately he averaged only 16.50 in his first ten first-class matches and scores of 98 and 190 in his penultimate game against Northamptonshire at Scarborough only partly made up for his disappointing season.

He will be best remembered for a bowling spell in a NatWest Trophy quarter-final at Old Trafford when he took three vital middle-order wickets in quick succession to turn the match Yorkshire's way.

Bloom, George Raymond

Born: 13/09/1941, Aston, Sheffield
LHB. Career: 1964

Although a wicket-keeper, George Bloom played his one match for Yorkshire as a batsman. He played for Scarborough from the age of 15 and in 1966 became the North Riding coach.

Bocking, Henry

Born: 10/12/1835, Sheffield
Died: 22/02/1907, Sharrow, Sheffield
?HB, Career: 1865

Henry Bocking was taken to The Oval in 1865 as umpire but found himself playing on the second day due to an illness to Luke Greenwood. He was given one more match for Yorkshire but spent most of his career playing for various Sheffield club sides.

Boden, John George

Born: 27/12/1848, Birstall, Leeds
Died: 03/01/1928, Ilkley
RHB, WK. Career: 1878. Amateur

John Boden was a stop-gap wicket-keeper between George Pinder and Joe Hunter when he had his one game – against the Australians. He played for several important clubs including Middlesbrough, Scarborough, Harrogate and Leeds.

Bolton, Benjamin Charles
Born: 23/09/1861, Cottingham, Hull
Died: 18/11/1910, Hull
RHB, RFM. Career: 1890-91.
Amateur

Ben Bolton's first victim in first-class cricket was WG Grace. He had previously played for Hornsea and had a long spell with Hull Town whom he captained for many years. He excelled at several sports and died in hospital after falling from an express train.

Bolus, John Brian
Born: 31/01/1934, Whitkirk, Leeds
RHB, SLA/LM. Career: 1956-62
Cap No 103, 1960

Despite having his best season for Yorkshire in 1961, with 1,970 runs, Brian Bolus was deemed surplus to requirements 12 months later. An aggressive stroke-player, he was strong off his legs and could cut and cover-drive well. In 1959 he became the first Yorkshire batsman to score over 1,000 runs in a second eleven season. By nature an opening

batsman (he played in this role in all of his seven Tests) he was also happy to bat in the middle-order.

After being released by Yorkshire he moved to Nottinghamshire for the 1963 season, his England career also starting in the same year. He played for his new county for ten years, captaining it in his final season, and then moved to Derbyshire in 1973, leading it in all of his three seasons there. In his full first-class career he scored over 25,000 runs and later played for Bradford, Cleckheaton, Brighouse and Farsley as well as becoming an England selector.

Booth, Arthur
Born: 03/11/1902, Featherstone, Wakefield
Died: 17/08/1974, Rochdale, Lancashire
RHB/LHB, SLA. Career: 1931-47.
Cap No 80, 1946

For one glorious season, Arthur Booth showed everyone what they had been missing. In 1946 he topped the national first-class averages with 111 wickets at 11.61 and Yorkshire won the Championship. He was aged 43.

Two games in 1931 had been followed by a 14-year gap while he played for Northumberland, Littleborough and Spen Victoria. A good coach, he spent time on the Lancashire committee and scouted for Warwickshire.

Booth, Major William
Born: 10/12/1886, Lowtown, Pudsey
Died: 01/07/1916, La Cigny, Serre, France
RHB, RMF. Career: 1908-14.
Cap No 46

A young, successful all-rounder when the 1914-18 War broke out, Major (his Christian name) Booth had completed the double in 1913 and played in two Tests in the following winter in South Africa. Tragically, he fell in action during the battle of the Somme, dying in the arms of Abe Waddington.

Fulneck School, Pudsey St Lawrence and Wath Athletic were where Booth's pre-county career took place. Tall, he used his full height in his bowling and he moved the ball late and quickly. His 181 wickets in 1913 were the most in the country. When batting he was very strong on the off-side and made a double century against Worcestershire in 1911.

Booth received many tributes on his death and he is remembered by a memorial tablet in St Lawrence's Church, Pudsey.

Booth, Paul Antony
Born: 05/09/1965, Crossland Moor, Huddersfield
LHB, SLA. Career: 1982-89

Paul Booth made his Yorkshire debut just three days after his 17th birthday as a very promising spinner. However, he played in only 28 matches in both formats in eight seasons with the county despite being the second eleven's leading wicket-taker in three successive seasons. In his youth he played for Meltham, and later for Farsley while with Yorkshire, but then moved to Warwickshire. That county gave him more opportunities over his four years with it but he took only one five-for in a total of 60 first-class matches.

Booth, Roy
Born: 01/10/1926, Marsden, Huddersfield
RHB, RM, WK. Career: 1951-55

After playing for Golcar, Roy Booth had seven seasons as professional with Lightcliffe but his unfulfilled five years in the unhappy Yorkshire side of the time were followed by 15 very successful ones with Worcestershire. While with the west-midland county Booth twice took 100 dismissals in a season and his batting improved so much that he scored over 1,000 runs in 1959 and eventually finished his career with a tally of over 10,000. An undemonstrative 'keeper he took over 1,100 dismissals in his 20-year career and enjoyed his new county winning its first Championship titles in 1964 and 1965. Following retirement he served on Worcestershire's committee.

Bore, Michael Kenneth
Born: 02/06/1947, East Hull
Died: 02/05/2017, Knaresborough
RHB, LFM/M. Career: 1969-77

An average county player who became a good coach, Mike Bore's early cricket was with Hull Town, Leeds and Bradford. An accurate bowler, he never gained a regular place in the Yorkshire team and it was a similar case when he moved to Nottinghamshire although he played a full season in 1979 and was awarded

his cap the following year. He finished his career in 1988 with 372 wickets in 159 first-class matches and 139 in 147 List A games.

He moved into coaching with his second county and played for one season with Lincolnshire but was persuaded to return to Yorkshire in 1990 and put in charge of youth coaching at the indoor school. During this time he captained East Bierley to victory in the Priestley Cup.

Borrill, Peter David

Born: 04/07/1951, Burmantofts, Leeds
RHB, RMF. Career: 1971

A useful pace bowler in club cricket, David Borrill played in only two games for Yorkshire (both first-class) but had a long career with Leeds. Other clubs included Darlington, as professional, Hanging Heaton and Old Modernians.

Bosomworth, William Edward

Born: 08/03/1847, Carlton Husthwaite, Thirsk
Died: 07/06/1891, Norton, Malton
RHB, RRMF. Career: 1872–80

A tall, but gangling rather than athletic bowler, William Bosomworth never played for Yorkshire in more than one match per season. He played in several games for the Yorkshire United XI and his main clubs were Malton and Scarborough.

Bottomley, Isaac Henry

Born: 09/04/1855, Spring Hall, Shelf, Halifax
Died: 23/04/1922, Morecambe, Lancashire
RHB, RRF/MF. Career: 1878-80. Amateur

Isaac Bottomley was an aggressive and attacking batsman who played the ball late. He twice played for Bradford against the Australians in 1880 and also played for Low Moor. Five of his nine games for Yorkshire came in 1879.

Bottomley, Thomas

Born: 26/12/1910, Rawmarsh, Rotherham
Died: 19/02/1977, Rotherham
RHB, RM. Career: 1934-35

Tom Bottomley played in five games for Yorkshire in the middle-order in 1934 but in only one the following season, usually when Maurice Leyland was on England duty. His only half-century came against Essex at Southend. A success with Sheffield United, he also played for Thorncliffe and Wath.

Bower, William Henry

Born: 17/10/1857, Bradford
Died: 31/01/1943, Nelson, Lancashire
RHB, WK. Career: 1883

After playing for Keighley, William Bower moved to Lancashire, becoming groundsman at Nelson in 1881. He had the briefest possible career with Yorkshire but played four games for Lancashire then continued his long club career by captaining both Nelson and Colne, also playing for Burnley as well as returning to Keighley.

Bowes, William Eric

Born: 25/07/1908, Elland, Halifax
Died: 04/09/1987, Otley
RHB, RMF. Career: 1929-47.
Cap No 67, 1930. Benefit: 1947

Bespectacled and unathletic, Bill Bowes was an unlikely-looking sportsman but he was one of the dominant bowlers during the 1930s. Yorkshire won the Championship seven times in nine seasons and Bowes was in the top three of the competition's national bowling averages six times.

Success for West Leeds High School and Kirkstall Educational was followed by a spell on the Lord's ground staff,

him making his first-class debut for MCC a year prior to his first game for Yorkshire. Tall (6 ft 5 in) he gained considerable and disconcerting bounce on hard and responsive pitches and also bowled a very effective yorker. Although his natural ball was the in-swinger he developed the away-swinger as well and many batsmen found him difficult to face. A total of 193 wickets in the wet summer of 1935 – his best season – testifies to his ability to make the most of different types of conditions.

In 1932 Bowes made his Test debut but also played an important part in the development of 'Bodyline' by strengthening a leg-side field for Jack Hobbs in a game against Surrey in which Douglas Jardine was also playing. Bowes was included in the party for the infamous tour of Australia in the following winter; as captain, Jardine preferred his faster bowlers and Bowes played in only one Test but did take the wicket of Don Bradman, the outstanding batsman for whom the theory was instigated.

Bill Bowes in his days as a journalist.

A total of 15 Tests, in which he took 68 wickets, was scant reward for a bowler of Bowes' ability but his fielding and batting were both poor, him taking more wickets (1,639) than he scored runs (1,531) in his first-class career. His career-best performance came on a hot day at Scarborough when he persevered for three-and-a-half hours to take nine for 121 in 40 overs against Essex in 1932. His Test-best was six for 33 against West Indies at Old Trafford in 1939.

The Second World War had a lasting effect on Bowes; he spent two years in prison camps, lost over four stones but played on for two more seasons, belatedly being awarded a benefit in 1947. In retirement he was cricket correspondent of the *Yorkshire Evening News* and later the *Evening Post* until 1973. Of those amongst Yorkshire's greatest bowlers who have taken over 500 wickets only two players in the post-1918 era have an average lower than his.

Boycott, Geoffrey

Born: 21/10/1940, Fitzwilliam, Wakefield
RHB, RM. Career: 1962–86
Cap No 108, 1963. Benefit: 1967
Testimonial: 1984

Of the 63 batsmen to have scored over 30,000 runs in first-class cricket Geoffrey Boycott has the highest average. But no one has been involved in controversy with Yorkshire CCC more than he over the last 60 years. Even as recently as 2016 when he stood for re-election to the county's Board, members were asked not to vote for him and this after a hugely successful presidency over the 2012-13 seasons including the Club's 150th anniversary celebrations.

Early cricket at Hemsworth Grammar School and with Ackworth, Barnsley and Leeds was a prelude to Boycott winning his Yorkshire and England caps in successive years. At the end of the 1965 season he played a knock of 146 at Lord's to help defeat Surrey in the Gillette Cup final. Other than on the England tour of Australia in 1979-80 did he rarely play with such freedom as befits List A cricket. Another famous innings – in 1967 – was better-known for him being dropped afterwards. At Headingley against India he made 246 not out, his highest Test score, but, being out of form, scored slowly on the first day.

Although he had frequently been criticised for batting selfishly Boycott was appointed Yorkshire captain in 1971. Runners-up spot in the Championship in 1975 was the high point but his management skills were often questioned and he was sacked, tactlessly between the death and funeral of his mother, in 1978. This was just one year after a triumphant return to Test cricket, following a self-imposed exile, when he scored his 100th first-class century in the Headingley Test against Australia. In India in 1980/81 he became the highest run-scorer in Test cricket and then played in his 108th and final match.

His Yorkshire career continued but he was again badly treated when, in 1983, he was awarded a testimonial at the same time as being told that his contract would not be renewed. This brought about a huge dispute and there were many recriminations.

A batsman with an outstanding technique, Boycott was very solid in defence and scored mostly with very correct square cuts and drives. His knowledge and understanding of the game were never questioned and his presence on the Yorkshire committee and Board was valued. In retirement he became a strident but astute commentator.

Brackin, Thomas
Born: 05/01/1859, Thornes, Wakefield
Died: 07/10/1924, Darton, Barnsley
RHB, RS. Career: 1882

An opening batsman, Tom Brackin was given a brief run in the Yorkshire side but so abject was his performance that he was demoted in the order and concluded his career at number ten. Three of his six innings were ducks.

Geoffrey Boycott in 1964, the year of his Test debut.

Brathwaite, Kraigg Clairmonte

Born: 01/12/1992, Belfield, Black Rock,
St Michael, Barbados
RHB, OB. Career: 2017

Kraigg Brathwaite made his first-class debut for Barbados at the age of 16 and played in his first Test match for West Indies when 18. A solid opening batsman, he is a long-form specialist. In the Headingley Test of 2017 he scored 134 and 95 and was then signed by Yorkshire for the last two Championship games of the season.

Brayshay, Peter Beldon

Born: 14/10/1916, Headingley, Leeds
Died: 06/07/2004, Leeds
RHB, RMF/F. Career: 1952.
Amateur

Educated at Bootham School, York, Peter Brayshay served with the RAF in Asia and made his first-class debut in 1946 for Europeans against Hindus at Bombay (now Mumbai). This match and two for Yorkshire were his only such games. A successful bowler in league cricket with Leeds, he played badminton for Yorkshire and England.

Brearley, Horace

Born: 26/06/1913, Heckmondwike,
Batley
Died: 14/08/2007, Birmingham
RHB. Career: 1937. Amateur

More famous as the father of Mike, Horace Brearley played for Middlesex 12 years after his one appearance for Yorkshire. He topped the Yorkshire League averages while with Sheffield United in 1939 and later played for Brentham, Ealing. He was president of both the Central Yorkshire League and the Heavy Woollen Cup and coached at City of London School.

Brennan, Donald Vincent

Born: 10/02/1920, Eccleshill, Bradford
Died: 09/01/1985, Ilkley
RHB, WK. Career: 1947-53.
Amateur. Cap No 83, 1947

Yorkshire's only amateur wicket-keeper of note, Don Brennan was a fast bowler when at Downside School but developed into a stylish 'keeper even briefly taking the place of Godfrey Evans in the England team in 1951.

A brief spell with Eccleshill after the Second World War soon led to Brennan taking over the gloves in the county side from Paul Gibb who had moved to Essex. Although tall, he was especially brilliant when standing up to the wicket to Yorkshire's spinners and kept particularly well down the leg-side.

Brennan toured India, Pakistan and Ceylon (now Sri Lanka) with the MCC but he did not add to his two Test caps although he did have the satisfaction of making his only first-class half-century. He was well-respected for his dogged qualities as a batsman but had a limited range of strokes.

Unfortunately, Brennan's 'keeping deteriorated over his last couple of seasons and he retired to concentrate on his business activities. He retained his connection with Yorkshire cricket and was an outspoken committee member during the controversies of the 1970s-80s.

Don Brennan on his wedding-day.

Tim Bresnan bowling against Middlesex at Scarborough in 2014.

Bresnan, Timothy Thomas

Born: 28/02/1985, Pontefract
RHB, RFM. Career: 2001-
Cap No 165, 2006. Benefit: 2014

Strong and well-built, Tim Bresnan started his career as an effective seam and swing bowler and a lower-order batsman. The latter aspect of his play improved so much that he became one of the best all-rounders in the country.

A total of 68 wickets, including 47 in first-class cricket, in 2005 led to Bresnan's ODI debut in 2006 and his first Test came three years later. He played very important roles in the Ashes victory of 2010/11 and the Test series win over India in 2011 which saw England rise to number one in the rankings. At Trent Bridge a knock of 90 and innings figures of five for 48 brought him the man-of-the-match award.

Bresnan's international career of 23 Tests, 85 ODIs and 34 T20Is (which involved a World Cup winner's medal in the West Indies in 2011) was followed by County Championship winner's medals in 2014 and 2015 as well as a BBL winner's medal with Perth Scorchers in 2016/17. He features in two of Yorkshire's highest record partnerships and his career-best of 169 not out at Chester-le-Street in 2015 came in sharing an unbeaten 366 with Jonny Bairstow. His career-best with the ball was five for 36 against Nottinghamshire at Scarborough in 2016. He holds Yorkshire's record in T20 matches – six for 19 in the Roses game at Headingley in 2017, the year in which he became the first player to achieve the 1,000-run and 100-wicket double for the county in that format. Having been appointed Yorkshire's vice-captain for the 2017 season he led the side in 11 of its 12 T20 matches as well as two Championship games.

Britton, George

Born: 07/02/1843, Hunslet, Leeds
Died: 03/01/1910, Leeds
RHB. Career: 1867

George Britton opened the batting for several clubs as a sound and reliable batsman; he was mostly with Hunslet and Leeds. A professional musician, he played violin in the Leeds Grand Theatre Orchestra for over 30 years up until the time of his death.

Broadbent, Arthur

Born: 07/06/1879, Armley, Leeds
Died: 19/07/1958, Aberdeen, Scotland
RHB, RMF. Career: 1909-10

A bowling all-rounder, Arthur Broadbent played for Leeds and then Uddingston in Scotland. His first-class debut came in 1907 for his adoptive country but a brief return to Yorkshire saw him become the first – he remains the only - bowler to take 100 wickets in a season for the county's 2nd XI. His final club was Aberdeenshire whom he captained for five seasons.

Broadhead, Wilfred Bedford

Born: 31/05/1903, East Ardsley, Wakefield
Died: 02/04/1986, Wath-on-Dearne, Rotherham
RHB, LB. Career: 1929

Wilfred Broadhead was a prolific batsman in league cricket scoring a record 906 runs for Barnsley in 1947 and also captaining both Mexborough and Swinton.

Broadhurst, Mark

Born: 20/06/1974, Worsborough
Common, Barnsley
RHB, RF/FM. Career: 1991-94

Mark Broadhurst made his debut for Yorkshire two weeks before his 17th birthday as a very promising fast bowler. He played in 19 games for England U-19s but none of his six first-class matches were in the County Championship. After being released by Yorkshire he moved to Nottinghamshire but appeared in only one first-team game in three seasons.

Brook, Harry Cherrington

Born: 22/02/1999, Keighley
RHB, RM. Career: 2016-

A promising top-order batsman, Harry Brook played for England U-19 while still at Sedburgh School and had five seasons with the Academy before making his first-class debut at the age of 17, a List A debut a year later and first Championship match in 2017 in which season he also captained the England U-19 ODI team.

Brook, James William

Born: 01/02/1897, Ossett, Wakefield
Died: 03/03/1989, Selby
RHB, RMOB. Career: 1923

One of the best batsmen in his area in the 1920s, 'Jimmy' Brook became, in 1921, the first batsman to score 1000 runs in a season for Ossett. He scored about 20 centuries for the club and had also played for Lidget Green, Elland and Dewsbury but had a very short career for Yorkshire.

Brooke, Bernard

Born: 03/03/1930, Newsome,
Huddersfield
RHB, RMF. Career: 1950

Bernard Brooke became a professional with Armitage Bridge when aged 17, was Yorkshire second eleven's leading wicket-taker in the 1949 season but made little impact on the first team. He played for several league clubs including Lightcliffe, Bingley and Pudsey St Lawrence.

Brooks, Jack Alexander

Born: 04/06/1984, Oxford
RHB, RFM. Career: 2013-
Cap No 173, 2013

Jack Brooks moved to Yorkshire after four seasons with Northamptonshire, him previously having played for the county of his birth for five seasons from 2004. He

Jack Brooks bowling against Durham at Headingley in 2014.

toured Bangladesh with the England Lions in 2011/12, an honour repeated in South Africa three years later.

Although at times expensive, he regularly took wickets in his peak years through clever variations of length and he was Yorkshire's leading bowler for three consecutive seasons in which he took at least 60 wickets in each, a feat that no Yorkshire bowler had previously achieved more than once since the Championship's reduction in 1993. These years included each of the two Championship-winning campaigns of 2014 and 2015 in which he was a vital member of the team.

Brophy, Gerard Louis

Born: 26/11/1975, Welkom, Orange Free State, South Africa
RHB, WK. Career: 2006-12.
Cap No 162, 2008. Benefit: 2011

After four seasons with Northamptonshire, Gerard Brophy came to Yorkshire as a wicket-keeper/batsman. His first experience of first-class cricket had come in the country of his birth with Transvaal B in 1996 and he also represented Gauteng and Free State. His first cricket in England had been for Nottinghamshire 2nd XI, also in 1996,

and he became England-qualified when he moved to Yorkshire.

Brophy played a vital role within the team in all three forms of the game and often played important innings especially in white-ball cricket in which he occasionally opened the batting. His best innings in List A matches was 93 not out off 70 balls against Derbyshire at Headingley in 2010. An undemonstrative but efficient 'keeper his best season was in 2008 when he made 82 dismissals including 49 in first-class matches.

Broughton, Peter Norman

Born: 22/10/1935, Castleford
RHB, RFM. Career: 1956

A tall pace bowler who could make the ball lift awkwardly, Peter Broughton played for Castleford, before representing Yorkshire, then for Idle (as professional) and Leeds. In 1960 he moved to Leicestershire for three years and then had seven seasons with Cumberland. In his full career he took 85 wickets in his 30 first-class matches, his best performance being six for 38 against Somerset at Taunton in 1956.

Brown, Alfred

Born: 10/06/1854, Old Malton
Died: 02/11/1900, Malton
RHB, RRMF. Career: 1872

Both of Alfred Brown's games for Yorkshire were against Surrey, the first starting just seven days after his 18th birthday. He was a well-built, all-rounder who also excelled in athletics, but ill-health prevented him from being able to stand up to the rigours of the three-day game. He played for Malton for 25 years but mainly on an irregular basis.

Brown, John Thomas

Born: 20/08/1869, Driffield
Died: 04/11/1904, Pimlico,
Westminster, London
RHB, LB. Career: 1889-1904.
Cap No 17. Benefit: 1901

For ten seasons, during which Yorkshire won the Championship five times, 'Jack' Brown was one of a pair of regular opening batsmen whose exploits have acquired almost legendary status. He and John Tunnicliffe shared 19 century opening partnerships together including one which broke the world record for any wicket - 554 against Derbyshire at Chesterfield in 1898, Brown scoring exactly 300.

Appearing for Driffield at the age of 12, Brown topped its batting and bowling averages just two years later. Two years with Perth, Scotland, acted as a prelude to him gaining a place in the Yorkshire side. Unfortunately a severe bout of influenza prevented him playing regularly for two seasons but he managed to act as professional for Brighouse in 1892.

The first of Brown's ten (consecutive) 1,000-run seasons came in 1894 and he went to Australia in the following winter where he came top of England's Test batting averages with 343 runs in the five Tests at 42.47. In his innings of 140 in the final game at Melbourne his first 50 runs came in 28 minutes – a world record which stood for 112 years. It was his only Test century and he played only three more times for his country.

Short in stature but powerfully-built, Brown played the cut and pull particularly effectively, always looked neat and stylish and was a fine fielder in the covers. His leg-breaks looked innocent but brought him occasional success including a hat-trick against Derbyshire at Derby in 1896 and a best of six for 52 against Sussex at Bradford in 1898. His best season with the bat was in 1896 when he scored 1,873 runs in all first-class matches at 35.33. His career-best score of 311 came against Sussex a year later at Sheffield when he shared a stand of 378 with Tunnicliffe.

Aside from cricket, Brown played rugby for Driffield and also ran a sports shop in Halifax for eight years. Sadly, ill-health struck him again after the turn of the century; a heavy smoker who also suffered from asthma, the onset of heart trouble caused him to stop playing in May 1904 and although he was still only 35 by the time autumn came along recovery did not ensue and the addition of 'congestion of the brain' caused the inevitable at a tragically early age.

Brown, John Thomas

Born: 24/11/1874, Darfield, Barnsley
Died: 12/04/1950, Duckmanton,
Chesterfield, Derbyshire
RHB, RF. Career: 1897-1903.
Cap No 31

A genuine fast bowler, 'Jack' Brown would have achieved more but for injury. Tall and powerfully-built, he took 57 wickets in 1899, including eight for 40 against Gloucestershire at Huddersfield, but a damaged knee restricted his county appearances. Managing to play league cricket, he was professional with Barnsley for four years and for two with Bacup. In his last season with Yorkshire he dislocated a shoulder at Taunton and played no more cricket thereafter. The elder brother of William, he fathered 14 children.

Brown, William

Born: 19/11/1876, Darfield, Barnsley
Died: 27/07/1945, Barnsley
RHB, RMF. Career: 1902-08

Two games, spaced six years apart, was the extent of William Brown's career in first-class cricket. In playing successfully for a number of clubs he forged a career in league cricket which included seven years with Barnsley, some as professional, and six with Farsley for whom he took 363 wickets.

Brownhill, Thomas

Born: 10/10/1838, Ecclesfield,
Sheffield
Died: 06/01/1915, Wortley, Sheffield
RHB. Career: 1863-71

Tom Brownhill played for several clubs in the Sheffield area as well as Ossett and Holbeck. His first appearance for 'Yorkshire' was in 1862, starting with a 'king pair', and he was a brilliant cover-point but had an undistinguished time for the county with the bat. He later spent four seasons in first-class cricket as an umpire.

Brumfitt, Jack

Born: 18/02/1917, Guiseley, Leeds
Died: 16/03/1987, Ilkley
RHB. Career: 1938. Amateur

A solid and reliable opening batsman in league cricket, Jack Brumfitt played mostly for Bradford and Ilkley and just once for Yorkshire. In his main sport of rugby union, he played for Ilkley, Otley and Coventry as well as Yorkshire and Warwickshire.

Buller, John Sydney

Born: 23/08/1909, Wortley, Leeds
Died: 07/08/1970, Edgbaston,
Birmingham
RHB, WK. Career: 1930

The presence of Arthur Wood as wicket-keeper in the Yorkshire side gave Syd Buller little opportunity and his one game was not in the Championship. He played for the second eleven for six seasons but then moved to Worcestershire in 1935 where he played in 110 matches until the end of 1946 scoring 1,732 runs and making 248 dismissals.

The following season Buller became a first-class umpire and was the most respected of his era. Playing a prominent role in the throwing controversy of the time he no-balled South African Geoff Griffin in the Lord's Test of 1960 and Harold Rhodes five years later, when playing for Derbyshire, and needed a police escort as a result. One of the first incidences of 'joke bowling' was reported by him to Lord's when Clive Inman made an eight-minute half-century for Leicestershire against Nottinghamshire in 1965. That was also the year in which he received the MBE.

Buller stood in over 600 first-class and List A matches, including 33 Tests from 1956, and collapsed and died during a rain-break when Warwickshire were playing Nottinghamshire.

Bulmer, John Robert Leopold

Born: 28/12/1867, Guisborough
Died: 20/01/1917, Werneth, Oldham, Lancashire
RHB, RFM. Career: 1891

John Bulmer's only game for Yorkshire was a Roses match. He played for several league clubs in Lancashire including four-year spells as professional with both Lancaster and Royton.

Burgess, Thomas

Born: 01/10/1859, Harrogate
Died: 15/02/1922, Harrogate
RHB, RMF. Career: 1895

Although he had four seasons with Batley, Tom Burgess played for most of his career – almost 20 years - for Harrogate. He was appointed groundsman and professional there in 1892 and in the following season took 100 wickets at 9.57. His only first-class match was also at Harrogate.

Burgin, Eric

Born: 04/01/1924, Pitsmoor, Sheffield
Died: 16/11/2012, Sheffield
RHB, RMF. Career: 1952-53

One of Fred Trueman's many opening partners, Eric Burgin made a good contrast with his slower-paced in-swing. He twice took five wickets in an innings and these were against Yorkshire's greatest rivals of the time – Lancashire and Surrey. He spent a long time with Sheffield United as successful player and coach. As a soccer player he played for and captained York City as a centre-half.

Burman, John

Born: 05/10/1838, Bramham, Leeds
Died: 14/05/1900, Halton, Leeds
?HB. Career: 1867

John Burman played for at least eight different clubs, including Dewsbury, Knaresborough, Ossett and Scarborough. He took part in 11 games against the All-England XI but appeared only once for Yorkshire.

Burnet, John Ronald

Born: 11/10/1918, Saltaire, Bradford
Died: 06/03/1999, Greenhow, Pateley Bridge
RHB, OB. Career: 1958-59. Amateur.
Cap No 100, 1958

After several years of dressing-room divisions, Ronnie Burnet was given the leadership of Yorkshire with the instruction to sort matters out. Although never having played first-class cricket and being aged 39, he had captained the second eleven from 1953, this including victory in the Minor Counties Championship in 1957.

Burnet had previously led Baildon to three consecutive titles but in his first season with Yorkshire the county finished only eleventh. However, the sacking of Johnny Wardle and the retirement of Bob Appleyard restored harmony and Yorkshire won the Championship in the following season.

After retiring, Burnet joined the Yorkshire committee but was ousted in the revolution of the 1980s. Following his services as chairman of Yorkshire's Sports Council he was awarded the OBE.

Burrows, Matthew

Born: 18/08/1855, Chesterfield, Derbyshire
Died: 29/05/1893, Beeston, Leeds
RHB, RRFM. Career: 1880

A solid opening batsman, Matt Burrows was professional with Friarmere in 1879-80 before playing for Dewsbury and Savile as well as Holbeck. He also played one match for Derbyshire in 1884 and had one season with Galashiels, Scotland, in 1886. He was given several opportunities in his one season with Yorkshire.

Burton, David Cecil Fowler

Born: 13/09/1887, Bridlington
Died: 24/09/1971, Chertsey, Surrey
RHB. Career: 1907-21. Amateur.
Cap No 45

In captaining Yorkshire to the County Championship in 1919 and top-four finishes in each of the next two seasons, Cecil Burton laid the foundations for the successful 1920s.

After Rugby School, Burton played both cricket and rugby at Cambridge but gained a Blue in neither sport. In 1910/11 he went on MCC's first tour of West Indies but did not establish himself in Yorkshire's side before the First World War. However, because he was a fine sprinter he set an example with his fine out-fielding and this contributed to his post-War appointment.

Burton scored his first century - 142 not out, which remained a career-best - in 1919 against Hampshire at Dewsbury; he shared in a seventh-wicket stand of 254 with Wilfred Rhodes and this stood as Yorkshire's record for 96 years.

In 1956 Burton established an indoor cricket school at Sunningdale, Berkshire.

Burton, Robert Claude

Born: 11/04/1891, Bridlington
Died: 30/04/1971, Stone Cross,
Pevensey, Sussex
RHB, RM/S. Career: 1914. Amateur

Brother of Cecil, Claude Burton attended Malvern School and Oxford. He played for the University for three seasons without gaining a Blue and also for irregular sides such as Authentics, Free Foresters and Harlequins. His subtle variety of pace made him a deceptive bowler but his Yorkshire career was very short.

Butterfield, Edward Banks

Born: 22/10/1848, Keighley
Died: 06/05/1899, Keighley
RHB. Career: 1870. Amateur

A solid opening batsman, 'Ted' Butterfield's only first-class match was against Nottinghamshire, and he also played for Keighley for over ten seasons.

Byas, David

Born: 26/08/1963, Kilham, Driffield
LHB, RMF. Career: 1986-2001.
Cap No 131, 1991. Benefit: 2000

On August 24th, 2001 Yorkshire skipper David Byas stood under a high ball on his home ground of Scarborough waiting for a catch which would soon take the county to its first Championship title for 33 years.

While still a schoolboy at Scarborough College, Byas joined Scarborough CC and, at the age of 22, was appointed captain. He had seemed destined to one day lead Yorkshire and he did so for six seasons. In first coming to prominence as a very powerful batsman he scored 1,394 runs for his club in his fifth season of 1984. Once with Yorkshire he developed into one of the best left-handers in the country, made the number three position his own and provided solidity.

Byas came close to Test cricket in 1995 when he was put on stand-by in what was his best season – 1,913 runs including a career-best of 213 against Worcestershire at Scarborough. Limited-overs cricket also produced an outstanding record and only Geoff Boycott has scored more runs for Yorkshire than he. Added to this was his brilliant slip-fielding and as an all-round sportsman he also played hockey for Yorkshire and England.

Officially, Byas retired after 2001 but had one season with Lancashire before being Yorkshire's Director of Cricket for four years and then coaching at Pocklington School.

Byrom, John Lewis

Born: 20/07/1851, Saddleworth
Died: 24/08/1931, Delph
RHB, RRM. Career: 1874. Amateur

The winners of the Huddersfield League each year receive the Byrom Shield and it was John Byrom who donated it and whom it is named after.

After having played briefly for Yorkshire he built a terrace of 12 houses for the members of Friarmere

David Byas, Yorkshire's captain, with the 2001 County Championship trophy at Scarborough.

CC for which he was, in turn, captain, secretary and president. His ambitious plans came to full fruition in 1921 when the club won both the League title and the Sykes Cup. The houses still stand and so does the club's pavilion which he also had erected. The places where he was born and died are now part of Oldham, Lancashire.

The Byrom Shield.

Callis, Elliot

Born: 08/11/1994, Doncaster
RHB, LB. Career: 2014

Educated at Worksop College, Elliot Callis played for Sheffield Collegiate in two spells – before having four years with the Yorkshire Academy and after playing for Bedfordshire in 2015. His one game for the county was a List A match against Sri Lanka A.

Cammish, James William

Born: 21/05/1921, Scarborough
Died: 16/07/1974, Napier, New Zealand
RHB, LBG. Career: 1954

James Cammish took 22 wickets in five first-class matches for Auckland in 1950/51 before returning to Scarborough and then playing for Leeds. One of his two matches for Yorkshire was in the Championship.

Carrick, Phillip

Born: 16/07/1952, Armley, Leeds
Died: 11/01/2000, Steeton, Keighley
RHB, SLA. Career: 1970-93.
Cap No 117, 1976. Benefit: 1985
Testimonial: 1994

The most recent significant member of Yorkshire's long line of quality left-arm spinners, Phil Carrick served the county long and well. So much early promise was shown that he played for Farsley at the age of 14 and for Yorkshire when only 18. After spells as professional with Guisborough and Pudsey St Lawrence he gained a regular place in the county side in 1973 taking what remained a career-best eight for 33 against Cambridge University. Two years later he played a vital role in the county gaining runners-up spot in the County Championship by being the side's leading wicket-taker with 79 wickets; this remained his best season.

In Carrick's early career he gave the ball air and aimed to deceive the batsman with flight as well as spin. His career coincided with the increased covering of pitches, however, and so he developed into a more defensive bowler, aiming close to leg stump. This policy made him very effective in limited-overs matches and he bowled economically in this form of the game.

One of the survivors of the controversies which were so disruptive to Yorkshire during the first part of his career, Carrick was appointed Yorkshire captain for the 1987 season and immediately led his team to victory in the Benson and Hedges Cup, in a nail-biting final at Lord's, as well as eighth place in the Championship – the county's best for seven years. He skippered the side for three seasons and such was his concern for Yorkshire's well-being that he tried to encourage the committee to abandon its only-Yorkshire-born policy.

Brief experiences in South African cricket with Eastern Province and Northern Transvaal led to several seasons coaching in that country and he played for Cheshire after retirement from the first-class game.

Carrick often batted in a determined manner (he scored three centuries), especially when others had failed, and he scored over 10,000 runs in all first-class matches as well as taking over 1,000 wickets. The second

of only three players to do the 2,000-run and 200-wicket double for Yorkshire in List A matches, he was on the reserve list of first-class umpires when he met his tragically early death at the age of 47. A quiet and unassuming man, he was a most popular player and captain.

Carter, Edmund Sardinson
Born: 03/02/1845, Malton
Died: 23/05/1923, Scarborough
RHB, RF, Lobs, WK.
Career: 1876-81. Amateur

A colourful and influential character, 'Teddy' Carter gained a Blue at Oxford for cricket, as well as rowing, in 1865-67 and also played for Victoria, Australia, in 1868/69 where he was convalescing.

Carter helped to form Ealing CC after joining the clergy in the London suburb but from 1875 worked in York, firstly at the Minster, and from 1908 at Thwing, Scarborough. With Lord Londesborough he staged the early Scarborough Festivals – where he introduced Lord Hawke - and his main club was Yorkshire Gentlemen for whom he played for 36 years.

Cartman, William Henry
Born: 20/06/1861, Skipton
Died: 16/01/1935, Skipton
RHB. Career: 1891

William Cartman played for the town of his birth for at least 15 years; he was professional there for a time as well as for two years at Enfield, Lancashire. A free-scoring batsman, he played in three games in the County Championship. He played rugby union for Skipton, whom he also captained.

Carver, Karl
Born: 26/03/1996, Northallerton
LHB, SLA. Career: 2014-

Karl Carver made his first-class debut for Yorkshire in the season prior to making first appearances in both of the white-ball competitions. He had four seasons in the Academy team and played in club cricket for Sessay and Sheriff Hutton Bridge. He varies his bowling style according to the format but he created an unwanted record in 2017 by becoming the first Yorkshire bowler to be struck for six sixes in an over, courtesy of Ross Whiteley for Worcestershire in a T20 match at Headingley.

Cawthray, George
Born: 28/09/1913, Brayton, Selby
Died: 05/01/2001, Leeds
LHB, RMF. Career: 1939-52

Best-known as Headingley's groundsman for 12 years from 1964, George Cawthray scored over 8,000 runs and took over 800 wickets for Hull in a 20-year spell. The club employed him as a professional cricketer as well as groundsman from 1946; his earlier clubs were Cawood and Selby Londesborough and he later joined Leeds. His four games for Yorkshire consisted of two in each of his two seasons and were all in the County Championship.

George Cawthray when with Leeds CC in 1964, the year he became Headingley's groundsman.

Unfortunately, Cawthray was at the forefront of controversies which affected two Headingley Tests against Australia. In 1972 the pitch was attacked by a fungus, the game finishing in fewer than three days, and three years later the pitch was vandalised before the final day's play. Following retirement he worked in a consultation capacity for several clubs.

Chadwick, John Peter Granville
Born: 08/11/1934, Pateley Bridge
RHB, RM. Career: 1960-65
Peter Chadwick's first club was Pateley Bridge and he returned there in the 1980s but between times played for Harrogate for 31 years, including two as captain, as well as Great Horton. For Harrogate he scored over 20,000 runs and took over 600 wickets and was also a brilliant slip fielder. He played for Yorkshire only in first-class cricket and very irregularly.

Champion, Albert
Born: 27/12/1851, Hollins End, Handsworth, Sheffield
Died: 26/06/1909, Sheffield
LHB, RRM. Career: 1876-79
Although, as a batsman, Albert Champion averaged fewer than eight for Yorkshire his first-class career ended when he had two ribs broken by a fast ball. He played for clubs on each side of the Pennines, including Accrington, Batley, Bacup, Longsight and Pitsmoor as well as United North of England XI. His other first-class teams were Lancashire and Liverpool & District.

Chapman, Colin Anthony
Born: 08/06/1971, Bradford
RHB, WK. Career: 1990-98
Colin Chapman played in a total of 18 first-class and List A matches for Yorkshire as a substitute wicket-keeper/batsman for Richard Blakey. Small in stature, he was an attacking batsman who occasionally opened. His only half-century was in the Roses match of 1997 at Headingley and his clubs were Bingley and Pudsey Congs. He later coached at Southport and Birkdale CC.

Charlesworth, Albert Percy
Born: 19/02/1865, Chapel Allerton, Leeds
Died: 11/05/1926, Hull
RHB. Career: 1894-95
Albert Charlesworth started with a pair, when he opened the batting, and was soon dropped but batted better in his second season when he made his top score of 63 against Nottinghamshire at Trent Bridge. His clubs included Morley but he was also professional with Harrogate, Hull and Rawtenstall.

Chichester-Constable, Raleigh Charles Joseph
Born: 21/12/1890, Great Marlow, Buckinghamshire
Died: 26/05/1963, Burton Constable, Hull
RHB, RF. Career: 1919. Amateur

Raleigh Chichester-Constable, CBE made only one appearance for Yorkshire but played for the second eleven for 13 seasons – all as captain - from 1926. Of his 24 first-class matches 19 were for MCC. He was made an honorary life member of Yorkshire CCC and continued to serve the Club on the committee after his playing days which included leading Hull Town to its first Yorkshire League title in 1936. He was awarded the DSO in both World Wars.

Clarkson, Anthony
Born: 05/09/1939, Killinghall, Harrogate
RHB, RM/OB. Career: 1963

Tony Clarkson had a very brief career with Yorkshire but in six seasons with Somerset he played in 104 first-class matches, scoring 4,378 runs, and 50 List A matches. In 1969 at Northampton he became the first English player to score a century in the Sunday League. He also played for Devon, while with Torquay, and

other clubs included Darlington RA, Harrogate, Middlesbrough and Windhill. He umpired in first-class cricket from 1992 to 2004.

Claughton, Hugh Marsden
Born: 24/12/1891, Guiseley, Leeds
Died: 17/10/1980, Middleton-in-Wharfedale, Ilkley
RHB, RMF. Career: 1914-19

An all-rounder whose short Yorkshire career was badly interrupted by the First World War, Hugh Claughton played for many clubs on both sides of the Pennines and in Scotland. These included Baildon Green, Darwen, Ramsbottom, Stockton-on-Tees, Tong Park, Werneth and Windhill. A great-nephew, John Claughton, played for Warwickshire.

Claydon, Mitchell Eric
Born: 25/11/1982, Fairfield, New South Wales, Australia
LHB, RMF. Career: 2005-06

England-qualified, despite his birthplace, Mitch Claydon's 17 games for Yorkshire all came in the first half of the 2006 season except for one first-class game, which was his debut match in that format. Although a useful bowler he took only 16 wickets and most of his appearances were in white-ball cricket. He joined Durham in 2007 and after six seasons moved to Kent where he achieved much greater success.

Clayton, Robert Owen
Born: 01/01/1844, Penygroes, Carmarthenshire, Wales
Died: 26/11/1901, Gainsborough, Lincolnshire
RHB, RF/MF. Career: 1870-79

In taking eight wickets in his first

match, against Surrey, Bob Clayton clearly demonstrated his potential. Although he took 18 five-fors in his 12-season first-class career, which included 33 games for MCC, his promise remained largely unfulfilled, despite a career-best eight for 66 against Lancashire at Old Trafford in 1877. Tom Emmett, his skipper, believed that he did not think enough about each batsman's weaknesses.

Originally thought to have been born near Otley it is now known that Clayton is another of Yorkshire's 'foreigners'. He joined the Lord's ground staff in 1872 and remained there until his death. His final years included 25 as a first-class umpire and coaching at several schools.

Cleary, Mark Francis

Born: 19/07/1980, Moorabbin, Melbourne, Australia
LHB, RFM. Career: 2005

A useful pace bowler, Mark Cleary played in just six games for Yorkshire in first-class and List A cricket at the end of the 2005 season as a replacement for batsman Phil Jaques. An itinerant cricketer, he also played for Leicestershire, Netherlands, South Australia, Victoria and Wellington as well as Colne in league cricket.

Clegg, Henry

Born: 08/12/1850, High Town, Dewsbury
Died: 30/12/1920, Dewsbury
RHB. Career: 1881

A middle-order batsman, Henry Clegg played briefly for Yorkshire but for several clubs especially Dewsbury in the 1890s but also including Batley, Bury, Bradford and Saltaire. At Little Lever he combined playing with being groundsman.

Clifford, Christopher Craven

Born: 05/07/1942, Hovingham, Malton
RHB, OB. Career: 1972

Chris Clifford played for Yorkshire while fellow off-spinner Geoff Cope was suspended and Warwickshire later gave him a second chance, him remaining with them for three seasons. A stalwart with Scarborough for over 30 years he was in the side which won the National Club Knock-out in 1976. He trained as a PE teacher, coached in South Africa and taught in Scarborough.

Close, Dennis Brian

Born: 24/02/1931, Rawdon, Leeds
Died: 14/09/2015, Baildon
LHB, RM/OB. Career: 1949-70.
Cap No 91, 1949. Benefit: 1961
Testimonial: 1970

One of Yorkshire's greatest cricketers, Brian Close was an outstanding all-rounder and brilliant captain. He led the county from 1963 for eight seasons (only Lord Hawke and Brian Sellers have led it for longer) during which there were four Championship successes and two Gillette Cup wins.

Close made his Yorkshire debut at the age of 18, became England's youngest-ever Test cricketer in the same season and remains the youngest player to complete the double of 1,000 runs and 100 wickets. A naturally-talented sportsman – he played soccer for Leeds United, Arsenal and Bradford City – he was one of the best-left-handed batsmen in the country for many years, demonstrating real power in his attacking strokes. He bowled off-spin or at medium pace with a high action and often took wickets when the

main bowlers failed to do so. A legendary fielder, he stood in what others would consider to be suicidal positions and took many blows but never flinched.

However a story of 22 Tests spread over 28 seasons was the consequence of the selectors not being sure how best to use him. His longest sequences were five against the West Indies in 1963, when he memorably held a fierce pace attack at bay, and a run of seven games as captain (six won, one drawn) in 1966/67. Time-wasting in a county match, for which he refused to apologise, led to his sacking but he returned to play at the age of 45, again against West Indies, and suffered even

more attacks on his body from a merciless battery of fast bowlers.

By this time he was leading Somerset, having been sacked by Yorkshire in highly controversial circumstances, and helped to launch the careers of Viv Richards and Ian Botham. The latter, in his funeral oration, described Close as 'the best captain a young player could ever have'. A positive approach was the hallmark of his leadership; he always wanted to try something new or different in order to force a result.

His final first-class match came at the age of 55 by which time he had scored almost 35,000 runs, taken over 1,100 wickets and more than 800

Close batting in the Headingley Test of 1963 against West Indies. Lance Gibbs is at short- leg.

catches. He had already returned to Yorkshire, captained the Academy team and acted as chairman of the cricket committee. He was awarded the CBE in 1975 – a richly-deserved honour.

Clough, Gareth David
Born: 23/05/1978, Leeds
RHB, RM. Career: 1998

Gareth Clough played in just one match for Yorkshire, after two years with the Academy. Three years later he began an eight-season career with Nottinghamshire for whom he became a limited-overs specialist especially with his economical bowling. He played in 135 such games for his new county but in only 11 first-class matches. After leaving Nottinghamshire in 2008 he had two seasons with Lincolnshire.

Coad, Benjamin Oliver
Born: 10/01/1994, Harrogate
RHB, RMF. Career: 2013-

Ben Coad attended Thirsk School and was with the Academy for four seasons before playing for Yorkshire initially mainly in white-ball cricket, him not making his first-class debut until 2016. However, he made a big impact in 2017 with his skilful swing and seam bowling and took 50 wickets in the Championship, him being easily Yorkshire's leading bowler. He has played club cricket for Studley Royal and Harrogate.

Collinson, Robert Whiteley
Born: 06/11/1875, Moss Side, Halifax
Died: 26/12/1963, Thorpe St Andrew, Norwich
RHB. Career: 1897. Amateur

A good all-round sportsman, Robert Collinson was with Keighley before his two games with Yorkshire. He moved to Norfolk shortly afterwards, playing for that county for 14 seasons as well as Carrow. Having represented Yorkshire at rugby union he later played soccer for Norwich City!

Cooper, Howard Pennett
Born: 17/04/1949, Great Horton, Bradford
LHB, RMF. Career: 1971-80

Successful more in List A than first-class cricket, Howard Cooper's bowling often restricted the attacking instincts of opposing batsmen in this form of the game; his career rate of conceding fewer than four runs per over clearly indicates this. However, he carried a persistent back injury and this caused him to modify his action as well as bowl 'within himself' – economy rather than penetration.

A slow surface would present Cooper's bowling as tricky and at Cardiff in 1975 he took eight for 62 in a Championship match against Glamorgan. Figures of six for 14 at Worcester in a JPL match in 1975 have been beaten only twice for Yorkshire in List A games. His main clubs were Bankfoot, Bradford and Pudsey St Lawrence.

Cooper, Philip Edward

Born: 19/02/1885, Rotherham
Died: 21/05/1950, Hoveton,
Wroxham, Norfolk
RHB. Career: 1910. Amateur

Later known as Peter Whiteoak-Cooper, Philip Cooper made a pair, did not bowl nor take a catch in his one game for Yorkshire. He had earlier played for Rotherham and Sheffield United and captained Kent second eleven for two seasons in the early-1920s.

Cope, Geoffrey Alan

Born: 23/02/1947, Burmantofts, Leeds
RHB, OB. Career: 1966-80.
Cap No 114, 1970. Benefit: 1980

Geoff Cope bowling in the nets in 1968.

After appearing for Leeds and Otley, Geoff Cope first played for Yorkshire at the age of 19. For his first three seasons he played mostly when Ray Illingworth was unavailable but when the senior off-spinner left at the end of 1968 the role was his. Two years later he justified the faith placed in him with a season's haul of 83 first-class wickets.

Unfortunately, Cope's career was dogged by controversy over his action and he was twice suspended by the TCCB – in 1972 and 1978. Between these two actions he had the best period of his career taking at least 50 first-class wickets in each of four consecutive seasons from 1974 and formed a very effective partnership with Phil Carrick. When Yorkshire gained the runners-up spot in the County Championship in 1975 the pair took 47% of their opponents' wickets.

Cope played in three Tests – all against Pakistan in 1977/78 – and two ODIs. After retirement he played for Lincolnshire, for four seasons, and Yeadon. Having been elected on to the county committee in 1998, he was a founder-member of the Board when it was formed in 2002 and worked as Operations Director for three years.

Corbett, Alexander Melvin

Born: 25/11/1855, Aston, Rotherham
Died: 07/10/1934, Kimberworth, Rotherham
RHB. Career: 1881

After early cricket with Elsecar and Rotherham, Alexander Corbett made a pair in his only game for Yorkshire. In his first innings he was caught off bat and forehead by WG Grace.

Coverdale, Stephen Peter

Born: 20/11/1954, York
RHB, WK. Career: 1973-80

Playing for Sheriff Hutton Bridge and York while at St Peter's School gave Stephen Coverdale good experience before gaining Blues (1974-77) at Cambridge University. Deputising for David Bairstow, he played for Yorkshire once in 1973 and eight times in 1980 in both forms of the game. After playing for Harrogate he moved to Northamptonshire where he was chief executive for 19 years.

Coverdale, William

Born: 08/07/1862, Pickering
Died: 23/09/1934, Bridlington
?HB, WK. Career: 1888

William Coverdale's league clubs were Bridlington, Pickering, whom he captained, and Rotherham Town. He was one of a few wicket-keepers who Yorkshire tried in 1888 between the Hunter brothers.

Cowan, Michael Joseph

Born: 10/06/1933, Leeds
RHB, LFM. Career: 1953-62
Cap No 104, 1960

One of Fred Trueman's several opening partners, Mike Cowan suffered much from injuries and 1960 was his only full season. A back injury caused him to return home early from Pakistan when touring with MCC in 1955/56 and he later missed the whole of the 1959 season.

While with Yorkshire Cowan played for Bingley for two seasons and came first or second in each in the Bradford League averages. Other clubs included Littleborough, Rochdale and Doncaster Town whom he captained in 1970-74 and he also played for Northumberland. A negligible batsman, he has the very rare distinction, in first-class cricket, of taking more wickets than scoring runs. He later became a brilliant after-dinner speaker.

Cownley, John Michael

Born: 24/02/1929, Wales, Sheffield
Died: 07/11/1998, Stalybridge, Cheshire
LHB, RMF, LBG. Career: 1952

Ten years after playing for Yorkshire Michael Cownley put in two appearances for Lancashire but only one of his total of four first-class matches was in the County Championship. He also played for the UAU and represented Sheffield University as a boxer. Originally a pace bowler he switched to spin and captained Timperley, Cheshire.

Coxon, Alexander

Born: 18/01/1916, Huddersfield
Died: 22/01/2006, Roker, Sunderland, Durham
RHB, RMF. Career: 1945-50.
Cap no 81, 1947

After playing for Brighouse and Saltaire, amongst others, Alec Coxon had to wait until the end of World War II before making his Yorkshire debut. He duly first played in the County Championship at the age of 30 but then gave his all. In making a real impact in his first full season he took a career-best of eight for 31, including the hat-trick, against Worcestershire at Headingley.

Coxon's one Test came in 1948 at Lord's against the all-conquering Australians when he took three top-

order wickets but they cost him 172 runs. He bounced back by taking 100 wickets in each of his final two seasons and then settled in Durham where he played for the (then minor) county for four years as well as Sunderland, South Shields and Wearmouth. He died just four days after his 90th birthday.

Craven, Victor John

Born: 31/07/1980, Harrogate
LHB, RM. Career: 2000-04

An opening and middle-order batsman as well as useful bowler Vic Craven played in 81 games for Yorkshire in all three forms of the game without ever really establishing himself in the team. He played in more List A games than in any other type of cricket where his bowling often came in handy – his best of four for 22 against Kent at Scarborough in 2003 was a match-winning performance.

Craven never made a century for Yorkshire but continued to be a prolific batsman in league cricket. His main club was Harrogate, with whom he had two spells, before moving to Bilton, where he later became captain, but he also played for Methley and had three seasons with Cumberland. He retired from the game in 2017.

Crawford, George Henry

Born: 15/12/1890, Hull
Died: 28/06/1975, Cottingham, Hull
RHB, RFM. Career: 1914-26

Nine matches spread over three seasons were the sum total of George Crawford's experience in first-class cricket. A good pace bowler, his best of five for 59 was against Surrey at Sheffield in 1926. Always based in Hull, he played for Hull Town and ran a sports shop in the city.

Crawford, Michael Grove

Born: 30/07/1920, Moortown, Leeds
Died: 02/12/2012, York
RHB. Career: 1951. Amateur

Michael Crawford in his administrative days with Yorkshire.

Michael Crawford led the second eleven for three seasons during which time he captained Yorkshire in his only first-class match. After Shrewsbury School he failed to make the first team at Cambridge but gained a Blue at soccer. He captained Leeds for about 15 seasons including its first Yorkshire League title in 1958. He served Yorkshire CCC for 21 years as treasurer and then chairman until ousted in the controversies of 1984.

Creighton, Ernest

Born: 09/07/1859, Hemsworth, Wakefield
Died: 17/02/1931, Leeds
?HB, SLA. Career: 1888

In taking ten wickets in four consecutive matches Ernest Creighton seemed to have established himself in the Yorkshire side but Bobby Peel was the preferred bowler of his type so that was the end of his first-class career. He was very successful in club cricket with Accrington, Bacup, Burnley and Ramsbottom and he took over 900 wickets in nine seasons with Todmorden.

Crick, Harry

Born: 29/01/1910, Ecclesall, Sheffield
Died: 10/02/1960, Lower Wyke, Bradford
RHB, WK. Career: 1937–47

In a career interrupted by the War, during which he made 70 flights over Germany and became a flight-lieutenant, Harry Crick was given a run of games in 1947 but age was against him. He continued to work for the RAF and was killed in a road accident.

Crookes, Ralph

Born: 09/10/1846, Sheffield
Died: 15/02/1897, Ecclesall, Sheffield
?HB. Career: 1879

Ralph Crookes played just one match for Yorkshire - against Kent at Maidstone – in which he scored two runs and bowled ten wicketless overs.

Crossland, Samual Moorhouse

Born: 16/08/1851, Leeds
Died: 11/04/1906, Wakefield
RHB, WK. Career: 1883–86

Son of Andrew Crossland (see Appendix 1), Sam was a useful reserve 'keeper for Yorkshire. He played much of his club cricket in the Wakefield area including for Hodgson's and Simpson's.

Crowther, Arthur

Born: 01/08/1878, Leeds
Died: 04/06/1946, East Bierley, Bradford
RHB. Career: 1905

Arthur Crowther made a pair in his only game for Yorkshire, against Warwickshire at Edgbaston. His early clubs were Staincliffe and Dewsbury but in 1911 he made 244 for Batley in the Heavy Woollen Cup final. He later played for Heckmondwike and Ossett.

Cuttell, William

Born: 28/01/1835, Sheffield
Died: 10/06/1896, Sheffield
RHB. Career: 1863-71

William Cuttell played in one match for 'Yorkshire' in 1862; his best season was in 1865 when he recorded both his only half century – against Kent at Cranbrook - and his best bowling figures of six for 48 against Surrey at The Oval. He played for a host of clubs including Accrington, Scarborough, Darlington and Buxton.

Dalton, Andrew John

Born: 14/03/1947, Horsforth, Leeds
RHB. Career: 1969-72

A highly promising, attractive and attacking batsman, Andrew Dalton played in 38 matches for Yorkshire in two forms of the game. On three occasions he passed 50 in first-class cricket and scored a century each time. Captain of Leeds Grammar School first eleven for two seasons, he also played for Newcastle University. After leaving Yorkshire through not wishing to play full-time he was professional with South Northumberland as well as Undercliffe and Leeds.

Darnton, Thomas

Born: 12/02/1836, Stockton-on-Tees
Died: 18/10/1874, Stockton-on-Tees
RHB, RRM. Career: 1864-68

An opening batsman and good all-round cricketer, Tom Darnton's one half-century was a score of 81 not out in a total of 144 against the All England XI in Sheffield in 1865. A colourful character, he played for a host of clubs mostly in the north-east, the main ones being Darlington and Middlesbrough, but also ventured as far south as Dewsbury. His death, at the age of 38, was caused by consumption.

Davidson, Kenneth Richard

Born: 24/12/1905, Calverley, Leeds
Died: 25/12/1954, Prestwick, Ayrshire, Scotland
RHB. Career: 1933–35.
Cap No 72, 1934

Ken Davidson's early cricket was with Bingley and Leeds, whom he captained. He played for Yorkshire in 1933 as an amateur but then turned professional and scored 1,231 runs in 1934 including his two centuries. A stylish middle-order batsman, he forsook cricket for badminton, at which he also played professionally, and represented Yorkshire. He tragically met his death in an air crash at Prestwick aerodrome while accompanying the USA badminton team on a world tour.

Dawes, Joseph

Born: 14/02/1836, Hallam, Sheffield
Died: unknown
RHB, RRF. Career: 1865

Joe Dawes made his debut for Yorkshire while coach at Eton – a post he held for four years. A useful all-rounder, his club cricket took place mostly in the south of the county, including appearances for Sheffield and Derbyshire in its pre-official days. He later coached with the Royal Artillery at Woolwich.

Dawood, Ismail

Born: 23/07/1976, Dewsbury
RHB, WK. Career: 2004-05

A successful wicket-keeper with the Academy, Yorkshire's first team did not have a vacancy at the time so Ismail Dawood tried his luck with three other counties (Northamptonshire, Worcestershire and Glamorgan) in six years. He settled with Herefordshire and followed a university course which gave opportunity to play for Leeds/Bradford. Yorkshire then came knocking and he became the first British-born Asian to play for the county in the Championship but after 56 games in all three formats he was released. One season with Cheshire was succeeded by club cricket with East Bierley and Hanging Heaton.

Dawson, Edwin

Born: 01/05/1835, Dalton, Huddersfield
Died: 01/12/1888, Bradford
RHB, RM. Career: 1863-74

'Ned' Dawson had one game for 'Yorkshire' in 1862 and in the following season appeared in the County Club's first-ever game. Tall, he never bowled in first-class cricket but was a hard-hitting batsman who played for many clubs, his longest spells being with Leeds and Bradford.

Dawson, Richard Kevin James

Born: 04/08/1980, Doncaster
RHB, OB. Career: 2001-06.
Cap No 154, 2004

Richard Dawson played for Devon, while studying at Exeter University, when aged 18 and made his debut for Yorkshire two years later followed by the first of his seven Tests at the age of 21, gaining his England cap before his Yorkshire one.

As an off-spinner of potential he played in nine Championship matches in his first season and took 30 wickets – the third-best in a title-winning season. A total of 40 wickets in 2002 were followed by a decline, sadly, and after 2006 he spent one season with Northamptonshire and

then four with Gloucestershire. Thereafter he went into coaching and for 2014 returned to the county of his birth to oversee the second eleven. In 2015, however, he became Head Coach of Gloucestershire and helped it win the Royal London Cup in his first season in the post.

Dawson, William Arthur

Born: 03/12/1850, Bradford
Died: 06/03/1916, Ilkley
RHB, RM. Career: 1870. Amateur

William Dawson made a pair, did not bowl and took one catch in his only game for Yorkshire. His clubs included Bradford and Leeds Clarence. A talented sportsman, he gained a Blue in athletics at Cambridge in 1872 and played rugby union for Bradford and Yorkshire.

Day, Albert George

Born: 20/09/1865, Dewsbury
Died: 16/10/1908, Dewsbury
RHB. Career: 1885-88. Amateur

Only two of Albert Day's six

matches for Yorkshire were county games. He batted in the middle-order and had a long connection with the Dewsbury and Savile club.

Dennis, Frank

Born: 11/06/1907, Holbeck, Leeds
Died: 21/11/2000, Christchurch, New Zealand
LHB, RFM. Career: 1928-33
Cap No 64, 1929

The 1929 season was Frank Dennis' first full campaign and he took 76 wickets in the County Championship with his lively bowling. Although given his county cap, he never again gained a regular place in the side. Awkward when bowling a full length, his main suit was complemented by his aggressive batting.

Dennis spent the last five seasons before the War with Cheshire and he also played for Oxton, as professional, in the same county. His other clubs included Hickleton Main, Hull, Baildon and Undercliffe. In 1948 he emigrated to New Zealand and was a selector for Canterbury CA. His brother-in-law was Len Hutton and Simon Dennis was a nephew.

Dennis, Simon John

Born: 18/10/1960, South Cliff, Scarborough
RHB, LFM. Career: 1980-88
Cap No 125, 1983

Simon Dennis showed considerable promise as a 16-year-old when he played for Yorkshire U-25 and also on his debut three years later. In 1983 he gained a regular place in the Yorkshire side but both injuries and illness took their toll. His bowling lost its rhythm and pace and, on his release, joining Glamorgan for three seasons produced no better results.

After leaving the first-class scene Dennis had one season with Lincolnshire and captained Bingley. Len Hutton and Frank Dennis were both uncles and Richard Hutton a cousin.

Denton, David

Born: 04/07/1874, Thornes, Wakefield
Died: 16/02/1950, Thornes, Wakefield
RHB, RMF. Career: 1894-1920.
Cap No 25 Benefit: 1907

Only Herbert Sutcliffe has scored more runs for Yorkshire than David Denton who made the number three position his own for a quarter of a century. Although slightly-built, he was a stylish and adventurous batsman – one of the most polished professionals of his time - who scored equally-well all round the wicket. With strong yet flexible wrists his off-side driving and leg-side shots could be used to great effect when the situation demanded and he usually scored quickly.

D. DENTON.

Denton first played for his home-town club and then Castleford before making his debut for Yorkshire just 12 days after his 20th birthday. He played in only four matches in 1894 but in the following season not only established himself in the first-choice eleven but passed 1,000 runs for the first time – a feat which he would go on to achieve on a total of 21 occasions. His best season came in 1905 when he scored 2,405 runs and this led to his Test debut in the same year at Headingley against Australia.

That game was the only one of Denton's 11 Tests on home soil. His other ten games were all in South Africa and he made his only Test century at Johannesburg on the 1909/10 tour when he scored an enterprising 104 in only 100 minutes. In 1912 he made the highest score of his first-class career – an innings of 221 against Kent at Tunbridge Wells – which was one of his three double-centuries and he also scored two centuries in a match three times.

An excellent outfielder, Denton only very rarely dropped a catch and his quick covering of the ground and fast returns made him one of the best of his time. Despite passing the 1,000-run mark yet again in 1920 he was aged 46 and ill-health forced his retirement. His incapacity meant the turning-down of the offer of a coaching position but in 1925 he returned to the field of play as an umpire and stood regularly in first-class matches for six seasons, continuing to do so occasionally until 1937 by which time he had begun to act as Yorkshire scorer. A long and varied career for a dedicated cricketer.

Denton, Joe
Born: 03/02/1865, Thornes, Wakefield
Died: 19/07/1946, Purston Jaglin, Wakefield
RHB. Career: 1887-88

Elder brother of David, Joe Denton was given a run in the Yorkshire side in 1887 but responded with only one half-century – against Sussex at Bradford. He had a long career with Hodgson's and Simpson's CC.

Dewse, Henry
Born: 23/02/1836, York
Died: 08/07/1910, York
RHB, RS Lobs, WK. Career: 1873

Henry Dewse, always known as Harry, spent the early part of his career keeping wicket for York for whom he played for over 30 years. He also had 14 seasons with Malton and played for Northumberland and Tynemouth as well. He was aged 37 when he played his one game for Yorkshire.

Deyes, George
Born: 11/02/1878, Southcoates, Hull
Died: 11/01/1963, Tipperlin, Edinburgh
RHB, RF. Career: 1905-07

A hostile fast bowler, George Deyes took a five-for on his debut against Somerset at Harrogate but took only one more in the Championship. Of his 17 games for Yorkshire 11 came in his final season. As a batsman he was a genuine number eleven, once scoring a mere three runs in 14 successive innings. Professional at Stone, he was with Staffordshire for five seasons from 1910 having previously played for Thirsk and Hull. He later became groundsman at George Watson's College, Edinburgh.

Dick, Robert Douglas

Born: 16/04/1889, Middlesbrough
Died: 14/12/1983, Guisborough
RHB, RFM. Career: 1911. Amateur

Robert Dick took 19 wickets in two second eleven matches and then played in one game in the County Championship. Those three appearances were his only ones for Yorkshire. His club cricket was for Redcar and Middlesbrough.

Dobson, Arthur

Born: 22/02/1854, Ilkley
Died: 17/09/1932, Horsforth, Leeds
RHB, RM. Career: 1879

In just two matches for Yorkshire Arthur Dobson scored one run in three innings, in two of which he opened the batting, did not bowl and took one catch. A good cover-point fielder, he was a useful bowler in club cricket mainly with Ilkley and Horsforth.

Doidge, Matthew James

Born: 02/07/1970, Horsforth, Leeds
LHB, SLA. Career: 1990

Matthew Doidge first played for Yorkshire's second eleven as an 18-year-old but in his one appearance in first-class cricket he did not bat and took no wickets in 24 overs. His early cricket was with Pudsey St Lawrence and Bowling Old Lane and he later played for, and captained, Pudsey Congs. He also represented YCB in six List A matches, scoring one half-century, but did not bowl.

Dolphin, Arthur

Born: 24/12/1885, Wilsden, Bradford
Died: 23/10/1942, Heaton, Bradford
RHB, WK. Career: 1905-27.
Cap No 42 Benefit: 1922

In the pantheon of Yorkshire's great wicket-keepers, Arthur Dolphin stands, chronologically, between David Hunter and Arthur Wood. He was unfortunate to be a contemporary of Herbert Strudwick otherwise he might well have played in more than one Test.

Dolphin first played for Wilsden as a 14-year-old and became the first county player – when aged 19 - from the Bradford League, duly taking over from Hunter in 1910. Short and lively, he had to deal with a wide variety of bowling in the Yorkshire side. Five significant left-arm bowlers, including George Hirst, Wilfred Rhodes and Roy Kilner, brought their own challenges of differing paces as well as spin and swing. Even right-arm bowlers such as George Macaulay delivered medium-paced off-breaks and so standing up to the stumps presented regular difficulties.

However, Dolphin practised his art with the minimum of fuss and was praised for his quick brain and exceptional eyesight which enabled him to create a huge number of stumpings, 31% of his dismissals coming in this way. His most successful season was in 1919 when he made 82 dismissals. As a lower-order batsman, often obstinate, he scored six of his seven half-centuries in the three seasons of 1914-20. His two highest innings were both against Essex at Leyton: in 1914 he made his highest score of 66 which he started in the role of nightwatchman and in 1919 he contributed 62 not out towards a century tenth-wicket stand which averted the follow-on.

Dolphin's one Test was at Melbourne on the disastrous 1920/21 tour and he also played in India with MCC in 1926/27 on a non-Test visit. He suffered from sciatica and had to retire at the age of 41 but umpired for ten seasons in first-class cricket, including standing in seven Tests, until 1939.

Douglas, Joseph Stanley

Born: 04/04/1903, Bradford
Died: 27/12/1971, Paignton, Devon
LHB, LM.
Career: 1925-34

As a left-arm bowler Stan Douglas was a useful reserve for Wilfred Rhodes and Hedley Verity. Of his 23 appearances, only six came in the 1925-32 period but he took exactly 20 wickets in each of 1933 and 1934. He twice topped the second eleven bowling averages three years in a row and took over 1,000 wickets in the Bradford League when with various clubs as a professional. A good coach, he helped develop Bob Appleyard's bowling.

Drake, Alonzo

Born: 16/04/1884, Parkgate,
Rotherham
Died: 14/02/1919, Honley,
Huddersfield
LHB, LSM. Career: 1909-14.
Cap No 48. Grant: 1919 (to widow)

To 'Lonza' Drake falls the distinction of being the first Yorkshire player to take ten wickets in an innings. At Weston-super-Mare in 1914 against Somerset his match-figures of 15 for 51 included a second-innings analysis of 10 for 35.

Early cricket with Sheffield United, Honley and Harrogate preceded Drake's short Yorkshire career. An authentic all-rounder with a batting average higher than his bowling, he scored over 1,400 runs in 1911 and completed the double two years later.

As a batsman he was a powerful stroke-player with a strong off-drive. Although he bowled at the pace of a spinner he gave the ball a natural swing in either direction. A good soccer player, his clubs included Sheffield United and Huddersfield Town. He died of ill-health mainly caused by him being a heavy smoker.

Drake, John

Born: 01/09/1893, Tong Park, Baildon, Bradford
Died: 22/05/1967, Meanwood, Leeds
RHB, RMF. Career: 1923-24

Despite being a pace bowler of note in club cricket, Jack Drake took only one wicket in his three games for Yorkshire. He began his career with Tong Park, became professional at Saltaire and was later with Guiseley and Windhill. He spent 35 years in London as player and groundsman in Highbury.

Driver, Jeremiah

Born: 16/05/1861, Keighley
Died: 10/12/1946, Keighley
RHB, WK. Career: 1889

Jeremiah Driver was a good batsman who scored over 2,500 runs in six successive seasons with Keighley but played for Yorkshire as a deputy for wicket-keeper David Hunter. He played for Keighley for at least ten seasons and other clubs included Gildersome, Skipton, Bradford – as professional - and Nelson for whom he gave long service as captain and groundsman.

Dury, Theodore Seton

Born: 12/06/1854, Ripley, Harrogate
Died: 20/03/1932, Kensington, London
RHB, RRM. Career: 1878-81. Amateur

Appearances for Yorkshire followed Theo Dury's earlier cricket for Harrow

and Oxford for whom he gained a Blue in 1876. He also played for MCC and scored 565 runs in a total of 24 first-class matches. He spent at least eight years with Harlequins and made occasional appearances for Esher, Harrogate and Southgate. A second Blue was won in racquets.

A solicitor by profession, Dury eventually became Chief Master of the Supreme Court.

Dyson, William Lord

Born: 11/12/1857, Rastrick, Halifax
Died: 01/05/1936, Brighouse, Huddersfield
RHB. Career: 1887

William Dyson had a short and unsuccessful career with Yorkshire. A professional with Brighouse, he also played for Low Moor.

Earnshaw, Wilson

Born: 20/09/1867, Morley, Wakefield
Died: 24/11/1941, Lowtown, Pudsey
RHB, WK. Career: 1893-96

Only two of Wilson Earnshaw's six matches for Yorkshire were in the County Championship. He deputised for David Hunter as wicket-keeper and had five seasons with Accrington, seven with Chickenley and also played for Dewsbury and Savile, Ossett and Barnoldswick.

Eastwood, David

Born: 30/03/1848, Lascelles Hall, Huddersfield
Died: 17/05/1903, Sheepridge, Huddersfield
RHB, RSM. Career: 1870-77

David Eastwood may have played more for Yorkshire but for his fielding and his connection with the Lascelles Hall club which dominated contemporary county teams. He was, though, good enough to represent the North and the Players.

Eastwood played for both Durham and Northumberland during a four-year stint as professional with Sunderland and represented all three counties in 1875. His other clubs included Rusholme, Heckmondwike, Elland and Leeds Clarence. From 1893 to 1897 he coached at Oxford University and umpired in first-class cricket including the County Championship in 1895.

Eckersley, Ronald
Born: 04/09/1925, Bingley, Bradford
Died: 30/05/2009, Salford,
Manchester, Lancashire
RHB, LMF. Career: 1945

Ron Eckersley played in non-first-class matches for Cambridge University during the War and came top of its bowling averages in 1944. His only appearance for Yorkshire was in a non-Championship season but he later spent nine seasons with Accrington.

Elam, Frederick William
Born: 13/09/1871, Hunslet, Leeds
Died: 19/03/1943, Headingley, Leeds
RHB, RF. Career: 1900-02. Amateur

Originally with Holbeck, Fred Elam played for Leeds, whom he captained for a time, as an opening batsman until 1920. His two matches for the county were two years apart but both were in the Championship in title-winning seasons.

Elliott, Matthew Thomas Gray
Born: 28/09/1971, Chelsea, Victoria,
Australia
LHB, RM. Career: 2002

A tall opening batsman, Matthew

Elliott first appeared at Headingley in the Test of 1997 and made 199 for Australia. This remained his highest Test innings, him scoring 1,172 runs in his 21 matches. His brief Yorkshire career came at the end of a season and he scored a match-winning innings of 128 not out in the C&G Trophy final at Lord's against Somerset.

Ellis, John Ernest
Born: 10/11/1864, Sheffield
Died: 01/12/1927, Walkley, Sheffield
RHB, WK. Career: 1888-92.
Amateur

Tried as a successor to Joe Hunter in the wicket-keeping position, John Ellis made eight appearances in 1888 and just three more four years later. A negligible batsman, his tally of dismissals is higher than his total of runs. He also played for Shiregreen and Sheffield United.

Ellis, Samuel
Born: 23/11/1851, Dewsbury
Died: 28/10/1930, Sandal Magna,
Wakefield
RHB. Career: 1880. Amateur

Sam Ellis played in just three first-class matches including one for an England XI. He also played for Dewsbury and Savile for 14 seasons.

Elms, John Emanuel
Born: 24/12/1874, Pitsmoor, Sheffield
Died: 01/11/1951, Fir Vale, Sheffield
RHB, RFM/OB/LB. Career: 1905

'Jack' Elms had the briefest of careers for Yorkshire but took over 2,000 wickets in the Yorkshire Council. During his 47 years with Sheffield United as player and then coach he changed his bowling style from pace to spin. Devoted to

Bramall Lane, he painted the ground in the winter and acted as assistant trainer to the football club.

Elstub, Christopher John

Born: 03/02/1981, Dewsbury
RHB, RMF. Career: 2000-02

A useful pace bowler in limited-overs matches, Chris Elstub's three seasons with Yorkshire began one year before his three at Leeds Metropolitan University when he played for the UCCE but not in first-class cricket. He did, however, have one such game for British Universities against the Pakistanis in 2001. He was with Kent second eleven in 2003 and later played for East Bierley, having begun his career as a PE teacher.

Emmett, Thomas

Born: 03/09/1841, Halifax
Died: 29/06/1904, Leicester
LHB, LRF. Career: 1866-88. Cap No 2

Tom Emmett made an immediate impact with Yorkshire, taking a five-for on his debut, and in forming an opening partnership with George Freeman the pair soon gained a reputation for their hostility.

Although fast, Emmett learned that speed alone was not enough and he soon mastered the art of swing bowling. One of the first to use the full width of the crease to change the angle of attack, he was also an early exponent of bowling outside the off-stump to induce an edge.

Emmett's batting also improved and he gradually became a genuine all-rounder. Pervading all his cricket, though, was his sense of humour. 'There's an epidemic here and it ain't catching' was one retort to some dropped chances and, having bowled

when WG Grace scored 318, stated that 'he should be made to play with a littler bat'.

Emmett played in seven Tests, including the very first one, the last coming at the age of 42. By this time the Yorkshire Committee had decided 'That T Emmett be made captain in the absence of a Gentleman'. The county, after some fallow years, improved under his leadership but his powers were on the wane and he retired at the age of 46. He had led the county for five years and gradually handed over to Lord Hawke.

Emmett had played for a host of clubs including Bradford, Halifax, Keighley and Otley. In retirement he coached at Rugby School and for Leicestershire; his tragic end came when he died after a fit of apoplexy in Leicester Asylum. He was the first Yorkshire bowler to take 1,000 wickets but it was how he played the game that mattered most, Lord Harris stating that he had 'never known a keener or merrier cricketer.'

Farrar, Albert

Born: 29/04/1883, Brighouse, Halifax
Died: 25/12/1954, Salterhebble,
Halifax
RHB. Career: 1906

Despite a nine-season career in the Yorkshire second eleven 'Alty' Farrar played in only one first-class match. He also played rugby league for Rochdale Hornets.

Fearnley, Michael Carruthers

Born: 21/08/1936, Horsforth, Leeds
Died: 07/07/1979, East Bierley,
Bradford
LHB, RM. Career: 1962-64

Mike Fearnley could move the ball in either direction via seam or swing. This resulted in a tally of over 1,500 wickets in the Bradford League in which he played for Farsley, from the age of 16 and later as captain, and Bradford and Bingley. A well-respected coach, he was the elder brother of Duncan, the famous bat-maker. He died while playing in a match.

Featherby, William Dixon

Born: 18/08/1888, Goodmanham
Lodge, Market Weighton
Died: 20/11/1958, Goodmanham
Lodge, Market Weighton
RHB, RMOB. Career: 1920

Bill Featherby batted in neither of his two first-class matches and bowled only four overs despite being a useful off-spinner. He also played for Bridlington, East Riding and for Londesborough Park at least until the age of 65.

Fellows, Gary Matthew

Born: 30/07/1978, Halifax
RHB, RM. Career: 1998-2003

A very valuable player in limited-overs matches, Gary Fellows made

his first-class debut for Matabeleland at the age of 18. He played in 12 of the 16 games in the Championship-winning team of 2001 and scored his one century in the 2002 Old Trafford Roses match, but never really established himself in the first-class game.

As a lower-middle-order batsman and good containing bowler Fellows turned in several important performances in List A cricket. His best efforts both came at Headingley in winning causes: 80 not out against Surrey in 2001 in the C & G Trophy and four for 19 against Durham in the Norwich Union League a year later.

Fellows played for Shropshire in 2005 and had five years with Wrenthorpe before moving to Hanging Heaton for whom he has scored over 6,000 runs and where he became captain.

Fiddling, Kenneth

Born: 13/10/1917, Hebden Bridge,
Halifax
Died: 19/06/1992, Shaw Hill,
Halifax
RHB, WK. Career: 1938-46

Of Ken Fiddling's 18 matches for Yorkshire 14 came in 1946 when he was tried as Arthur Wood's successor as wicket-keeper. From 1947 he had seven seasons with Northamptonshire, scored over 1,000 runs and made 266 dismissals in 142 matches. His club cricket was with Todmorden, Bowling Old Lane and Lightcliffe.

Finch, Aaron James

Born: 17/11/1986, Colac, Victoria, Australia
RHB, SLA. Career: 2014-15.
Cap No 176, 2014

Aaron Finch arrived in Yorkshire as an opening batsman with a brilliant record in short-form cricket having scored the highest innings in T20I matches - 156 for Australia against England at Southampton in 2013. His one century for Yorkshire, however, came in a first-class game. He has played in over 100 internationals for Australia, scoring more than 4,000 runs, but no Tests, and in 2017 he captained his country in some T20 matches.

Firth, Alfred

Born: 03/09/1847, Dewsbury
Died: 16/01/1927, Wyke, Bradford
?HB. Career: 1869. Amateur

Alfred Firth's only first-class match was against Surrey at The Oval. His club cricket was with Heckmondwike, Scarborough, Leeds and Bradford.

Firth, Edgar Beckwith

Born: 11/04/1863, Malton
Died: 25/07/1905, Matjesfontein, Cape Province, South Africa
?HB. Career: 1894. Amateur

Edgar Firth was a stalwart of Yorkshire Gentlemen, but played in only one first-class match - in the Scarborough Festival. Having being

ordained he was a minor canon at York Minster before emigrating.

Firth, Edward Loxley

Born: 07/03/1886, Hope, Derbyshire
Died: 08/01/1949, Syracuse, New York, USA
?HB. Career: 1912. Amateur

Edward Firth, also known as Edward Loxley-Firth, was a middle-order batsman who, after one season in the first eleven at Charterhouse, played in two non-Championship matches ending his career with a pair against the Australians. He also played for Sheffield United. His subsequent colourful life included divorce, bankruptcy and imprisonment.

Firth, Jack

Born: 26/06/1917, Cottingley, Bingley
Died: 06/09/1981, Bradford
RHB, WK. Career: 1949-50

Jack Firth deputised behind the stumps for Don Brennan but then moved to Leicestershire with whom he had eight seasons. He played until the age of 40 and scored over 3,000 runs and made 444 dismissals in 223 matches for the midland county. His 52 victims in 1952 was, at the time, a Leicestershire record. He played soccer for York City.

Fisher, Horace

Born: 03/08/1903, Featherstone, Wakefield
Died: 16/04/1974, Middlestown, Wakefield
LHB, LMS. Career: 1928-36
Cap No 75, 1935

In 1932 Horace Fisher made history by performing the first hat-trick in which all three victims were dismissed 'lbw'. Despite this, and figures of six for 11 against Leicestershire at Bradford in the same season he was given a lengthy run in the side only in 1935.

As a left-arm bowler, Fisher was in the shadow of Hedley Verity but performed effectively for the second eleven and was its leading wicket-taker three times in five successive seasons from 1930. He was also a success in league cricket and his considerable number of clubs included Barnsley, Middleton, Bacup, Baildon and Huddersfield.

Fisher, Ian Douglas
Born: 31/03/1976, Bradford
LHB, SLA. Career: 1995/96–2001

When Ian Fisher took ten wickets in just two first-class matches on Yorkshire's tour of Zimbabwe, making his debut the day after his 20th birthday, it was assumed he had a bright future. In his seven seasons with Gloucestershire, from 2002, he was given more opportunities and took 114 wickets in 55 first-class games, as well as 67 in 74 white-ball matches (both forms). One year with Worcestershire was followed by him

moving into back-room work and in 2013 he became Yorkshire's Strength and Conditioning Coach and played for New Farnley. Early in his career he had been with Denholme and Pudsey St Lawrence, amongst other clubs.

Fisher, Matthew David
Born: 09/11/1997, York
RHB, RFM. Career: 2013–

When Matt Fisher made his debut for Yorkshire at Scarborough against Leicestershire in a Yorkshire Bank 40 match he was aged 15 years and 212 days. This meant that he was the youngest cricketer to play in any inter-county match. He also played for England U19 from the age of 15, took part in two World Cups and captained the side in India in 2017.

Fisher's early cricket was with Easingwold School, Sheriff Hutton Bridge and the Academy (seven seasons). By 2015 he had established himself in both of Yorkshire's white-ball teams as a lively and economical bowler, made his Championship debut in the same season and was the county's leading T20 wicket-taker. Unfortunately he missed the whole of the 2016 season due to injury but was starting to re-establish himself in the side in 2017.

Flaxington, Samuel
Born: 14/10/1860, Otley
Died: 10/03/1895, Otley
RHB. Career: 1882

Samuel Flaxington was given four games in one month but only one half-century was not enough for him to be kept on. He also played for Bradford, Yeadon and Otley and became a teacher but committed suicide when his wife left him for another man.

Fleming, Stephen Paul

Born: 01/04/1973, Christchurch, New Zealand
LHB, RSM. Career: 2003

Widely regarded as one of New Zealand's best-ever captains, Stephen Fleming played for Yorkshire for just two months. In 18 games in all three formats, he made most impact in List A matches especially when he scored 139 not out against Warwickshire under lights at Headingley. A strong and powerful top-order batsman, he led his country in 80 of his 111 Tests and also Nottinghamshire to the County Championship title, relegation and promotion in successive seasons.

Fletcher, Stuart David

Born: 08/06/1964, Keighley
RHB, RMF. Career: 1983-91.
Cap No 131, 1988

A bustling and hard-working bowler, Stuart Fletcher made his debut when aged only 19. Although he had only four good seasons in first-class cricket he was more consistent in limited-overs matches and was the leading wicket-taker in Yorkshire's successful Benson & Hedges Cup campaign of 1987.

His best performance in the Championship was an innings analysis of eight for 58 against Essex at Sheffield in 1988. That performance came in what was easily his best season when he took 59 wickets but thereafter he was troubled by back injuries and was never again the same bowler. Even so he had two seasons with Lancashire after leaving Yorkshire and then had three years with Lincolnshire. His early cricket had been with Rastrick and Lascelles Hall.

Fletcher, William

Born: 16/02/1866, Whitkirk, Leeds
Died: 01/06/1935, Knaresborough
RHB, RF/MF. Career: 1891-92

Playing against MCC at Lord's in 1892, William Fletcher became only the fifth from the county to take a hat-trick and only Fred Trueman has taken one since against MCC. A noted all-rounder, he made a pair in his next match against Sussex and never really rediscovered his form. His long career in club cricket included spells with Colne, Rishton, Leeds and Middlesbrough.

Foord, Charles William

Born: 11/06/1924, Scarborough
Died: 08/07/2015, Scarborough
RHB, RMF. Career: 1947-53

One of Fred Trueman's many opening partners, Bill Foord was an unlikely-looking sportsman. Rather unathletic, he was an average fielder and batsman and his wearing of spectacles plus the fact that he took more wickets than scored runs, made him reminiscent of Bill Bowes.

Foord developed well during his time with Yorkshire and his final season, during which he took six for

63 against Hampshire at Bournemouth, was easily his most successful. He had a potent out-swinger and this helped him to take 61 wickets that year. Although he played briefly for York he was with Scarborough for most of his life as player and administrator.

Foster, Ernest
Born: 23/11/1873, Bramley, Leeds
Died: 16/04/1956, Moor Allerton, Leeds
RHB, RMF. Career: 1901. Amateur

One game at Lord's against MCC was the sum total of Ernest Foster's games for Yorkshire as he did not even play for the second eleven. As a good all-rounder, his club cricket was with Wortley, Dewsbury and Leeds.

Foster, Michael James
Born: 17/09/1972, Leeds
RHB, RFM. Career: 1993-94

A powerful striker of the ball, Michael Foster made a century in his first season – 118 at Leicester in a Sunday League match – but that was his only such score although his stand of 190 with Richard Blakey remains a record for Yorkshire's fifth wicket. His time with the county, in both forms of the game, was followed by one season with Northamptonshire and three years with Durham.

Foster, Thomas William
Born: 12/11/1871, Birkdale, Southport, Lancashire
Died: 31/01/1947, Dewsbury
RHB, RMF. Career: 1894-95

The second Lancashire-born Yorkshire player, 'Tommy' Foster had a short but brilliant career. The highlight was an innings-analysis of nine for 59 at Lord's against the MCC in only his second game. His

excellent 1894 figures speak for themselves but despite already being established with Dewsbury it is believed that Lord Hawke duly discovered his birthplace. He also played, as professional, for Rawtenstall.

Frank, Joseph
Born: 27/12/1857, Helmsley
Died: 22/10/1940, Helmsley
LHB, RF. Career: 1881. Amateur

Only one of Joseph Frank's seven first-class games was for Yorkshire, three being for the Gentlemen. Against the Australians he damaged one of Fred Spofforth's fingers putting him out of a Test. The tourists objected to his action and this may well have led to his further lack of opportunity. A cousin of Robert Frank, most of his club cricket was for Duncombe Park.

Frank, Robert Wilson
Born: 29/05/1864, Pickering
Died: 09/09/1950, Pickering
RHB, LB. Career: 1889-1903.
Amateur. Cap No 18

In the first 15 years of the 20th century 'Roberty' Frank was, in his role as captain of the second eleven, a most influential member of Yorkshire CCC. In this capacity he had a huge influence on the great players who

made up the successful teams of the 1920s.

Frank's first 17 first-team matches were spread over seven seasons but Lord Hawke knew that he had an eye for a good player. He also served the Club as committee-man, vice-president and attended the Scarborough Festival for 64 consecutive years.

Freeman, George
Born: 27/07/1843, Boroughbridge
Died: 18/11/1895, Sowerby Grange, Thirsk
RHB, RF. Career: 1865-80

The first of Yorkshire's great fast bowlers, George Freeman formed a formidable opening partnership with Tom Emmett. It was short-lived, however, as Freeman played 33 of his 44 first-class matches in just a four-year span from 1867 during which he was a vital part of a team which was twice declared 'champion county'.

Hostile in the extreme, even good batsmen could not escape being struck on the body and WG Grace, many years later stated that Freeman was the best bowler he ever faced.

Andrew Gale batting against Sussex at Hove in 2013.

Gale, Andrew William
Born: 28/11/1983, Dewsbury
LHB, LB. Career: 2004-16.
Cap No 163, 2008. Benefit: 2016

One of Yorkshire's longest serving captains, Andrew Gale had the distinction of leading the county to its first consecutive Championship wins since 1968 when the title was won in 2014 and 2015. In addition, in each of his first and last seasons of captaincy one more win would have secured the title. However, a run of 26 consecutive Championship matches without defeat in 2014-15 was Yorkshire's best since 1946.

A free-flowing batsman with a wide range of strokes, Gale has twice scored over 1,000 first-class runs in a season; the first and better of these, 2013, contained an innings of 272 against Nottinghamshire at Scarborough.

Appointed captain in 2010, the tenure of office was for all three forms of the game but Gale's teams were less successful in the shorter versions, other than the Twenty20 semi-final success in 2012, and he resigned from being in charge in white-ball cricket during the 2015 season. One year later he concluded his playing career when he was appointed Yorkshire's First Eleven Coach for the 2017 season. With only 12 defeats in 98 Championship matches Gale's record is inferior to only two other Yorkshire captains.

Geldart, Callum John
Born: 17/12/1991, Huddersfield
LHB, RM. Career: 2010-11

Callum Geldart played for the Academy for four seasons and each of his two games for Yorkshire were both University first-class matches. His club cricket was with Streethouse, Undercliffe, Pudsey Congs, whom he also captained, and Hanging Heaton.

Gibb, Paul Antony
Born: 11/07/1913, Acomb, York
Died: 07/12/1977, Guildford, Surrey
RHB, WK. Career: 1935-46.
Amateur. Cap No 76, 1936

The only player to score a century in his first match for Yorkshire as well as in his first Test, Paul Gibb had

made his first-class debut for Scotland in 1934. After St Edward's School, Oxford he gained a Blue in all four years at Cambridge.

A steadfast opening batsman, Gibb played in all five Tests in South Africa in 1938/39 but when tried as a 'keeper after the War he was soon replaced. He then left the first-class game but re-appeared in 1951 for Essex as a professional.

From 1957 Gibb umpired for ten seasons in first-class cricket. In this capacity he aroused considerable controversy by no-balling Derbyshire's Harold Rhodes six times in the county match against the South Africans in 1960.

Gibbs, Herschelle Herman
Born: 23/02/1974, Green Point, Cape Town, South Africa
RHB, LB. Career: 2010

A brilliant opening batsman who represented his country in 90 Tests and 248 ODIs, Herschelle Gibbs played for Yorkshire only in T20 matches. He was the county's leading run-scorer in his one season, his record including a century at Northampton. He also played for Glamorgan but most of his first-class cricket was for Western Province.

Gibson, Barney Peter

Born: 31/03/1996, Leeds
RHB, WK. Career: 2011

Although Barney Gibson played in only one match for Yorkshire it was at the age of 15 years 27 days and this made him the youngest cricketer ever to play in a first-class match in England. He had five seasons with the Academy and Pudsey Congs and later played for Methley.

Gibson, Ryan

Born: 22/01/1996, Middlesbrough
RHB, RM. Career: 2013-

Tall, Ryan Gibson had four seasons in the Academy team and played for Yorkshire mainly in the two short forms as a useful bowler. In 2017 his only game was a non-competitive List A match. His clubs were Marton, Normanby Hall, Pudsey Congs and Stamford Bridge.

Gifkins, Charles John

Born: 19/02/1856, Thames Ditton, Surrey
Died: 31/01/1897, Albuquerque, New Mexico, USA
RHB, RMF. Career: 1880. Amateur

Charles Gifkins opened the batting in each of his two matches for Yorkshire. His other cricket was with Hull Town as well as Chicago and other clubs in that area.

Gilbert, Christopher Robert

Born: 16/04/1984, Scarborough
RHB, RM/OB. Career: 2006-07

Despite scoring a half-century in his only first-class innings – against Loughborough UCCE – the career of Chris Gilbert was otherwise restricted to 18 games in the two short forms. He had two seasons with the Academy and his club cricket was

for Heywood, Doncaster Town and Scarborough.

Gill, Fairfax

Born: 03/09/1883, Wakefield
Died: 01/11/1917, Boulogne, Pas de Calais, France
RHB. Career: 1906

'Fairy' Gill tragically died in hospital from wounds suffered in the War. He always lived in Wakefield, played for his home club but scored over 3,500 runs in seven seasons as professional with Ossett. He had a very short career in first-class cricket.

Gillespie, Jason Neil

Born: 19/04/1975, Darlinghurst, Sydney, Australia
RHB, RF/MF. Career: 2006-07.
Cap No 158, 2007

An outstanding bowler in Test cricket, Jason Gillespie was a regular member of the highly-successful Australian side of the turn of the century. His first appearance at Headingley was in the 1997 Test when he took seven for 37 – still the record for an overseas bowler at the ground.

Jason Gillespie as Yorkshire's coach.

Darren Gough bowls against Australia in the Edgbaston Test of 1997.

Past his best when he came to play for Yorkshire, his most notable achievement was in sharing in the county's record stand for the ninth wicket. However, he later became an exceptional coach and re-joined the Club in that capacity in 2012 guiding the team to two Championship titles, losing only seven of the competition's 80 matches in his five seasons in charge. On his return to Australia he soon became a member of the national side's coaching team and has since coached both Kings XI Punjab and Kent.

Gillhouley, Keith

Born: 08/08/1934, Crosland Moor, Huddersfield
RHB, SLA. Career: 1961

Keith Gillhouley took 91 wickets for the second eleven in 1960 – the second-best haul of all-time – and replaced the injured Don Wilson in the first team during the following season. Despite taking 77 wickets in 24 matches, with only Fred Trueman and Ray Illingworth taking more, he was not tried again. The best performance of his brief but successful career was seven for 82 against Middlesex at Bradford. He moved to Nottinghamshire and took 170 wickets in four seasons and later played for Ashton-under-Lyne.

Gough, Darren

Born: 18/09/1970, Monk Bretton, Barnsley
RHB, RFM. Career: 1989-2008.
Cap No 139, 1993. Benefit: 2001

England's best pace bowler of the 1990s, Darren Gough will always be remembered for the way he played the game. Enthusiastic and with a smile on his face, he was popular the world over. Although he took 229 wickets in 58 Tests and created a new England record with 234 ODI wickets, his proneness to injury restricted his appearances.

Following time with Monk Bretton and then Barnsley, Gough first played for Yorkshire at the age of 18 and had his breakthrough season in 1993 when he achieved match-figures of ten for 96 against Somerset at Taunton. An England A tour followed and his Test debut a year later. With his ability to swing the ball late, he was a handful in all conditions, overseas Test highlights including a hat-trick at Sydney in 1998/99 and a man-of-the-series award for his 14 wickets in three games in Sri Lanka in 2000/01. His best performance in England was a match-winning six for 42 against South Africa at Headingley in 1998.

A committed stroke-maker, it was always hoped that Gough would develop into a genuine all-rounder but his batting prowess tailed-off somewhat after making a century against county champions Warwickshire at Headingley in 1996.

In 2004 Gough moved to Essex, but was persuaded to return to Yorkshire as captain three years later. Although no trophies were won he kept the side in the Championship's first division and led the team with his usual energy and commitment. He later won BBC TV's Strictly Come Dancing, forged a career in the media and in 2017 assisted with the England U-19 teams.

Goulder, Alfred

Born: 16/08/1907, Attercliffe, Sheffield
Died: 11/06/1986, Sheffield
LHB, SLA. Career: 1929

Alfred Goulder played for Rawmarsh and had a long career with Sheffield United as a bowler who spun the ball a great deal but not quickly enough for success in the first-class game. He was tried as a possible successor to Wilfred Rhodes but played in only one match in the Championship.

Gray, Andrew Kenneth Donovan

Born: 19/05/1974, Armadale, Western Australia
RHB, OB. Career: 2001-04

Andy Gray was born to English parents and emigrated to the country of their birth to attempt a career in first-class cricket. Unfortunately, despite playing in 57 games in all three formats and being an all-rounder, he failed to establish himself in the side. He never took a five-for but did score one century, at Taunton in the Championship in his best season of 2003. After his time with Yorkshire he had two seasons with Derbyshire and then seven with Shropshire, also playing for Shifnal in the Birmingham League.

Grayson, Adrian Paul

Born: 31/03/1971, Ripon
RHB, SLA. Career: 1990-95

Paul Grayson played for Bedale, Pudsey Congs and Yorkshire Bank before making his county debut. Unfortunately, he did not really fulfil his promise until he moved to Essex. There he scored 6,589 first-class runs in his nine seasons but his bowling also improved, especially in limited-overs cricket, so much so that he played in two ODIs in the early 2000s as a lower-middle-order all-rounder.

Grayson became Essex coach in 2007 but his nine seasons in that role went without a trophy, eight of them being spent in the Championship's second division. In 2016 he was appointed coach of Durham UCCE and from 2017 fulfilled this role in combination with, in the women's game, being head coach of Yorkshire Diamonds.

Greenwood, Andrew

Born: 20/08/1847, Cowmes, Huddersfield
Died: 12/02/1889, Huddersfield
RHB. Career: 1869-80

Andrew Greenwood played for several representative teams, including the Players, and also had the honour of being involved in what later became known as the first two Test matches in Australia. They were on his only tour abroad. Although he was a capable batsman and a regular member of the Yorkshire side for seven seasons his only century was for United North of England against the South at Huddersfield in 1876. His highest score for Yorkshire came a year later when he made 91 against Gloucestershire at Sheffield.

A very good outfielder, Greenwood played for several clubs but was associated mostly with Lascelles Hall for about 15 years. This was along with his uncle, Luke, who also played for Yorkshire.

Greenwood, Frank Edwards

Born: 28/09/1905, Birkby,
Huddersfield
Died: 30/07/1963, Lindley,
Huddersfield
RHB, RM. Career: 1929-32.
Amateur. Cap No 68, 1931

Frank Greenwood led Yorkshire to the title in 1931 in his first season as skipper. There was a repeat performance in the following season but he played in only six of the 28 matches and then left the game.

Greenwood was in the first eleven at Oundle School and his first club was Slaithwaite. He later joined Huddersfield where he became captain. Of his 57 games for Yorkshire, 33 came in 1931 but he

scored only 745 runs, his only century having come in his first season against Glamorgan at Hull. A good hockey player, he died on holiday having moved to the Isle of Man.

Greenwood, Luke

Born: 13/07/1834, Cowmes,
Huddersfield
Died: 01/11/1909, Morley
RHB, RRMF. Career: 1864-74

An effective all-rounder, Luke Greenwood played for 'Yorkshire' in two seasons before the Club was formed. A regular in the county's early years, taking eight for 35 against Cambridgeshire at Dewsbury in 1867, he also played for various representative sides, mostly for United North of England Eleven.

Greenwood led Yorkshire for one season – 1874 – and then coached at schools, including Winchester, as well as umpiring in first-class cricket for three seasons in the 1880s including the famous Oval Test match of 1882. He later became groundsman at Morley.

Grimshaw, Charles Henry

Born: 12/05/1880, Calverley, Leeds
Died: 25/09/1947, Calverley, Leeds
LHB, SLA. Career: 1904-08

Despite being a good all-rounder in club cricket, 'Harry' Grimshaw was given little opportunity to bowl for

Yorkshire. His success as a batsman for the second eleven led to him playing 18 games for the first team in 1905 but fewer chances came his way thereafter.

Apart from two seasons as professional with Dudley, Grimshaw spent most of his career with Bowling Old Lane. His tally of 1,273 wickets created a new record for the Bradford League.

Grimshaw, Irwin
Born: 04/05/1857, Farsley, Bradford
Died: 18/01/1911, Farsley, Bradford
RHB, WK. Career: 1880-87

Regarded by some as one of the best professional batsmen in England, Irwin Grimshaw was a middle-order player who drove and cut particularly well. Two of his four centuries came in his best season of 1885 which included his career-best 129 not out against Cambridge University at Sheffield. Unfortunately he was never consistent enough though he did play for several representative sides including the North as well as an England XI for whom he scored 77 against the Australians in 1884.

In a varied club career, Grimshaw played for Farsley United and Bingley prior to his county career which he followed with stints as professional with Holmfirth, Nelson, Cudworth and Dobcross. He kept wicket regularly at this level, a skill only occasionally used in first-class cricket in which he was known as a fine outfielder.

Guy, Simon Mark
Born: 17/11/1978, Rotherham
RHB, WK. Career: 2000-11

A neat and tidy wicket-keeper, Simon Guy spent his time with Yorkshire on the periphery of the first eleven. He deputised for regular 'keepers as well as competing with others but also played, especially in Twenty20 cricket, as a specialist batsman.

Guy suffered a serious setback in 2008 when he underwent an operation for a cerebral abscess on his brain; so determined was he to return to action that he had designed a special mask to protect his face while playing. His club cricket was with Rotherham Town, Darlington, Marske, Sheffield Collegiate and Wickersley. He also had four seasons with Suffolk and in 2015 became Director of Cricket at Denstone College, Uttoxeter, Staffordshire.

Haggas, Stell

Born: 18/04/1856, Keighley
Died: 14/03/1926, Werneth, Oldham,
Lancashire
RHB. Career: 1878-82

A strong leg-side player, Stell Haggas learnt his early cricket with Thwaites and then Keighley before playing in 31 matches for Yorkshire, 27 of them in 1878 and 1879. He moved to Lancashire to play for Bacup and Werneth but also represented the Red Rose county in three games over two seasons from 1884. His son, Walter, also played for Lancashire.

Haigh, Schofield

Born: 19/03/1871, Berry Brow,
Huddersfield
Died: 27/02/1921, Taylor Hill,
Huddersfield
RHB, RFM. Career: 1895-1913.
Cap No 28. Benefit: 1909

One of Yorkshire's best-ever bowlers, Schofield Haigh arrived at the county club by a circuitous route having played for Aberdeen and Perth as a young professional. Prior to this he had played for Berry Brow Salem and Armitage Bridge. Having taken seven for 12 for Scotland against his home county in 1895 he was persuaded to return and in only his sixth game for Yorkshire he came up against the 1896 Australians at Bradford but took ten wickets including eight for 78 in the second innings.

From then on Haigh's place in the side was assured and, along with George Hirst and Wilfred Rhodes, provided the trio of wicket-taking bowlers who dominated seven of their county's first nine official Championship-winning seasons

which included a hat-trick of titles from 1900. He had made his Test debut on the previous winter's tour of South Africa, where he took six for 11 at Cape Town but his home Test appearances were sporadic although he did play in all five games on another tour of South Africa in 1905/06 but ended with only 24 wickets in his 11 Tests.

Haigh bowled fast-medium from a long stride and swung the ball prodigiously; he was able to vary his pace according to the conditions and included an off-break in his repertoire which made him almost unplayable on sticky wickets. His career-best was nine for 25 against Gloucestershire at Headingley in 1912 and he took over 100 wickets in a season on ten occasions, his best being 174 in 1906.

As a batsman Haigh enjoyed hitting the ball hard and possessed a pleasing off-drive but could defend solidly if needed and the highest of his four centuries was a score of 159 against Nottinghamshire at Sheffield in 1901.

A dedicated and popular county player, Haigh completed the double

in 1904, is one of only four Yorkshiremen to score over 10,000 runs and take over 2,000 wickets in all first-class cricket and his total of wickets for Yorkshire has been beaten by only two players – Hirst and Rhodes!

After his playing career Haigh coached at Winchester College but died close to his Huddersfield roots just 20 days short of his 50th birthday.

Hall, Brian

Born: 16/09/1929, Morley
Died: 27/02/1989, Doncaster
RHB, RMF. Career: 1952

Brian Hall's only first-class match was at Lord's against MCC. His bowling was very successful in club cricket: he took all ten in a match for East Brierley and took 112 wickets for British Ropes in 1956 when his club won two trophies. His first club was East Ardsley.

Hall, Charles Henry

Born: 05/04/1906, York
Died: 11/12/1976, Upper Poppleton, York
RHB, RMF. Career: 1928-1934

Charles Hall joined York, soon after leaving school, as a tall pace bowler. His two five-fors for Yorkshire, the best being six for 71 against Middlesex at Sheffield, both came in 1932 and he later was professional for Bradford before joining Woodhouse Grange.

Hall, John

Born: 11/11/1815, Nottingham
Died: 17/04/1888, South Retford, Nottinghamshire
RHB, RS/Lobs. Career: 1863

Having played three games for 'Yorkshire' in 1844-45, John Hall made his only appearance for Yorkshire CCC at the age of 47. An itinerant cricketer, he played firstly for Leicester and then Bradford where he ran the largest cricket clothing business in the north of England.

Hall, Louis

Born: 01/11/1852, Batley
Died: 19/11/1915, Morecambe, Lancashire
RHB, RS/Lobs. Career: 1873-94.
Cap No 3. Benefit: 1891

Louis Hall holds the record for carrying his bat on more occasions for Yorkshire – 14 – than any other player. A very dour batsman, his debut season was followed by four years when he did not play at all, except as professional for Perthshire in Scotland.

Once Hall had become a regular in the Yorkshire side he formed a reliable opening partnership with George Ulyett. At Hove in 1885 the pair became the first to score two century opening stands in the same match in all first-class cricket.

Solid and dependable, Hall sometimes batted exceptionally slowly but was a good stroke-maker on the leg-side. The 1887 season was his best, him scoring 1,240 runs and this included his career-best of 160 against Lancashire at Bradford. He was a brilliant fielder close to the wicket.

Away from cricket he was a Methodist preacher and teetotaller and this must have influenced him being able to captain Yorkshire on 40 occasions, despite being a professional, as Lord Hawke's deputy. The first Yorkshire player to be awarded a benefit, Hall later coached at Uppingham School and acted as a first-class umpire for seven seasons.

Halliday, Harry

Born: 09/02/1920, Pudsey
Died: 27/08/1967, Stanley, Wakefield
RHB, RM/OB. Career: 1938-53
Cap No 86, 1948. Testimonial: 1954

A stylish but tenacious middle-order batsman, Harry Halliday made his debut at the age of 18 but had to wait another nine years, mainly because of the War, before he could establish himself in the county side. One of several Yorkshire products of Pudsey St Lawrence, his best season was in 1950 when he scored 1,484 runs including his highest score of 144 at Chesterfield.

A good all-round cricketer with a batting average higher than his bowling, Halliday caught well at slip and his off-spinners came in very useful at times, none more so than when he took six for 79 against Derbyshire at Sheffield in 1952.

Harry Halliday (left) walks out to bat with skipper Norman Yardley against MCC at Scarborough in 1952.

On leaving Yorkshire Halliday had professional engagements with Church and Cumberland but having previously gained coaching experience in South Africa, he later put this to good use with Workington and Scarborough as well as at Scarborough College.

Halliley, Charles

Born: 05/12/1852, Earlsheaton, Dewsbury
Died: 23/03/1929, Ravensthorpe, Dewsbury
RHB. Career: 1872

Good performances for representative and local sides against England elevens brought him to the attention of Yorkshire but he met with little success. He later played for Boston Spa and New Wortley.

Hamer, Arnold

Born: 08/12/1916, Primrose Hill, Huddersfield
Died: 03/11/1993, Berry Brow, Huddersfield
RHB, OB. Career: 1938

Arnold Hamer played for Yorkshire as a spin bowler but after the War he was transformed into an opening batsman and success with Pudsey St Lawrence took him to Derbyshire at the age of 33. In 11 seasons there he scored over 15,000 runs. His other club cricket was with Primrose Hill, Spen Victoria and Windhill. He played for York City as a full-back before the War.

Hamilton, Gavin Mark

Born: 16/09/1974, Broxburn, West Lothian, Scotland
LHB, RFM. Career: 1994-2003
Cap No 145, 1998

In five years straddling the millennium Gavin Hamilton went from being the best all-rounder in the country to a former bowler and declining batsman. He came to Yorkshire via school and club cricket (Sidcup) in Kent and a first-class debut for Scotland in 1993. By 1998 his attacking batting and quality seam bowling had developed so well that 578 runs and 59 wickets in that season's first-class matches enabled him to be the only player to feature in the top 15 of both national averages.

A successful 1999 World Cup for Scotland led to his Test debut at Johannesburg but a pair and no wickets meant that he was to remain a one-cap wonder. In 2002 he suffered a most severe attack of the yips and, despite various attempts to overcome it he played most of the rest of his career as a specialist batsman. This included two years with Durham and further successes for Scotland.

Hampshire, Alan Wesley

Born: 18/10/1950, Rotherham
RHB, RM. Career: 1975

A product of Loughborough College, Alan Hampshire played for Harrogate and Sheffield Collegiate as well as Billingham Synthonia and Manningham Mills as professional. Brother of John Harry, he shared the same strong build and batting style.

Hampshire, John

Born: 05/10/1913, Goldthorpe,
Rotherham
Died: 23/05/1997, Rotherham
RHB, RFM. Career: 1937

As a successful professional with Hickleton Main, Barnsley and Rotherham, Jack Hampshire had a brief opportunity as an opening bowler at first-class level but his career was ended by a broken collar-bone. His two sons both played for Yorkshire and he also played soccer, as a centre-half, for Bristol City and Manchester City.

Hampshire, John Harry

Born: 10/02/1941, Thurnscoe,
Rotherham
Died: 01/03/2017, Rotherham
RHB, LB. Career: 1961-81
Cap No 109, 1963. Benefit: 1976

One of the most powerful batsmen ever to play for Yorkshire, John Hampshire was blessed with very strong shoulders and forearms with which he hooked and pulled to considerable effect. Driving attractively on both sides of the wicket, he was always a popular batsman to watch.

Hampshire's county debut came after representing Rotherham Town and he was tried as an opener before settling in the middle order where he contributed valuably to five Championship and two Gillette Cup victories. An England debut in 1969 saw him score a century and this meant that he was the first England player to achieve such a feat at Lord's. Unfortunately, he was dropped after his second Test and his remaining six Tests all came in four different series.

The break-up of the hugely successful Yorkshire squad of the

1960s saw Hampshire suddenly being cast in the role of a senior player, under the captaincy of Geoff Boycott. The 1978 season was his best in terms of runs – 1,596 – but he deliberately batted slowly at Northampton in protest at his skipper's tactics. The county committee's reaction was to criticise him, sack Boycott and give him the captaincy! By now, though, because of the members' pro-Boycott faction, the post was no longer the honour it once was. Hampshire drank from the poisoned chalice for two years with reliability rather than flair but led Yorkshire to two semi-finals and two top-seven finishes in the

Championship. He returned to the ranks in 1981 for just one season before spending three years with Derbyshire.

Devoted to the game he loved, Hampshire spent some time coaching in Tasmania, where he had played for the state side in the late-1960s, as well as for Zimbabwe, and soon became a first-class umpire. In fulfilling this role for 21 years so successful was he that he was asked to stand in 21 Test matches and 20 ODIs. Some of these came as a result of him being a member for four years of the ICC's international panel of officials.

In 2016 Hampshire was rewarded for his long-standing involvement in the game by being elected President of Yorkshire CCC. His enthusiasm and commitment to the post was reflected in his regular presence at matches but he sadly passed away shortly before the start of what would have been his second year in office.

Handscomb, Peter Stephen Patrick

Born: 26/04/1991, Melbourne, Australia
RHB, WK. Career: 2017

Peter Handscomb played for Yorkshire in all three formats for the first four months of the 2017 season. He played as a batsman in the Championship but also kept wicket in both of the white-ball competitions. An attractive stroke-maker, he was the county's leading run-scorer in the Royal London Cup. His Test and ODI debuts had come in the previous winter and he was only the second Australian to score a half-century in each of his first four Tests.

Hannon-Dalby, Oliver James

Born: 20/06/1989, Halifax
LHB, RMF. Career: 2008-12

Oliver Hannon-Dalby twice took five for 68 in consecutive matches in 2010, against Warwickshire and then Somerset, but that remained his only full season in first-class cricket. A very tall bowler with a slightly awkward run-up and action, he spent three seasons in the Academy side and four with Barnsley before moving to Warwickshire, and Lightcliffe, for the 2013 season. His new county turned him into a white-ball specialist and his effective changes of pace brought him 100 wickets in five seasons and helped win two trophies.

Harbord, William Edward

Born: 15/12/1908, Manton, Rutland
Died: 28/07/1992, Harrogate
RHB, RSM. Career: 1929-35.
Amateur

William Harbord was in the first eleven at Eton for one season and played one first-class match for Oxford University thus not obtaining a Blue. He played intermittently for Yorkshire as an attacking middle-order batsman but gained selection for the MCC tour of the West Indies in 1934/35. He was on the Yorkshire committee for several years and became a vice-president.

Harden, Richard John

Born: 16/08/1965, Bridgwater, Somerset
RHB, SLA. Career: 1999-2000.
Cap: 1999

In a long career with Somerset which had started in 1985, Richard Harden scored over 12,000 runs in first-class cricket and over 6,000 in limited-overs matches. He was brought to Yorkshire to bolster its middle-order and although a solid player, he was past his best by then and he contributed little in either form of the game. He remains one of the county's most odd signings.

Hardisty, Charles Henry

Born: 10/12/1885, Horsforth, Leeds
Died: 02/03/1968, Leeds
RHB. Career: 1906-09. Cap No 43A

Of Charles Hardisty's 38 matches for Yorkshire, 21 came in the 1908 season and after one more year of little opportunity he moved to Northumberland where he had two seasons. He played for several clubs, starting with Horsforth Hall Park and then Leeds before moving to

Consett and Wallsend. He later captained Horsforth and also played for Keighley and Whitkirk.

Hargreaves, Herbert Silvester
Born: 22/03/1912, Cinder Hill, Shireoaks
Died: 29/09/1990, Bury St Edmunds, Suffolk
RHB, RFM. Career: 1934–38

Born just 100 yards away from the Nottinghamshire border, Herbert Hargreaves was a most useful reserve pace bowler and contributed valuably to two Championship wins. He took a wicket with his first ball for Yorkshire, against Cambridge University at Fenner's, and later played for Suffolk. His earlier club cricket was with Hull Town and Sheffield United as well as Perth, Scotland as professional.

Harmison, Stephen James
Born: 23/10/1978, Ashington, Northumberland
RHB, RF. Career: 2012

For a brief period in 2004 Steve Harmison was at the top of the ICC Test bowling rankings. In that year and, famously, in 2005 he was at his peak and opened England's bowling in a record-equalling sequence of victories in which he took 97 wickets in 23 Tests. He played for Yorkshire when briefly on loan from his county, Durham.

Harris, William
Born: 21/11/1861, Greasborough, Rotherham
Died: 23/05/1923, Longsight, Manchester
LHB. Career: 1884–87

Bill Harris played in two matches in each of two seasons but with limited success. He had a long and successful career with several clubs including Worksop, Armley for seven seasons and Haslingden for 18 as well as Leeds.

Harrison, George Puckrin
Born: 11/02/1862, Scarborough
Died: 14/09/1940, Scarborough
RHB, RF/MF Career: 1883-92.
Cap No 9.

With exactly 100 wickets in his first season, George Harrison was already a successful fast bowler. Tragically, he suffered an arm injury and although he had some success at a slower speed, he was dropped in 1886 and did not play at all in either of the next two seasons.

Harrison took 11 for 76 in his first county game – against Kent at Dewsbury – and the 1883 season also included his career-best figures of seven for 43 at Old Trafford. He was very successful in club cricket, his teams including Bowling Old Lane, Ganton, Pickering, Scarborough and Idle. From 1907 he umpired for 13 seasons in first-class cricket.

Harrison, Harold
Born: 26/01/1885, Horsforth, Leeds
Died: 11/02/1962, Rawdon, Leeds
?HB, SLA. Career: 1907

A good spin bowler in league cricket, Harold Harrison had a brief career with Yorkshire but he enjoyed playing for clubs on both sides of the Pennines. He played for three clubs in Yeadon then Dewsbury, Rawtenstall, Enfield, Haslingden and Farsley before finishing as groundsman and professional at Ayr.

Harrison, William Hendy
Born: 27/05/1863, Shipley, Bradford
Died: 15/07/1939, Lister Hills,
Bradford
?HB. Career: 1888

Two of William Harrison's three games for Yorkshire were county matches and his only other first-class cricket was one match in the USA in 1892.

Hart, Herbert William
Born: 21/09/1859, Cottingham, Hull
Died: 02/11/1895, Hull
LHB, LF. Career: 1888. Amateur

As a bowler of high pace, 'Herbie' Hart was a great success for Hull Town for many years and placed many batsmen in danger. For Yorkshire, however, his experience was brief. His early death was from typhoid.

Hart, Philip Richard
Born: 12/01/1947, Seamer,
Scarborough
RHB, SLA. Career: 1981

Philip Hart's short spell with Yorkshire, only in first-class cricket, came relatively late in his career but he continued to be an effective spin bowler for Scarborough for about 20 years. He also played for Normanby Hall as professional and spent one winter coaching in Transvaal (now Gauteng). He is brother-in-law to Martyn Moxon and wrote an interesting autobiography

Hartington, Harry Edmondson
Born: 18/09/1881, Dewsbury
Died: 16/02/1950, Pontefract
RHB, RFM. Career: 1910-11

All of Harry Hartington's ten games for Yorkshire were in the Championship and they followed spells with Dewsbury and Chickenley.

As a good pace bowler he later played for Ossett and was professional with Haslingden. His longest association was with Featherstone for whom he first played in 1908 and became president in 1929. He was also a noted bowling coach.

Hartley, Peter John
Born: 18/04/1960, Keighley
RHB, RMF. Career: 1985-1997.
Cap No 130, 1987. Benefit: 1996

The exploits of Peter Hartley with Keighley, for whom he took seven for 20 at the age of 17, came to the notice of Warwickshire and he played three first-class matches for them in 1982. Three years later he became the first Yorkshire player to represent another county first.

A bowler with a stiff, angular action, Hartley moved the ball both ways via seam and swing especially when he took a career-best nine for 41, including a hat-trick, against Derbyshire at Chesterfield in his best season of 1995. As one of the county's best-ever bowlers in limited-overs cricket he played an important part in the successful Benson & Hedges Cup campaign of 1987. His best effort was five for 36 against Sussex at Scarborough in 1993.

Although not a genuine all-rounder, Hartley occasionally made an important contribution with the bat such as when his highest score rescued Yorkshire from 37 for six at Old Trafford. He had some strong strokes in his repertoire.

After his release by Yorkshire he had three seasons with Hampshire and became an umpire in 2003. On the International Panel from 2006 for three years, he has spent most of his time on the county circuit to which he contributed so much.

Hartley, Stuart Neil

Born: 18/03/1956, Shipley, Bradford
RHB, RM. Career: 1978-1989
Cap No 123, 1982. Benefit: 1992

Unusually, Neil Hartley captained Yorkshire before he had received his county cap. At the instigation of manager Ray Illingworth he led the side in a total of 14 matches in both forms of the game. A natural leader, he had captained the young Yorkshire Federation team in 1973 and later captained Bingley, which had been his first club as a boy.

Schooled at Beckfoot Grammar and in Perth, Australia, Hartley was a natural sportsman with a good eye and he developed into a useful all-rounder and brilliant fielder especially in limited-overs cricket. In the shorter form of the game his bowling, which did not trouble batsmen much in first-class cricket, brought rewards when batsmen took risks; as a batsman he was able to score quickly and more freely than in the longer form in which his technique was often found wanting.

Despite his shortcomings at first-class level Hartley was a loyal servant of the Club, playing in over 300 first-team matches, and spent some years as second eleven captain for which he was awarded, again unusually, a benefit in 1992.

Harvey, Ian Joseph

Born: 10/04/1972, Wonthaggi,
Victoria, Australia
RHB, RMF. Career: 2004-05

A short-form specialist (he played in 73 ODIs for Australia but no Tests), Ian Harvey scored each of Yorkshire's first two centuries in Twenty20 cricket with a best of 109 against Derbyshire at Headingley in 2005. A free-scoring batsman, he complemented this skill with very useful economical bowling. Although less effective in first-class cricket Harvey made a career-best double century against Somerset at Headingley in 2005.

Harvey came to Yorkshire after having made his name over five seasons with Gloucestershire to where he returned in 2015 as assistant coach.

Hatton, Anthony George

Born: 25/03/1937, Whitkirk, Leeds
LHB, RFM. Career: 1960-61

Tony Hatton was in the first eleven at Roundhay School and also learned the game with Whitkirk before moving to Colton, North Leeds and Castleford. A good bowler in club cricket, all of his three first-class games were in the Championship and he took four wickets in his first match including that of Colin Cowdrey.

Hawke, Lord

Born: 16/08/1860, Willingham by
Stow, Gainsborough, Lincolnshire
Died: 10/10/1938, West End,
Edinburgh
RHB, LM. Career: 1881-1911.
Amateur. Cap No 1

Martin Bladen Hawke succeeded to his family's title in 1887 by becoming the Seventh Baron as a descendant of Admiral Hawke who was created First Baron in 1776. Hawke's family had moved to Wighill Park, Tadcaster when his father inherited the title in 1874.

Being in the first eleven at Eton, Hawke played for Yorkshire Gentlemen in the holidays, and then Cambridge University. He gained a Blue in each of three years and led the team in 1885 when it beat Oxford by seven wickets. Meanwhile, not only had he made his county debut, he had even been appointed captain, in 1883 although in practical terms it applied only after the end of term. He held the post for a record 28 seasons but it is the changes which he put in place for which he will always be remembered.

On the field of play Hawke placed great emphasis on fielding and this became emblematic of his ambition to create more disciplined

887 which remains the highest by any county. He played in five Tests in South Africa, four as captain, and he also led tours to North America, India, West Indies and Argentina, him being very keen to globalise the game.

Hawke's contribution to cricket, which cannot be over-estimated, is also manifested in him being Yorkshire President for the last 40 years of his life as well as president and treasurer of MCC at different times from 1914. His high ideals were summarised by his statement that 'sometimes cricket is too serious…as a pursuit it loses its flavour. The moral character of my men is of infinitely more importance than their form'.

Hayley, Harry
Born: 22/02/1860, Heath, Wakefield
Died: 03/06/1922, St John's, Wakefield
RHB, RSM. Career: 1884–98

With a mere seven first-class matches, all for Yorkshire, spread over 15 seasons, Harry Hayley had an unusually protracted career. An unorthodox and hard-hitting batsman, he scored over 10,000 runs in 11 seasons as professional with Leeds and also played for Wakefield and Wakefield Trinity at rugby league. A noted coach, he founded a sports outfitters in his home town.

Haywood, William John
Born: 25/02/1841, Upper Hallam, Sheffield
Died: 07/01/1912, Walkley, Sheffield
RHB, RRMF. Career: 1878

William Haywood played his one game for Yorkshire aged 37 after leading the second eleven. He also played for Hallam, Sheffield and Hunslet.

performances. This bore fruit in 1893 when the county won its first title, official or otherwise, for 23 years, and was followed by a further seven under his leadership including a hat-trick of Championships from 1900. Away from the ground, Hawke was a benevolent autocrat and brought in far-reaching measures to improve the status of professionals. He came down hard on the heavy drinkers, introduced winter pay, bonuses based on performance and benefits, the investment of which had to be managed carefully. In addition, it was he who designed the White Rose emblem for Yorkshire CCC and which has been in use ever since.

As a player Hawke was not in the highest class but was a strong, hard-hitting batsman, mostly in the middle order and his top score of 166 at Edgbaston in 1896 came in a total of

Head, Travis Michael

Born: 29/12/1993, Adelaide, South Australia
LHB, OB. Career: 2016

Travis Head had a brief spell with Yorkshire and played in all three formats. In his first List A game, at Leicester, he scored 175 – only 16 short of the county record. His stand of 274 with Jack Leaning broke Yorkshire's record for any wicket. Captain of his native state, he made his international debut for Australia in early-2016.

Hicks, John

Born: 10/12/1850, York
Died: 10/06/1912, Holgate, York
RHB, RF. Career: 1872-76

An opening batsman and good fielder, John Hicks played in several representative games for the North but only irregularly for his county. His best season was 1875 when he played in nine of his 15 games and scored his only half-century, that being at The Oval.

Higgins, James

Born: 13/03/1877, Birstall, Leeds
Died: 19/07/1954, Wibsey, Bradford
RHB, WK. Career: 1901-05

A useful wicket-keeper, James Higgins acted as David Hunter's deputy for Yorkshire and played regularly for the second eleven for five years. He also played for Dewsbury.

Hill, Allen

Born: 15/11/1843, Kirkheaton, Huddersfield
Died: 28/08/1910, Leyland, Lancashire
RHB, RFM. Career: 1871-82

Allen Hill took the first wicket and the first catch in the very first Test match at Melbourne in 1877. One of the best pace bowlers in England, he took a total of 749 first-class wickets, relying mostly on accuracy and pace off a short run-up.

Following club cricket with Lascelles Hall, Kirkheaton, Dewsbury and Savile, Mirfield and Burnley, Hill had match figures of 12 for 54 (all bowled) in his first inter-county match, against Surrey. From 1874 he took 100 wickets in three successive seasons.

As well as his two Tests, Hill played in many other representative games including 11 for the Players and 16 for the North for whom he took a career-best eight for 48 at Prince's in 1874. He umpired until 1891, his experience over several years including one Test, and he coached in Lancashire and at Stoneyhurst College.

Hill, Henry

Born: 29/11/1858, Thornhill, Dewsbury
Died: 14/08/1935, Headingley, Leeds
RHB. Career: 1888-91. Amateur

On his debut Henry Hill opened the batting and made almost half of Yorkshire's runs in a low-scoring game against MCC at Lord's. He played only irregularly for the county and his club cricket was with Yorkshire Gentlemen and Dewsbury and Savile, whom he captained, and he was also on the Yorkshire committee.

Hill, Lewis Gordon

Born: 02/11/1860, Manningham, Bradford
Died: 27/08/1940, Heaton, Bradford
RHB. Career: 1882. Amateur

Lewis Hill's only known recorded involvement in cricket is his one first-class match and this took place at Derby. He batted at number three.

Hirst, Edward Theodore

Born: 06/05/1857, Deighton, Huddersfield
Died: 26/10/1914, Barnwood, Gloucestershire
RHB. Career: 1877-88. Amateur

A talented sportsman, Edward Hirst was in the first eleven at Rugby School for three seasons before gaining Blues at Oxford in both cricket and rugby. Despite having a sound defence and an attacking approach he scored only one half-century for Yorkshire – against the Australians at Bradford in 1888 although he did score a century for Oxford University. His appearances were spasmodic and he missed the whole of three successive seasons from 1885. His club cricket was mainly for Lascelles Hall and Huddersfield and he also played rugby and tennis for Yorkshire.

Hirst, Ernest William

Born: 27/02/1855, Deighton, Huddersfield
Died: 24/10/1933, Evershot, Dorchester, Dorset
RHB, RFM. Career: 1881. Amateur

Brother of Edward, Ernest Hirst was captain of Huddersfield and also played for Lascelles Hall. He batted for Yorkshire both as opener and in the middle order.

Hirst, George Herbert

Born: 07/09/1871, Kirkheaton, Huddersfield
Died: 10/05/1954, Lindley, Huddersfield
RHB, LMF. Career: 1891-1929.
Cap No 22. Benefit: 1904.
Testimonial: 1921

The name of George Hirst will always be associated with two unique and remarkable 'doubles', one of which, it is safe to say, will never be repeated. In his annus mirabilis of 1906 he scored over 2000 runs, took over 200 wickets and at Bath scored two centuries as well as twice taking five wickets in an innings - all in the same match! Scores of 111 and 117 not out allied to figures of six for 70 and five for 45 enabled Yorkshire to beat Somerset by the huge margin of 389 runs. In a season of 35 matches (including 28 in the Championship) he scored 2,385 runs and took 208 wickets. He was at the peak of his powers, it being the only season in which he passed 200 wickets, and was the third of three successive seasons in which he scored over 2,000 runs.

Hirst played for Kirkheaton from the age of 13 and was soon engaged professionally at Elland, Mirfield and Huddersfield. Initially his bowling was his strongest suit and he learnt to swing the ball devastatingly late, his repertoire being later completed with a slower ball and accurate yorker. Batting in the middle-order, his quick eye and feet enabled him to play short bowling on the leg-side with comfort and his aggressive approach served him well.

Another of Hirst's many records is Yorkshire's highest individual innings – 341 at Leicester in 1905. His best bowling was nine for 23 in the Headingley Roses match of 1910.

An international debut came at Sydney in 1897/98 but Hirst was generally less successful in his 24 Tests (790 runs and 59 wickets) though he made crucial contributions in the Ashes series of 1902. In all first-class cricket he ended his career with 36,356 runs and 2,742 wickets making him one of only nine players to score over 20,000 runs and take 2,000 wickets. He retired in 1921 to coach at Eton but returned for just one match eight years later and also to coach with Yorkshire. He umpired in the Scarborough Festival in every season from 1922 to 1938 and also on Yorkshire's tour of Jamaica in 1936.

Short in stature but strongly built, Hirst's success was allied to him being a most popular figure - always genial and good-humoured. A great cricketer in every sense.

Hirst, Thomas Henry
Born: 21/05/1865, Lockwood , Huddersfield
Died: 03/04/1927, Meltham, Huddersfield
RHB, RFM. Career: 1899

Thomas Hirst was chosen for his only game for Yorkshire after the match had started, deputising for an injured player. His only other first-class match was for Scotland, having been professional with Uddingston for four seasons. He also played for Colne.

Hodd, Andrew John
Born: 12/01/1984, Chichester, Sussex
RHB, WK. Career: 2012-
Cap No 178, 2016

Originally on loan to Yorkshire, Andy Hodd later became a more regular wicket-keeper in the county side due to Jonny Bairstow's increasing involvement with England.

After Bexhill High School, Hodd made his debut for Sussex at the age of 18 then studied at Loughborough University before having one season with Surrey. On returning to Sussex he had only three seasons of regular cricket before making the move north. An efficient and enthusiastic wicket-keeper in all three formats he is also a very reliable batsman. He scored four centuries for Sussex but his best for Yorkshire was when he ran out of partners on 96 not out against Nottinghamshire at Scarborough in 2016. In 2017 he lost his place in the white-ball formats but remained a very reliable performer in the Championship and for New Farnley.

Andrew Hodd in action against Somerset at Scarborough in 2017.

Hodgson, Daniel Mark

Born: 26/02/1990, Northallerton
RHB, WK. Career: 2012-15

After earlier cricket with Richmond School, Durham Academy, Darlington and Leeds/Bradford MCCU, Dan Hodgson contributed very usefully for Yorkshire in both short forms of the game. He was an important member of the side which competed in the Champions League in 2012/13 and later played for Northumberland and Farsley. Most of his first-class cricket was for Mountaineers in Zimbabwe.

Hodgson, Geoffrey

Born: 24/07/1938, Lepton, Huddersfield
RHB, WK. Career: 1964

An excellent wicket-keeper, it was unfortunate for Geoff Hodgson that his career coincided with that of Jimmy Binks but he did have one opportunity albeit not in the Championship. He was very successful in his seven seasons in Yorkshire's second eleven and also played one game for Lancashire. In league cricket he played mainly for Kirkheaton and Spen Victoria.

Hodgson, Isaac

Born: 15/11/1828, Bradford
Died: 24/11/1867, Bowling, Bradford
RHB, LRS. Career: 1863-66

'Ikey' Hodgson was one of the county's first great bowlers and played for 'Yorkshire' from 1852 and then in 21 of the official Club's first 23 games.

Hodgson first came to prominence as an 18-year-old playing against the All England XI and he played in some such matches for 'England' itself. He probably bowled faster than his successors in the style but had a slower ball which broke effectively.

Sadly, Hodgson had to retire through ill-health and died just nine days after his 39th birthday.

Hodgson, Lee John

Born: 29/06/1986, Middlesbrough
RHB, RFM. Career: 2009-11

Lee Hodgson made his debut for Surrey in first-class and List A cricket in 2008 before playing occasionally in all three formats for Yorkshire as a useful all-rounder. His club cricket was with Saltburn, Marton and Marske.

Matthew Hoggard in action for England.

Hodgson, Philip

Born: 21/09/1935, Todmorden
Died: 30/03/2015, Hornsea, Hull
RHB, RFM. Career: 1954-56

Philip Hodgson was a very tall pace bowler who could make the ball rise unexpectedly. He took a five-for in his third game, at Hove, but lost form thereafter. He also played in four first-class matches for the Combined Services and his main clubs were Sheffield United, Pudsey St Lawrence, York and Hull.

Hoggard, Matthew James

Born: 31/12/1976, Leeds
RHB, RFM. Career: 1996-2009
Cap No 149, 2000. Benefit: 2008

The climax of Matthew Hoggard's career was undoubtedly The Ashes series of 2005 when he opened the bowling and often made the crucial, initial breakthrough. He had made his Test debut in 2000 and when established in the side four years later he then played in 40 consecutive matches.

Hoggard's Yorkshire debut came in the year after his one season with the Academy team; he became a regular in 1998 and two winters with Free State in South Africa saw further development. A very skilful swing bowler he could take wickets in all types of conditions as success in India and Australia demonstrated.

His dry sense of humour prompted him to once state that he was allergic to the white-ball and the most expensive analysis in T20 cricket, worldwide, was a brief unwanted record but with 42 wickets in 2000 he is still Yorkshire's leading wicket-taker in a List A season.

Hoggard's Yorkshire appearances were, overall, restricted by his England commitments and it was a shame that he left the county in acrimonious circumstances. In concluding his career with Leicestershire, he led them for three of his four seasons there, including to victory in the Friends Life t20 in 2011. An unexpected finale for an honest and hard-working bowler.

Holdsworth, William Edgar Newman

Born: 17/09/1928, Armley, Leeds
Died: 31/07/2016, Garforth, Leeds
RHB, RMF. Career: 1952-53

One of several bowlers to partner Fred Trueman in his early years, Bill Holdsworth was strong and hard-working. After Woodhouse Grove School he joined Lidget Green then was professional with Stalybridge and Chester-le-Street (one season at each). His front-on action tended to restrict his success at first-class level and his 35 wickets in 15 games in 1953 were not enough for him to receive further opportunities. His later club cricket was with Farsley and Bradford.

Holgate, Gideon

Born: 23/06/1839, Sawley, Barnoldswick
Died: 11/07/1895, Accrington, Lancashire
RHB, WK. Career: 1865-67

A very fine wicket-keeper, Gideon Holgate also played for Lancashire in his final two seasons with Yorkshire, there being no registration restrictions at the time. He scored just two half-centuries – both in the same match for Lancashire against Surrey in 1866. Most of his club cricket was with Burnley, Accrington and Scarborough.

Holmes, Percy

Born: 25/11/1886, Oakes, Huddersfield
Died: 03/09/1971, Marsh, Huddersfield
RHB, RM. Career: 1913-33.
Cap No 52, 1919. Benefit: 1928.
Grant: 1933

A brilliant opening batsman, Percy Holmes was unfortunate to be a contemporary of Jack Hobbs otherwise he would certainly have played more than his seven Tests spread over 12 seasons. But he was hugely fortunate to be a contemporary of the great Herbert Sutcliffe with whom he formed the greatest opening partnership in the history of all first-class cricket. The pair shared a world record 74 century stands together; 69 of these were for Yorkshire and included 64 in the Championship.

Paddock, Golcar and Spen Victoria were Holmes' early clubs and his first games for Yorkshire were in the middle-order, his alliance with Sutcliffe starting in 1919. The record for either county in Roses matches fell to them in that season – a record they improved on later - and both, remarkably, were members of *Wisden's* Five Batsmen of the Season. One of the main features of the pair's batting together was their running between the wickets. They developed a virtually telepathic understanding and seemed to trust each other implicitly. With neither having a recognised technical weakness against any type of bowling they were always able to score at a good speed.

Holmes was short in stature but dapper and very quick on his feet, this enabling him to get into position early. He possessed strokes all around the wicket excelling in particular in the cut. In 1925 with 2,453 runs he had his best season and this included his career-best of 315 not out against Middlesex at Lord's. Although this broke the 105-year old record for the highest innings made at the ground it was surpassed only one year later.

His most famous achievement, however, was to share in the world record stand, for any wicket, of 555 with Sutcliffe against Essex at Leyton in 1932. Holmes' share was 224 not out. At Test level, his most successful time was in South Africa in 1927/28 when he opened with Sutcliffe in all five matches and made four half-centuries.

Although aged 46 at the time of his retirement from Yorkshire he felt he could have played for longer and took up a professional appointment with Swansea and umpired in first-class cricket in 1947. Thereafter he coached at Scarborough College until past his 70th birthday.

With five of Yorkshire's top 11 innings, Holmes stands as one of its greatest batsmen.

Horner, Norman Frederick

Born: 10/05/1926, Queensbury, Bradford
Died: 24/12/2003, Driffield
RHB. Career: 1950

After club cricket with Queensbury, Norman Horner found himself surplus to requirements after his two matches for Yorkshire. In 15 seasons with Warwickshire, though, as an opening batsman he scored over 18,000 runs in over 350 first-class matches. He later was groundsman at Warwick School.

Houseman, Ian James

Born: 12/10/1969, Harrogate
RHB, RFM. Career: 1989-91

After being in the first eleven at Harrogate Grammar School for five seasons, Ian Houseman made his county debut aged only 19 while at Loughborough College. Although obviously showing much potential as a pace bowler, three wickets in five first-class matches were not convincing enough. He had one season with Cumberland and also played for Harrogate and Undercliffe.

Hoyle, Theodore Hind

Born: 19/03/1884, Halifax
Died: 02/06/1953, Hull
?HB, WK. Career: 1919

Theo Hoyle gained his one chance to play for Yorkshire when regular 'keeper Arthur Dolphin was representing the Players. His club cricket was with Halifax, Morley and Elland.

Hudson, Bennett

Born: 29/06/1851, Sheffield
Died: 11/11/1901, Wortley, Sheffield
RHB, RFM. Career: 1880

After playing for a few Yorkshire clubs, including Elland and Batley, as well as the county side, Bennett Hudson took up engagements in Lancashire with, amongst others, Bacup and Burnley. As a hard-hitting batsman, he also played five games for the Red Rose county.

Hunter, David

Born: 23/02/1860, Scarborough
Died: 11/01/1927, Northstead, Scarborough
RHB, WK. Career: 1888-1909.
Cap No 14. Benefit: 1897

Almost certainly the best wicket-keeper never to have played for England, David Hunter – who succeeded his brother Joseph in the Yorkshire line-up - stood in that position for the county during a 16-year period when it won no fewer than eight Championship titles. He had to keep to probably the best trio of bowlers in the White Rose county's history in Schofield Haigh, George Hirst and Wilfred Rhodes.

All three posed enormous difficulties for the batsmen and these were often made even more challenging for the man standing behind the stumps.

Despite this, Hunter stood up to the wicket for much of the earlier part of his career. Although he was tall, especially for a wicket-keeper, at over six feet, his agility and alertness allied to his acute sense of timing meant that he was virtually always in the right place at the right time. The fact that over 27% of his dismissals were stumpings shows how ready he was to pounce on the slightest error made by the batsman. His total of 1,186 victims for Yorkshire gives him the pre-eminent position, his nearest rival having 142 dismissals fewer.

A senior figure in the side during the latter part of his career, Hunter captained Yorkshire on six occasions, mainly in 1908, when the side emerged with four wins and two draws. Other honours which came his way were several games for the Players as well as the North but Dick Lilley, who was regarded as a better batsman, but an inferior 'keeper, kept him out of the Test team.

With regard to his batting, Hunter's place was as part of the tail but he could be very stubborn and took part in four century stands for the tenth wicket. None of these were when he made his only half-century but his partnership of 148 with Lord Hawke against Kent at Sheffield in 1898 stood as the county record for 84 years. His highest innings came at Worcester in 1900.

Hunter's first cricket was with Scarborough and he coached at the club in his retirement. His quiet and undemonstrative manner with younger players replicated his

approach as a player but those who fell victim to him certainly knew how quickly he could act.

Hunter, Joseph
Born: 03/08/1855, Scarborough
Died: 04/01/1891, Rotherham
RHB, WK. Career: 1878-88

The only Scarborough-born cricketer ever to play for England, Joseph Hunter succeeded George Pinder in the county side although it took four seasons for him to ensure a regular place as first-choice wicket-keeper. He had started with Scarborough mainly as an opening batsman.

A sound practitioner, Hunter was not as skilful as some of his contemporaries but he took nine catches in a match at Gloucester in 1887 and this stood as a Yorkshire record for 95 years. His highest innings came against the same county at Bradford in 1885. All of his five Test matches had come in the previous winter in Australia.

Hunter was followed by his brother David in the Yorkshire team. Although only 32 at the time of his last game, his health was declining rapidly and, tragically, he lived for only three more years.

Hutchison, Paul Michael

Born: 09/06/1977, Leeds
LHB, LFM. Career: 1996-2001
Cap No 146, 1998

When Paul Hutchison took seven wickets in a first-class innings for a third time and was still aged only 21 – a feat only previously achieved for Yorkshire by Fred Trueman - it was assumed that he had a great future ahead of him. His potential was confirmed with 59 wickets in 1998 and a career average at least five runs superior to four of his team-mates who all played for England. He went on his second England A tour but after playing in just one match in Zimbabwe he developed a stress fracture of the back and had to come home.

Once the fracture had healed Hutchison's action was remodelled but he was never as effective again. After Yorkshire had released him he had two seasons each with Sussex and Middlesex and later was with Pudsey St Lawrence, including being cricket chairman, then New Farnley as cricket manager. While working in sports retailing as well, he became consultant coach for Sweden in 2013 and head coach two years later.

Hutton, Leonard

Born: 23/06/1916, Fulneck, Pudsey
Died: 06/09/1990, Norbiton,
Kingston-on-Thames, Surrey
RHB, LB. Career: 1934-55.
Cap No 77, 1936. Benefit: 1950

By the age of 16, Len Hutton was opening the batting for Pudsey St Lawrence and him soon impressing Yorkshire's hierarchy resulted in his second team debut 30 days before his 17th birthday.

Promotion to the first eleven followed and in his first season he became Yorkshire's youngest-ever century-maker. In 1937 he played in the first of his 79 Tests and started with a duck! (His second and first-team debuts had been similarly marked.) The following season brought him his most famous innings; a marathon 13 hours and 17 minutes at the crease and 364 runs at

Len Hutton batting for Yorkshire in his last season of 1955.

The Oval against Australia gave him the world record for the highest score ever made in a Test match.

Unfortunately for Hutton the Second World War soon intervened and in 1941 an accident in training in a York gymnasium resulted in a fracture and dislocation to his left arm. Three operations followed but this resulted in his left arm being two inches shorter. The handicap of having to adjust his technique was overcome so well that in 1949 he became only the second – and last - Yorkshire player to pass 3,000 runs in a season. Furthermore the 1,294 runs which he scored in June remain the record for any month.

Hutton's exemplary technique enabled him to succeed on all types of pitches and conditions. His beautiful and graceful cover drive ranks with that of all the great batsmen and he played every shot to perfection. With his sound defence and remarkable powers of concentration he was able to build long innings almost instinctively.

Despite only having captained Yorkshire in one match, his elevation to the role with England was an obvious move. His status as a professional, however, caused controversy but he made history, yet again, when he led out the side to face India at Headingley, no less, in 1952. A year later, he famously triumphed in captaining his country to victory in the Ashes but probably even more impressively he became, 18 months later, the first captain to have won the Ashes at home and then successfully defend them in Australia.

In 1955 Hutton realised that he was a spent force and retired shortly after his 39th birthday. His outstanding contribution to cricket was rewarded with a knighthood in 1956. Sir Leonard was a Test selector for two years from 1975 and President of Yorkshire in 1990. Tragically, he lasted only a few months in office before passing away and his Memorial Service in York Minster was attended by a congregation of 2,000. There could not have been a more fitting tribute to a very great batsman and captain.

Hutton, Richard Anthony

Born: 06/09/1942, Pudsey
RHB, RFM. Career: 1962-1974
Cap No 111, 1964

The elder son of Sir Leonard, Richard Hutton was a fine cricketer in his own right – a genuine all-rounder good enough to represent his country. His bowling used his height (six feet, four inches) to enable him to achieve awkward lift and bounce and this was allied to good use of seam and swing. As a batsman he had a stylish off-drive and stood upright to deliver punishing blows. He was also an excellent slip-fielder.

Three years in the first eleven at Repton School were followed by Blues in each of three years at Cambridge University from 1962 onwards. The strength of the Yorkshire side in the 1960s prevented Hutton from gaining a regular place until 1968 but his consistency thereafter brought him his five Test caps in 1971. In the following winter he toured Australia with the Rest of the World.

In the first season of the John Player League Hutton had the remarkable bowling figures of 7.1-1-15-7 at Headingley against Worcestershire and this remains the record for Yorkshire in all List A cricket. There might have been more days like this but his retirement at the age of 31 appeared to have been caused by his clashes with Geoff Boycott. From 1991 he edited the *The*

Cricketer magazine for eight years and in 2017 was elected President of Yorkshire CCC.

Iddison, Roger

Born: 15/09/1834, Bedale
Died: 19/03/1890, York
RHB, RRF/Lobs. Career: 1863-76

Having captained 'Yorkshire' in some of the eight matches in which he played from 1855, it was natural that Roger Iddison should become Yorkshire CCC's first appointed skipper. Despite this honour the lack of regulations of the period meant that he could still play as many as 16 games for Lancashire. That county's first century came from his bat in 1866.

A member of the first touring party to go to Australia in 1861/62, Iddison was an all-rounder of note. A powerful batsman with a sound defence, he twice came third in the national averages and his bowling produced a strong break-back.

An important figure in the county's history, Iddison led Yorkshire to its first unofficial championship titles in 1867 and 1870 and was influential in the early days of the Scarborough festival.

Illingworth, Raymond

Born: 08/06/1932, Pudsey
RHB, OB. Career: 1951-83.
Cap No 96, 1955. Benefit: 1965

One of the best all-rounders in England, Ray Illingworth moved to Leicestershire after 1968 to become captain. An injury to Colin Cowdrey projected him to the England leadership and he enjoyed five years of considerable success including the famous Ashes triumph in Australia in 1970/71.

Illingworth was in Farsley's first eleven at the age of 15 and changed his medium-paced bowling to off-spin. It was in this role that he became accomplished in the county side. After a longish, slow run-up he would deliver the ball on a teasing line and length, very rarely being punished, and could spin it appreciably in the right conditions.

As a batsman, Illingworth eventually settled into the pivotal number six position from where he could keep the score moving or play a more solid role as needed. He was also an excellent fielder especially in the gully.

Ray Illingworth in 1969 – his first season as England captain.

Among Illingworth's highlights was 135 and 14 for 101 at Dover in 1964; a career-best nine for 42 at Worcester in 1957 and seven for six against Gloucestershire at Harrogate as Yorkshire clinched the County Championship in 1967.

Illingworth made his Test debut in 1958 but never gained a regular place in the team until he became captain.

Regarded as one of the best of all England's leaders, the team lost only five of his 31 matches in charge and he was only the fourth skipper to regain the Ashes in Australia. Tactically extremely astute, he also had good man-management skills bringing out the best in 'difficult' characters such as fast-bowler John Snow as well as those who were not so vital but had important roles to play.

Having initially left Yorkshire over a contract dispute, Illingworth returned as manager in 1979. Five controversial years in the post ended after he had taken over the captaincy during the 1982 season at the age of 50. The county won the John Player League in the next season but also came bottom of the Championship for the only time in its history. A new committee summarily sacked him.

A spell as a television commentator was followed by appointment as England manager in 1994 but this also is regarded as a period of failure. His methods were outdated, particularly in the 1996 World Cup, and some players appeared to find it difficult to relate to him.

One of only nine players to score over 20,000 runs and take over 2,000 wickets in first-class cricket, Illingworth was Yorkshire's president for two years from 2010. He will always be remembered in the county primarily for his vital all-round role in the great side of the 1960s.

Imran Tahir, Mohammad
Born: 27/03/1979, Lahore, Pakistan
RHB, LBG. Career: 2007

Imran Tahir made his Test debut aged 32 for South Africa rather than his native country. He represented his new nation in all three formats later becoming a white-ball specialist and playing in over 200 such games. He played for several teams in four countries, his other first-class counties being Middlesex, Hampshire, Warwickshire, Nottinghamshire and Derbyshire. His undistinguished career with Yorkshire consisted of one game in the Championship in which he took no wicket for 141.

Ingham, Peter Geoffrey
Born: 28/09/1956, Beauchief, Sheffield
RHB, OB. Career: 1979-81

Peter Ingham spent five seasons in the first eleven at Ashville College, Harrogate, being captain in the final two. Although he won the Cricket Society's award for the best all-rounder in private-school cricket he never bowled for Yorkshire in any of his 20 matches in two formats. An opening batsman and brilliant fielder, he later had three seasons with Northumberland and played for Birstall and Hanging Heaton, captaining both.

Inglis, John William
Born: 19/10/1979, Ripon
RHB, RM. Career: 2000

A product of Ripon Grammar School, John Inglis played for the Academy for two years prior to his two one-day games for England U-19 and his solitary (first-class) appearance for Yorkshire. He was with Harrogate for several seasons and later played for Methley, Wrenthorpe and Beckwithshaw before moving to Bilton in 2017.

Inzamam-ul-Haq
Born: 03/03/1970, Multan, Pakistan
RHB, SLA. Career: 2007

One of the best middle-order batsmen of his era, Inzamam played in 119 Tests and 375 ODIs for Pakistan and scored over 30,000 runs in first-class cricket and List A matches combined, this including a score of 329 against New Zealand at Lahore in 2002. He played six games in two formats for Yorkshire towards the end of the season and found the experience rather chilly.

Jackson, Frank Stanley

Born: 21/11/1870, Chapel Allerton, Leeds
Died: 09/03/1947, Hyde Park, London
RHB, RFM. Career: 1890-1907.
Amateur. Cap No 20

To come top of both the batting and bowling averages in a series against Australia, and – as captain - to win all five tosses and lead England to the regaining of the Ashes reads like a storybook scenario. This is what actually happened to Stanley Jackson in 1905 when he was at the height of his powers.

FS Jackson in his time as Yorkshire President.

Because of other commitments, Jackson played only four full seasons with Yorkshire but, batting in the upper order, his orthodox, attacking strokeplay and skilfully-varied bowling as well as brilliant fielding, especially at cover point, meant that he always seemed to be contributing to his side's success and performed the double in 1898. As Lord Hawke's occasional deputy with Yorkshire he won 18 and lost only two of his 30 games at the helm. His 20 Tests, in which he scored 1,415 runs, were all against Australia and all at home.

On his father's death Jackson became a Rt Hon and was knighted in 1927 when he became Governor of Bengal for five years. This was after having been MP for North Leeds, serving in the cabinet of the First World War and being chairman of the Tory Party. His interest in cricket continued, though: he was President of MCC in 1921 and of Yorkshire CCC from 1939 until his death. He was also a Test selector, twice being chairman. Did the Golden Age of cricket produce anyone who epitomised its spirit of flair and style more than Jackson?

Jackson, Samuel Robinson

Born: 15/07/1859, Ecclesall, Sheffield
Died: 19/07/1941, Leeds
RHB. Career: 1891. Amateur

About half of a Roses match at Old Trafford represented the total first-class career of Samuel Jackson. After lunch on day two he was, most unusually, allowed to substitute for an injured player. In May 1890 he had the honour of receiving the first ball ever bowled in a match at Headingley; this was for Leeds, whom he captained for many years. He was on the Yorkshire committee for several years and later became a vice-president.

Jacques, Thomas Alec
Born: 19/02/1905, Cliffe, Selby
Died: 23/02/1995, Selby
RHB, RF. Career: 1927-36. Amateur

A hostile pace bowler, 'Sandy' Jacques took five for 33 against Essex at Headingley in 1931; otherwise he had limited success and opportunity, playing more than four matches in only two of his seven seasons. He played professionally for Colne and also had several years with Undercliffe. A popular player who died four days after his 90th birthday, his other clubs were Saltaire, Eccleshill and York. In the Bradford League, he once took an 'all ten', all clean bowled, and took 28 out of 30 wickets to fall in four Priestley Cup Finals.

Jakeman, Frederick
Born: 10/01/1921, Holmfirth
Died: 17/05/1986, Lindley, Huddersfield
LHB. Career: 1946-47

The Second World War postponed Freddie Jakeman's first-class career until he was aged 26 but only one half-century in 16 innings with Yorkshire led to a move to Northamptonshire. There his aggressive batting produced over 5,000 runs in 119 matches in six seasons; his 258 not out against Essex at Northampton in 1951 was, at the time, the highest innings ever scored for his new county.

Jakeman had started his cricket with Holmfirth, topping the Huddersfield League averages in 1940; he later played for Lightcliffe, Salts and David Brown Tractors. He umpired in first-class cricket from 1961 to 1972.

James, Brian
Born: 23/04/1934, Darfield, Barnsley
Died: 26/05/1999, Honley, Huddersfield
RHB, LMF. Career: 1954

Brian James took only eight wickets in his four games for Yorkshire but was more successful in league cricket. He played most frequently for Honley but was also a professional with both Brighouse and Bankfoot.

Jaques, Philip Anthony
Born: 03/05/1979, Wollongong, New South Wales, Australia
LHB, SLC. Career: 2004-13.
Cap No 155, 2005

Phil Jaques played in a total of 130 games in all three formats in 2004, 2005, 2012 and 2013. Batting in the upper order, he was effective against both red and white ball and made his mark in his first season with 243 at Southampton to become the first batsman to score a double century both for and against Yorkshire.

Phil Jaques playing against Durham at Scarborough in 2013.

Jaques made over 1,100 first-class runs in 2004 but in his second season made over 200 runs more. His later two seasons were less successful. A strong and correct batsman he played in 11 Tests and six ODIs for Australia and his other counties were Northamptonshire, Worcestershire and Nottinghamshire.

Jarvis, Paul William

Born: 29/06/1965, Redcar
RHB, RFM. Career: 1981-93.
Cap No 127, 1986

When Paul Jarvis first played for Yorkshire in a List A match at the age of 16 years and 62 days he was, at the time, the county's youngest-ever player. His first-class debut followed just 13 days later.

Jarvis' early cricket was with Marske and Harrogate. Not being tall for a fast bowler, he made the ball skid onto the batsman and often gave the impression of being faster than he really was. With well-controlled seam movement he was very successful in the early part of his career. His peak came in 1987 when he took 81 wickets in first-class cricket and 36 in List A matches. The latter included four for 43 in the victorious Benson and Hedges Cup final against Northamptonshire at Lord's.

A Test debut came in the following winter but during a career of nine caps in five different series he became disillusioned and joined a 'rebel' tour to South Africa. He also played in 16 ODIs. A series of injuries did not help his progress and a move to give him a fresh start, to Sussex for whom he played for five seasons, was followed by two years with Somerset. He later became Director of Cricket at Framlington College, Suffolk.

Johnson, Colin

Born: 05/09/1947, Pocklington
RHB, RM/OB. Career: 1969-79
Testimonial: 1986

Although the career of Colin Johnson was relatively lengthy, he played regularly for Yorkshire in only one season. In 1972 he played in all but one of the county's 45 matches, this being despite him making only two half-centuries – one in each of the two formats.

Johnson spent four years in the first eleven at Pocklington School, his final one as captain and was successful in league cricket particularly with Harrogate and Pudsey St Lawrence both of whom he captained to several trophies. He also played for Bankfoot.

A sound middle-order batsman, Johnson had a good defensive technique and a good range of leg-side attacking shots. A most brilliant out-fielder, especially in the covers, it was often this part of his game which kept him in the side. His testimonial, unusually, was awarded seven years after his last game and, uniquely, this came in the form of an 'appreciation fund'.

Johnson, Joseph

Born: 16/05/1916, South Kirkby, Pontefract
Died: 16/01/2011, Netherthong, Holmforth
RHB, SLA. Career: 1936-39

Wicketless in the first two of his three matches, in which he played in three different seasons, Joseph Johnson then took five for 16 at Leicester, including two wickets with his last two balls in first-class cricket. He was professional with Clackmannan, Scotland and also played for David Brown Tractors as well as being their groundsman. He played football for Doncaster Rovers and Southport.

Johnson, Mark

Born: 23/04/1958, Gleadless, Sheffield
RHB, RFM. Career: 1981

Although primarily a bowler, Mark Johnson will be mostly remembered for a score of four not out! With David Bairstow, he took part in what is still Yorkshire's List A record tenth-wicket stand of 80, unbeaten, turning near-certain defeat at Derby into an amazing victory. In 1980 he captained Holmfirth to a double and also played for Elland, Guisborough and Darlington RA. He spent two winters coaching in South Africa.

Joy, Jonathan

Born: 29/12/1825, Farnham, Knaresborough
Died: 27/09/1889, Middlesbrough
RHB, RRMF. Career: 1863-67

In a first-class career covering 19 seasons Jonathan Joy played in four matches for 'Yorkshire' from 1849. His three games for the official Club included each of the first two Roses matches. A powerful batsman, he played representative cricket three times for the North and had an extensive career in club cricket. This began with Knaresborough and Harrogate and was followed by longer engagements with Stockton-on-Tees, Redcar and Middlesbrough where he was both captain and groundsman at different times.

Judson, Albert

Born: 10/07/1885, Cullingworth, Bingley
Died: 08/04/1975, Bingley
RHB, RFM. Career: 1920

The one Yorkshire match which Albert Judson played in lasted a mere 25 minutes. Against Kent at Sheffield his one over was his only contribution to the game. An accurate swing bowler in league cricket, he was professional at Keighley for three seasons from 1924 and then played for Bingley for 23 years.

Katich, Simon Matthew

Born: 21/08/1975, Middle Swan, Midland, Western Australia
LHB, SLC. Career: 2002

Of Simon Katich's four games for Yorkshire only one was in first-class cricket. Over a ten-year period he played in 56 Tests for Australia in the lower-middle order and later as an opening batsman. He scored over

20,000 runs in his first-class career, his other main teams being his home state as well as New South Wales, Durham, Hampshire, Lancashire and Derbyshire.

Kaye, Harold Swift
Born: 09/05/1882, Mirfield, Wakefield
Died: 06/11/1953, St John's, Wakefield
RHB. Career: 1907-08. Amateur

Harold Kaye was in the first eleven at Harrow for two years and had a long career for Yorkshire Gentlemen. A lieutenant-colonel in the army, he was awarded the DSO and Military Cross in 1916. Having captained Yorkshire on five occasions as a deputy for Lord Hawke, he later returned to the Club as a committee member.

Kaye, Haven
Born: 11/06/1846, Huddersfield
Died: 24/01/1892, Halifax
RHB, RRFM. Career: 1872-73

An opening batsman, Haven Kaye played representative matches for Colts of England and United North of England but not in first-class cricket. His first club was Lascelles Hall and he later played for Saddleworth but also occasionally for Halifax, Bradford and Elland. His highest innings for Yorkshire came in an opening stand of 90 at The Oval.

Keedy, Gary
Born: 27/11/1974, Sandal, Wakefield
LHB, SLA. Career: 1994

After only one match for Yorkshire, first-class, in which he scored one run but neither bowled nor took a catch, Gary Keedy had a long and very successful career with Lancashire. After Garforth School he played 14 times for England U-19.

He took 696 first-class wickets in his 18-season career with the Red Rose from 1995 before one year with Surrey and two with Nottinghamshire.

Keighley, William Geoffrey
Born: 10/01/1925, Nice, France
Died: 14/06/2005, Golden Vale, Sutton Forest, New South Wales, Australia
RHB, RFM. Career: 1947-51. Amateur. Cap No 90, 1949

The only Yorkshire cricketer in the 1946-91 period to be born outside the county, Geoffrey Keighley's parents were from Bradford. Having spent eight years of his boyhood in Australia, he went to Eton where he captained the first eleven and then to Oxford University where he twice gained a Blue. A batsman of class, he never had a full season with the county and left the game after touring Canada with MCC in autumn 1951. He emigrated to Australia and politics took him to the Upper House at Canberra.

Kellett, Simon Andrew
Born: 16/10/1967, Mirfield, Wakefield
RHB, OB. Career: 1989-95.
Cap No 135, 1992

Simon Kellett played in only two full seasons with Yorkshire; these were in 1991 and 1992 and he scored over 1,000 first-class runs in each as well as making over 500 runs in List A cricket in 1992. He began 1993 with half-centuries in each of the first two matches but then lost his place to Richie Richardson and never recovered form or favour. The winter of 1991/92 was spent with Wellington in New Zealand, his only other first-class team.

A stylish opening batsman, Kellett made several valuable contributions and his two highest innings in each format were both scored against Derbyshire. Following his release by Yorkshire he spent 15 seasons in the Minor County Championship with Cambridgeshire (mostly) and Herefordshire. His club cricket was with Undercliffe, Cambridge Granta and Dunnington whom he also captained. He later became cricket professional at Bradford Grammar School.

Kennie, George
Born: 17/05/1904, Bradford
Died: 11/04/1994, Poole, Dorset
RHB. Career: 1927

Despite not having a good season with either Yorkshire second eleven or Bowling Old Lane, George Kennie was called upon to replace Percy Holmes at Old Trafford at short notice. His brilliant fielding may have contributed to his selection but his first match for Yorkshire was also his last. He also played soccer for Bradford Park Avenue.

Kettleborough, Richard Allan
Born: 15/03/1973, Sheffield
LHB, RM. Career: 1994-97

After being in the first eleven at Workshop College, Richard Kettleborough played in 54 first-class matches in his two-county career. As a middle-order batsman his only first-class century came against Essex at Headingley in 1996 when his crucial innings helped turn potential defeat into comfortable victory.

Two seasons with Middlesex followed his time with Yorkshire and he then played for Sheffield Collegiate while starting an umpiring career in 2002. Promotion to the County Championship came two years later and to international cricket in 2009. Rapidly making a positive impression he was awarded ICC Umpire of the Year in three successive years from 2013. Having joined the Elite Panel in 2011, he has been an on-field offical in over 130 international matches.

Kilburn, Sam
Born: 16/10/1868, Dalton, Huddersfield
Died: 25/09/1940, Crosland Moor,
Huddersfield
RHB. Career: 1896

Sam Kilburn had an extremely short career with Yorkshire but an extensive one in club cricket. After time with Kirkheaton and Dalton he played as a professional for Church for three seasons before joining Lascelles Hall, much later winning the Huddersfield League batting prize at the age of 53.

Kilner, Norman

Born: 21/07/1895, Low Valley, Wombwell, Barnsley
Died: 28/04/1979, Alum Rock, Birmingham
RHB, RM. Career: 1919-23

Norman Kilner found it difficult to maintain a regular place in the Yorkshire side and so decided to move to Warwickshire where he was much more successful. A solid top-order batsman, he was the younger brother of Roy and first played for Mitchell Main and Barnsley.

Kilner spent 14 seasons with the midland county and scored over 16,000 runs in 330 matches with a top score of 228 at Worcester in 1933; he averaged almost 14 runs more than he had with Yorkshire. After umpiring in first-class cricket for three seasons from 1938 he remained with Warwickshire as coach and also coached at Birmingham University – golf as well as cricket!

Kilner, Roy

Born: 17/10/1890, Low Valley, Wombwell, Barnsley
Died: 05/04/1928, Kendray, Barnsley
LHB, SLA. Career: 1911-27.
Cap No 50. Benefit: 1925

One of the most popular players of his era, Roy Kilner's life was cut tragically short. A man of generosity and charm as well as humour he enlivened many a dull day.

Kilner, like his brother Norman, was a nephew of Irving Washington and also played for Mitchell Main. He began his career with Yorkshire as an aggressive batsman whose best strokes were the pull and the off-drive. After the First World War he found that his versatile spin bowling, which included the chinaman as well as variations in flight and pace, was needed to be used more and he became a genuine all-rounder completing the double on four occasions. He played nine times for England over a three-year period from 1924, making 59 on his debut against South Africa and 74 at Melbourne in 1924/25 having taken eight wickets in the previous Test at Adelaide.

Unfortunately, during a coaching visit to India in 1927/28, Kilner contracted enteric fever and, although fit enough to return home, never recovered and died in hospital. An estimated 100,000 lined the streets for the funeral of a player always held in high esteem.

King, Anthony Mountain

Born: 08/10/1932, Laughton-en-le-Morthern, Sheffield
RHB. Career: 1955

Tony King was in the first eleven at Bradford Grammar School for one season and also played for Salts and Bradford. A middle-order batsman, he scored 12 in his only first-class innings. A noted rugby union player, he captained Bradford in 1959/60.

Kippax, Peter John

Born: 15/10/1940, Huddersfield
Died: 17/01/2017, Harrogate
RHB, LB. Career: 1961-62

Peter Kippax was captain at Bedford Modern School in the last of his four years in the first eleven. An accurate bowler, five of his eight first-class wickets came in one innings – at Leicester in 1961. He played for Northumberland for three seasons from 1975 and then for Durham until 1990. His clubs included Lockwood, Luton Town, Leeds, West Hartlepool as professional, Idle and Harrogate. He coached at Woodhouse Grove School and Ashville College, Harrogate and later founded a cricket bat-making business.

Kirby, Steven Paul

Born: 04/10/1977, Ainsworth, Bolton, Lancashire
RHB, RFM. Career: 2001-04
Cap No 152, 2003

Steven Kirby arrived at Headingley via Leicestershire second eleven and made an immediate impact with his hostility and aggression. Coming in halfway through a match against Kent in early June as substitute for Matthew Hoggard he announced his presence with figures of seven for 50. The leading bowler in Yorkshire's Championship-winning campaign, he took 47 wickets in only ten matches.

A total of 67 first-class wickets in 2003 made it his best season but he soon moved to Gloucestershire for six seasons and then had three with Somerset. On taking up coaching he worked firstly in the south-west then with Oxford University and was appointed Head Coach for MCC at Lord's in 2016.

Kohler-Cadmore, Tom

Born: 19/08/1994, Chatham, Kent
RHB, OB. Career: 2017-

As a resident of East Yorkshire as a boy, Tom Kohler-Cadmore played for Yorkshire's age-group teams before taking up a sixth-form cricket scholarship at Malvern College. He joined the Worcestershire Academy before making his debut for the county side in 2013 in List A cricket and then in the other two formats a year later. A powerful stroke-maker he was successful in all three formats with his first county. He moved to Yorkshire during the 2017 season and played in the Championship and T20 matches, also joining Driffield.

Kruis, Gideon Jacobus
Born: 09/05/1974, Pretoria, Transvaal, South Africa
RHB, RFM. Career: 2005-09
Cap No 157, 2006

Deon Kruis made his debut aged 19 and had already taken 252 first-class wickets for Northern Transvaal, Griqualand West and Eagles. As Yorkshire's first Kolpak player his experience also included five seasons in Lancashire leagues. A total of 64 Championship wickets in his first season with Yorkshire was a major factor in the county winning promotion and also saw him as the country's leading wicket-taker. Unfortunately he never again produced such form and was injured for much of 2007.

Tall with an energetic action, Kruis was accurate, swung the ball and produced deceptive pace. He retired after his final season with Yorkshire having taken almost 600 wickets for all teams in all three formats.

Lambert, Greg Andrew
Born: 04/01/1980, Stoke-on-Trent, Staffordshire
RHB, RMF. Career: 2000

Greg Lambert played for the Academy in 1998 and the YCB in a List A match the following year. After his very short stint with Yorkshire he tried his luck elsewhere and, remarkably, played for no less than six county second elevens. Being very tall, his height often helped him in his bowling.

Lancaster, William Whiteley
Born: 04/02/1873, Scholes, Huddersfield
Died: 30/12/1938, Marsh, Huddersfield
RHB, RRFM. Career: 1895

A middle-order batsman, William Lancaster played in seven consecutive games but scored only one half century and they remained his only first-class matches. He played club cricket for Thongsbridge, Paddock and Burnley as professional in 1896. His elder brother, Tom, played for Lancashire.

Landon, Charles Whittington
Born: 30/05/1850, Bromley, Kent
Died: 05/03/1903, Ledstone Hall, Castleford
RHB, RRM. Career: 1878-82.
Amateur

Not only was Charles Landon born outside the county but he also made his first-class debut for Lancashire, in 1874. He had spent two years in the first eleven at Bromsgrove School as an all-rounder but his bowling was little used at county level and he never gained a regular place in the Yorkshire side. He also played for Yorkshire Gentlemen and the United North of England XI.

Law, William

Born: 09/04/1851, Rochdale,
Lancashire
Died: 20/12/1892, Rotherham
RHB, RMF. Career: 1871-73.
Amateur

William Law made his first-class debut for Oxford University in 1871 and led the side in his fourth year but made less than a handful of appearances for Yorkshire. Ministry in the C of E took him to Beverley and the mission at Harrow School where he had spent four years in the first eleven and later had a pavilion erected in his memory. His final posting was to Rotherham where he captained Rotherham CC. He was a successful pace bowler in club cricket.

Lawson, Mark Anthony Kenneth

Born: 24/10/1985, Leeds
RHB, LB. Career: 2004-07

With a five-for in only his third Championship match, Mark Lawson showed obvious promise. Competition from Adil Rashid, however, limited his appearances though he did take 26 wickets in seven first-class matches in 2006 with a best of six for 88 against Middlesex at Scarborough. He tried his luck with Middlesex, Derbyshire, Kent and Staffordshire and later played for New Farnley and Woodlands.

Leadbeater, Barrie

Born: 14/08/1943, Harehills, Leeds
RHB, RM. Career: 1966-79
Cap No 113, 1969. Benefit: 1980

Only the second player to score 1,000 runs in a season for Yorkshire's second eleven, Barrie Leadbeater often opened the innings. Although he possessed some attractive strokes he was consistent and steady. In his 147 first-class matches he scored only one century, an innings of 140 not out at Portsmouth in 1976.

Leadbeater's most famous knock came in the Gillette Cup final of 1969 when his 76 against Derbyshire secured him the man-of–the match award and also, unusually, his List A average was better than in first-class cricket. His playing career was followed by him becoming a very successful umpire who stood in county matches from 1981 to 2008. He also acted as a TV umpire in Tests and ODIs as well as being a training officer.

Leadbeater, Edric

Born: 15/08/1927, Lockwood,
Huddersfield
Died: 17/04/2011, Huddersfield
RHB, LB. Career: 1949-56

Capped by England but never by Yorkshire, Eddie Leadbeater played in two Test matches on the tour of India in 1951/52. Over 80 wickets in each of the previous two seasons had justified his selection.

Leadbeater gave the ball flight, despite his short stature, as well as varying his deliveries with a top-spinner. An analysis of eight for 83 at Worcester in 1950 remains the best performance by a Yorkshire leg-spinner but his form declined and he moved to Warwickshire for two years after being released by Yorkshire. His clubs were Liversedge, Pudsey St Lawrence and Royton but he was most associated with Almondbury for whom he played at the ages of 13 and 68.

Leadbeater, Harry

Born: 31/12/1863, Scarborough
Died: 09/10/1928, Scarborough
LHB, LM. Career: 1884-90. Amateur

None of Harry Leadbeater's ten first-class matches were against another county although he did play twice for the Gentlemen. A free-scoring batsman in club cricket he had a long association with Scarborough for whom he was also secretary.

Leaning, Jack Andrew

Born: 18/10/1993, Bristol, Gloucestershire
RHB, RMF. Career: 2012-
Cap No 180, 2016

Jack Leaning came to live in the county when his father became a coach at York City FC. He had three seasons with the Academy and played for York from 2013. A useful middle-order batsman, his breakthrough season for Yorkshire came in 2015 when he scored over 900 runs in first-class cricket. Since that year he has played less regularly but in 2017 returned to some of his best form in all three formats, particularly in T20 cricket.

Jack Leaning batting against Somerset at Taunton in 2017.

Three of his four first-class centuries came in 2015 but his best innings was 131 not out in a Royal London Cup match at Leicester in 2016 when he and Travis Head created a new record for any wicket in Yorkshire's entire List A history. In early-2017 he played for the North in a series of 50-overs matches in Abu Dhabi.

Leatham, Gerald Arthur Buxton

Born: 30/04/1851, Hemsworth Hall, Pontefract
Died: 19/06/1932, Dinas, Padstow, Cornwall
RHB, WK. Career: 1874-86.
Amateur

One of the best amateur wicket-keepers of his time, Gerald Leatham played only intermittently for Yorkshire but represented the Gentlemen eight times. One of six brothers, his family occasionally produced an eleven of their own to play in local matches.

Leather, Roland Sutcliffe

Born: 17/08/1880, Wyther, Kirkstall, Leeds
Died: 03/01/1913, Heliopolis, Egypt
RHB. Career: 1906. Amateur

The only first-class match in which Roland Leather played was when he opened the batting for a weak Yorkshire team against the non-Test playing West Indies. He was in the first eleven in his final year at Marlborough College in 1898 and played for at least ten years for Harrogate.

Lee, Charles

Born: 17/03/1924, Eastwood, Rotherham
Died: 04/09/1999, Leicester
RHB, RM. Career: 1952

Although Charles Lee was Yorkshire second eleven's leading run-scorer in both 1951 and 1952, competition for batting places was stiff. He moved to Derbyshire in 1954 where he spent 11 seasons as an opening batsman, scoring over 12,000 runs, and was appointed the county's first professional captain in 1963. His early club cricket was with Rotherham, where he returned as captain, and, later, Sheffield United and Swinton.

Lee, Frederick

Born: 18/11/1856, Baildon, Bradford
Died: 13/09/1896, Baildon, Bradford
RHB, WK. Career: 1882-90. Cap No 7

A stylish batsman who occasionally kept wicket, Fred Lee's best two seasons were in 1885, when he scored over 900 runs, and two years later when he made a career-best 165 against Lancashire at Bradford. He often batted in a free and enterprising manner close to the top of the order.

Lee topped Baildon's batting averages for three consecutive seasons from 1879 and later played for several other clubs including Bradford, Saltaire, Bowling Old Lane, Warrington and Bingley.

Lord Hawke felt that Lee did not always play for the team and so became one of the professionals to be dispensed with. Tragically he died from pleurisy and pneumonia more than two months before his 40th birthday.

Lee, George Henry

Born: 24/08/1854, Scarr,
Almondbury, Huddersfield
Died: 04/10/1919, Lockwood,
Huddersfield
?HB. Career: 1879

George Lee opened the batting in his only game for Yorkshire – a Roses match at Old Trafford. He is recorded as having played some games for Lockwood and Dalton.

Lee, Herbert

Born: 02/07/1856, Taylor Hill,
Huddersfield
Died: 04/02/1908, Lockwood,
Huddersfield
RHB. Career: 1885

After scoring 141 for the second eleven Herbert Lee was given a run of five matches, including four against other counties, but his highest score was a mere 12. He was brother to George and also played for Lockwood.

Lee, James Edward

Born: 23/03/1838, Soothill, Dewsbury
Died: 02/04/1880, Earlsheaton,
Dewsbury
?HB. Career: 1867. Amateur

James Lee's two games for Yorkshire, in which he batted in the middle-order, were his only first-class matches. He played club cricket for Dewsbury and Heckmondwike and also for Gentlemen of the North and Gentlemen of Yorkshire.

Lee, James Edward

Born: 23/12/1988, Sheffield
LHB, RMF. Career: 2006-09

James Lee's two Championship matches were four years apart, his other first-class appearances being for Leeds/Bradford MCCU in 2013. He also played in four List A matches

and these were all in 2009. He was a promising bowler in his three years in the Academy team and also for England in the U19 World Cup in 2008. He had one season with Suffolk and later played for Cleckheaton.

Lees, Alexander Zak

Born: 14/04/1993, Halifax
LHB, LB. Career: 2010-
Cap No 177, 2014

Having demonstrated a maturity beyond his years, Alex Lees became, in 2015, the third-youngest captain to lead Yorkshire in the County Championship when just two days short of his 22nd birthday. When Andrew Gale resigned the List A captaincy during that same season Lees took over and in 2016 became the county's youngest official captain since 1883. He led the team to two semi-finals but held the post for only one year.

Alex Lees batting against Warwickshire at Edgbaston in 2015.

A tall opening batsman with an array of powerful strokes, Lees scored over 1,000 first-class runs in each of 2014 and 2016 and his innings of 275 not out at Chesterfield in 2013 was Yorkshire's second-highest score since 1939. Although not always a first-choice in white-ball cricket, except when captain, he has played some effective innings in both formats. His club cricket was with Lightcliffe for whom he made the record Bradford League score of 227 not out in 2017.

Legard, Alfred Digby

Born: 19/06/1878, Scarborough
Died: 15/08/1939, Pentire, Newquay, Cornwall
RHB, RS. Career: 1910. Amateur

Alfred Legard made his first-class debut for MCC in 1904 having spent the last of his three seasons in Eton College's first eleven as captain. He also played for the Yorkshire Gentlemen. Rising to the rank of colonel, he served with distinction in the Boer War and the First World War and was awarded the CBE.

Lehmann, Darren Scott

Born: 05/02/1970, Gawler, South Australia
LHB, SLA. Career: 1997-2006.
Cap No 144, 1997

Comfortably the best of Yorkshire's overseas players, Darren Lehmann came originally as a second choice. After his seven years at the Club his first-class average of almost 70 was higher than any other Yorkshire player to have scored over 500 runs. His prodigious talent meant that he had so much time to play the ball as well as a considerable range of strokes.

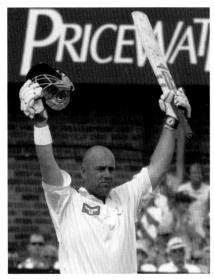

Darren Lehmann celebrates during his 252 against Lancashire at Headingley in 2001.

Lehmann was also a useful bowler; his cunning flight often deceived batsmen with innocuous-looking deliveries. The only blight on his time with Yorkshire was in 2002 when his one season as captain saw relegation from the Championship's first division.

In his home country, Lehmann played for South Australia and Victoria, his total of 13,635 runs in the Sheffield Shield being a record. He played in 27 Tests and 117 ODIs for Australia and, in his second career in the game, he became Australia's national coach in 2015.

Lehmann, Jake Scott

Born: 08/07/1992, Melbourne, Victoria, Australia
LHB, SLA. Career: 2016

Son of Darren, Jake Lehmann batted very consistently in his short spell with Yorkshire as temporary overseas player in first-class cricket. A good driver of the ball, his main first-class team was South Australia.

Ted Lester batting against Surrey. Roy Swetman is the wicket-keeper with skipper Stuart Surridge at slip.

Lester, Edward Ibson

Born: 18/02/1923, Scarborough
Died: 23/03/2015, Scarborough
RHB, OB. Career: 1945-64.
Cap No 87, 1948. Testimonial: 1956

One of Yorkshire's most loyal servants, Ted Lester spent 47 years with the Club. Spared war service because of a foot problem he played for Scarborough, Undercliffe and Keighley before making his county debut.

Lester established himself in Yorkshire's middle-order after the 1947 season and scored over 1,000 runs in six of the next seven seasons, his best being 1,801 in 1949. An unorthodox batsman, he hit the ball firmly with some ease, his best shot

being a pleasant late-cut. A brilliant outfielder (where his goalkeeping skills with Scarborough and the two Bradford clubs helped), he lost form in the mid-1950s but then became captain of the second eleven, a role which he fulfilled for four seasons from 1958.

Lester's final appointment, from 1962, was as first eleven scorer and he was employed in this important position on a full-time basis for 31 years. (It was during this time that he appeared in a Gillette Cup match in an emergency having retired eight years earlier.) He then spent a further ten years officiating only in home matches until he retired at the age of 69.

Leyland, Morris

Born: 20/07/1900, New Park, Harrogate
Died: 01/01/1967, Scotton Banks, Knaresborough
LHB, SLA. Career: 1920–46.
Cap No 59, 1922. Benefit: 1934

One of the best left-handed batsmen ever to play for Yorkshire, not to mention England, Leyland, always known as Maurice, was a solid, dependable middle-order player who always relished a battle.

Leyland's father was groundsman at Headingley and his early cricket was with Harrogate. Once he had established himself in the county side he batted with notable consistency and passed 1,000 runs in 17 consecutive seasons from 1923. Three times he passed the 2,000-run mark, his best being 2,317 in 1933, his highest innings of 263 against Essex at Hull coming three years later.

By this time Leyland had made his Test debut and his 41 matches were spread over the ten years from 1928. The tougher the challenge the more he responded: his Test average is higher than his first-class average and his average against Australia is higher than his Test average. Seven of his nine Test centuries came in Ashes matches and he scored a century in each of his first and last innings against Australia. The latter of these was his highest Test score of 187 made in the company of Len Hutton as the pair shared what remains England's second-wicket record stand of 382. Strong, rather than graceful, steady yet nimble, he was a hugely effective batsman.

Leyland's bowling may well have been used more but for the presence of Wilfred Rhodes and then Hedley

Verity in Yorkshire's side. However, he was good enough to take five wickets in an innings on ten occasions. His mixture of the orthodox with the chinaman and googly three times brought him over 50 wickets in a season and a hat-trick against Surrey at Sheffield in 1935. Although he had a stocky physique he was also a brilliant outfielder; he sped across the ground, picked up cleanly and threw in quickly.

A genial character, he often played with a smile and tales of his sense of humour are legendary. He brought these qualities with him into the way he coached young players for Yorkshire in the two decades after his retirement.

Lilley, Alexander Edward

Born: 17/04/1992, Halifax
RHB, LM. Career: 2011

Alex Lilley attended St Aidan's School, Harrogate, also later playing for Harrogate, and appeared in his only match for Yorkshire just ten days after his 19th birthday in the last of his four seasons in the Academy team. He also played in five games for Leeds/Bradford MCCU during the three seasons from 2014 while studying at Leeds Beckett University. He captained the team when it played against Yorkshire. His later club cricket was with Beckwithshaw where he became captain.

Linaker, Lewis

Born: 08/04/1885, Paddock, Huddersfield
Died: 17/11/1961, Paddock, Huddersfield
RHB, LMF. Career: 1909

Lewis Linaker made a pair but took one wicket in his only match for Yorkshire. He played club cricket for Paddock and Primrose Hill.

Lister, Benjamin

Born: 09/12/1850, Birkenshaw, Bradford
Died: 03/12/1919, Bradford
RHB, WK. Career: 1874-78. Amateur

Four of Benjamin Lister's six games for Yorkshire were in 1878 by which time he had turned professional. A wicket-keeper only in his early career his matches as a batsman produced no score above 20. His other first-class match was for Players of the North and, of his several clubs, he served Harrogate the longest.

Lister, Joseph

Born: 14/05/1930, Thirsk
Died: 28/01/1991, Harrogate
RHB. Career: 1954. Amateur

Nephew of George Macaulay, Joe Lister was in the first eleven at Cheltenham College for three years and made his first-class debut in 1951 for Combined Services. After a very brief career with Yorkshire he joined Worcestershire as assistant secretary, becoming secretary in 1956 but continued to play for the county side as well as captaining the second eleven.

Joe Lister as Yorkshire Secretary.

Lister returned to Yorkshire in 1971 to become secretary but his almost 20 years in the post were embroiled with a series of controversies none of which were of his own making. He battled on with integrity and neutrality and was one of the few to emerge from that period with honour intact.

Lister- Kaye, Kenelm Arthur

Born: 27/03/1892, Kensington,
London
Died: 28/02/1955, Tamboerskloof,
Cape Town, South Africa
RHB, LMF. Career: 1928. Amateur

Kenelm Lister-Kaye spent two years in the first eleven at Eton and played for Oxford University in 1912. His other first-class cricket was in India in the early-1920s and for Yorkshire at the age of 36. An erratic swing bowler, he took 37 wickets in his full career of 12 matches. In 1931 he became his family's Fifth Baronet thus inheriting a knighthood.

Lockwood, Ephraim

Born: 04/04/1845, Lascelles Hall,
Huddersfield
Died: 19/12/1921, Tandem, Lascelles
Hall, Huddersfield
RHB, RRMS. Career: 1868-84

With a score of 91 in an opening stand of 176 with his uncle John Thewlis at The Oval, Ephraim Lockwood made an excellent start to his first-class career. He eventually became one of the best batsmen in the country and played on over 30 occasions for both the North and the Players, scoring over 12,500 runs in his full career.

At the time of his debut Lockwood was professional with Cheetham Hill but had begun at Lascelles Hall before moving to Meltham Mills and Kirkburton.

He quickly established himself in the Yorkshire side and in 1872 became the first batsman in the Club's short history to score over 500 runs in a season. His cut shot was particularly effective and from 1874 he scored over 900 runs in nine out of the next ten seasons. Four times he

passed the 1,000-run mark, his best being 1,261 in 1876. The highest of his eight centuries was a knock of 208 at Gravesend in 1883.

Given the county captaincy in 1876, Lockwood's teams lost more matches than they won and he lasted only two seasons in the post.

Lockwood, Henry

Born: 20/10/1855, Lascelles Hall,
Huddersfield
Died: 18/02/1930, Lepton,
Huddersfield
RHB, RRFM. Career: 1877-82

Henry Lockwood, unlike his brother Ephraim, did not manage to establish himself in the Yorkshire side. A steady opening batsman, nine of his 16 matches came in 1881 when he scored both his half-centuries. His club cricket was with Lascelles Hall and, professionally, with Burnley St Andrews, Cockermouth and Little Lever.

Lodge, Joe Thomas

Born: 16/04/1921, Skelmanthorpe,
Huddersfield
Died: 09/07/2002, Skelmanthorpe,
Huddersfield
RHB, RMF. Career: 1948

An opening batsman, Tommy Lodge achieved more as a coach and in club cricket than for Yorkshire. In Scotland he coached at Strathallan School as well as for Perthshire with whom he also regularly made 1,000 runs in a season. He played soccer for Huddersfield Town and St Johnstone.

Love, James Derek

Born: 22/04/1955, Headingley, Leeds
RHB, RM. Career: 1975-89.
Cap No 122, 1980. Benefit: 1989

Jim Love will always be associated with his man-of-the-match performance in the Benson & Hedges Cup final in 1987. With an innings of 75 not out he guided Yorkshire to its first victory in a Lord's final for 18 years. A middle-order batsman, his attacking nature suited the shorter format and he was the first Yorkshire player to represent England in ODIs but not Test cricket.

In club cricket with Kirkstall Educational and Leeds, Love developed into a strong and powerful batsman whose best stroke was the off-drive. Not often given a full season in the first-class game he only twice passed 1,000 runs in a season, the better of these being 1,203 in 1983.

After three seasons with Lincolnshire,

Love went into coaching and was in charge of Scotland's national side when it played in the World Cup in 1999. For the first three years of his appointment, from 1993, he played club cricket for Edinburgh and in List A matches for Scotland. He later returned to Yorkshire, became cricket professional at Ampleforth College and co-ordinator for three of the county's junior teams.

Lowe, George Emanuel

Born: 12/01/1877, Guisborough
Died: 15/08/1932, Middlesbrough
?HB, WK. Career: 1902

George Lowe, (registered Low at birth) deputised as wicket-keeper for David Hunter in his only first-class (non-Championship) match. His only known club was Thornaby.

Lowe, Jordan Richard

Born: 19/10/1991, Rotherham
RHB, WK. Career: 2010

Jordan Lowe's only game for Yorkshire was a first-class fixture against India A. As a wicket-keeper, he had previously played for the Academy and had six seasons with Rotherham Town.

Lowson, Frank Anderson

Born: 01/07/1925, Bradford
Died: 08/09/1984, Pool-in-Wharfedale, Otley
RHB, OB. Career: 1949-58.
Cap No 92, 1949. Testimonial: 1959

Frank Lowson opened the batting with Len Hutton not only on a regular basis for Yorkshire but also, in 1951, in the first two of his seven Test matches. Because he had such a good technique and unflappable temperament it was often stated that it was difficult to distinguish between the pair.

At Bradford Grammar School Lowson was in the first eleven for five years and his first club was Bowling Old Lane. He quickly established himself in the Yorkshire team, scoring over 1,700 runs in each of his first three seasons including 2,152 in 1950, a total that remained his best. It took him only 65 days to complete 1,000 career-runs and no one from any county has ever achieved this feat more quickly.

Frank Lowson (right) walks out to bat with Len Hutton against Hampshire at Bournemouth in 1954.

Lowson's highest innings came in 1953 when he scored 259 not out at Worcester and he made over 1,000 runs in nine consecutive seasons including on the tour of south Asia in 1951/52. His stroke-play, especially his cuts and drives, was always admired as well as his solid defence.

Very slim, Lowson's last few years in the game were dogged by varicose veins. However, he followed his Yorkshire career with five years as professional with Brighouse and later played for Bradford and Bingley.

Lucas, David Scott

Born: 19/08/1978, Nottingham
RHB, LMF. Career: 2005

Lucas took eight wickets in his only first-class match for Yorkshire, against Bangladesh A, played also in List A matches but found more success elsewhere. In his full career, which included a combined total of 12 seasons with three other counties, he took 264 wickets in 95 games as well as over 100 wickets in the shorter formats.

Lumb, Edward

Born: 12/09/1852, Dalton,
Huddersfield
Died: 05/04/1891, Westminster,
London
RHB. Career: 1872-86.
Amateur. Cap No 5

Ten of Edward Lumb's 17 first-class matches came in 1883 when he scored his only two half-centuries. He represented the North and an England XI and most of his club cricket was for Lascelles Hall. Having suffered from consumption, he died from pleurisy at the age of 38. He was president of the Huddersfield League and donated the Lumb Cup.

Lumb, Michael John

Born: 12/02/1980, Johannesburg,
South Africa
LHB, RM. Career: 2000-06.
Cap No 153, 2003

A strongly-built batsman, Michael Lumb, son of Richard, was a punishing stroke-player with a wide range of shots. He passed the 1,000-run mark in a first-class season only once for Yorkshire although he took part in a triple-century stand with Darren Lehmann in 2006. He became a white-ball specialist during his five seasons with Hampshire and then Nottinghamshire. He made his T20I debut in 2010 and was a World Cup winner in the same year. He played in only three ODIs, despite scoring a century on debut, but a total of 27 T20Is.

A middle-order batsman in first-class matches, he developed into an opener in white-ball cricket and this took him into the IPL and the BBL. He played in over 200 matches in each of the three formats and scored well over 20,000 runs before retiring during the 2017 season due to an ankle injury.

Lumb, Richard Graham

Born: 27/02/1950, Doncaster
RHB, RM. Career: 1970-84
Cap No 116, 1974. Benefit: 1983
An opening batsman who partnered Geoff Boycott throughout his career, Richard Lumb was a tall and elegant player with a solid defence and a good-looking drive both straight and through the covers. His technique and temperament served him well in his role.

He promised much in his early career; he scored over 1,000 runs in the season in which he captained Yorkshire Schoolboys and also scored a double-century for ESCA, his club cricket at this time being with Brodsworth Main.

Lumb's first century for Yorkshire came in the Roses match of 1973 and he had his best season two years later when he scored 1,532 runs. He and Boycott shared 29 century partnerships together, a total exceeded only by Percy Holmes and Herbert Sutcliffe, and the pair provided some stability during a poor era for the county. Their best stand was 288 against Somerset at Harrogate in 1979 and Lumb's highest score was 165 not out against Gloucestershire at Bradford in 1984. He was also a good slip fielder, spent some winters coaching in South Africa and later emigrated there.

Lupton, Arthur William

Born: 23/02/1879, Bradford
Died: 14/04/1944, Carlton Manor,
Guiseley, Leeds
LHB, RFM. Career: 1908-26.
Amateur. Cap No 60, 1925

A major in the army, Arthur Lupton played in one match for Yorkshire in 1908 and other first-class teams for the next three years. It was not until 1925, at the age of 46, that he returned to first-class cricket – to captain Yorkshire! He led the county for three seasons during which time it came first, second and third, respectiveley, in the Championship and the team lost only two of the 92 games for which he was in charge.

Lupton was in the first eleven at Sedburgh School and also played for Yorkshire Gentlemen. Although a successful bowler in club cricket he did not take a single wicket for Yorkshire and never scored a half-century. Although well past his best, as a player and tactician, he did maintain the discipline of a successful side.

Lynas, George Goulton

Born: 07/09/1832, Coatham, Redcar
Died: 08/12/1896,
Skelton-in-Cleveland
RHB, RRF. Career: 1867

George Lynas remained in the north-east of the county and played for Stockton-on-Tees, Redcar and Darlington. In addition he kept wicket, despite being a burly figure, for Middlesbrough for at least 13 years and later was the club's manager.

Lyth, Adam

Born: 25/09/1987, Whitby
LHB, OB. Career: 2007-
Cap No 168, 2010

Adam Lyth fully established himself in the Yorkshire side as an opening batsman in 2010, having started in the middle-order. In that season he was the first batsman in the country to pass 1,000 first-class runs and was rewarded with a tour to West Indies, the first of his two trips with England Lions.

Lyth's best season of 2014, when he scored 1,619 first-class runs and was the country's leading fielder, was followed by him playing in all of the seven Tests of 2015. He scored a century in his second match, against New Zealand at Headingley and played in the whole of the Ashes-winning series.

By this time Lyth had an established partner in the Yorkshire side and he and Alex Lees shared 375 together at Northampton in their very successful year of 2014. Lyth's own highest score was 251 at Old Trafford in the same season. As an attractive stroke-player and brilliant fielder he was a very important part of the two Championship triumphs

Adam Lyth batting against Somerset at Taunton in 2017, Marcus Trescothick is at slip.

of 2014 and 2015. In white-ball cricket he was not always a regular fixture in the Yorkshire side but repaid more recent faith in his ability by smashing two Yorkshire T20 records in 2017: his season's total of 535 runs was 92 higher than the previous highest tally; a magnificent 161 against Northamptonshire at Headingley not only broke the Yorkshire record by 45 runs but was also the highest innings ever made in Britain.

Macaulay, George Gibson

Born: 07/12/1897, Thirsk
Died: 13/12/1940, Sullom Voe,
Lerwick,
Shetland Islands, Scotland
RHB, RFM/OB. Career: 1920-35.
Cap No 56, 1921. Benefit: 1931.
Grant: 1936

One of Yorkshire's greatest-ever bowlers, only three players have taken more wickets in first-class matches than Macaulay did. After playing for Barnard Castle School and club cricket with Thirsk Victoria, he began playing for Yorkshire as a pace bowler but was dropped halfway through his first season having taken only 24 wickets in ten games. George Hirst advised him to try to spin the ball and he became a most effective medium-paced off-spinner. He regained his place in 1921 and was never dropped again.

Macaulay toured South Africa in 1922/23 and played in the last four of the five Tests taking 16 wickets. Although he played in four more Tests – all in England – he was never as successful again. His first Test, at Cape Town, was the type of occasion of which schoolboy dreams are made. Opening the bowling, he took a wicket with his first ball and, at the end of the game, struck the winning run to give England a nail-biting victory by just one wicket.

An aggressive bowler, Macaulay's approach was full of intensity and he had a vigorous attitude towards the dismissal of all batsmen. A far from negligible batsman he often scored runs when they were most needed through his never-say-die attitude.

Macaulay was at his peak during the 1920s when Yorkshire won four successive Championship titles. He took over 100 wickets in each of the nine seasons from 1921 and again in 1933. His best seasons were the three consecutive ones starting in 1923 when he took 166 wickets (av 13.84), 190 (13.23) and 211 (15.48), respectively. His best match analysis was 14 for 92 against Gloucestershire at Bristol in 1926.

Macaulay retired because of a finger injury but was able to continue in league cricket with Wakefield, Ossett and Todmorden where he was professional for two seasons. During service with the RAF he died in tragic circumstances, suffering cardiac failure during the Second World War. His birthplace in Thirsk is marked by a plaque and his final resting place is in Lerwick Cemetery. Joe Lister, Yorkshire's Secretary for 19 years, was his nephew.

McGrath, Anthony

Born: 06/10/1975, Bradford
RHB, RM. Career: 1995-2012.
Cap No 148, 1999. Benefit: 2009

McGrath was a middle-order batsman who often held the innings together. Improving with age, he passed 1000 first-class runs for the first time in 2005, repeated this in

2006, averaging around the 60-mark in both seasons. In 2003 he was appointed as Yorkshire's youngest captain for 70 years but appearances for England led him to believe that he could play more Test and ODI cricket and so he resigned after just one season.

Sadly, in 2006, he decided to leave Yorkshire in the middle of his contract but after a stand-off lasting several months the return to Yorkshire of Darren Gough and Martyn Moxon made him reverse his decision. His final six seasons included one more - 2009 - as captain making

him the only Yorkshire player to be appointed twice but he resigned at the end of the year as his batting form had suffered.

When a thumb injury forced him to retire McGrath had played successfully in all three forms of the game, his away-swing bowling and good slip fielding also contributing valuably. After two years as Yorkshire's consultant coach he was appointed Assistant Head Coach at Essex in late-2015 and helped the county win promotion and then the County Championship.

McKay, Clinton James

Born: 22/02/1983, Melbourne, Australia
RHB, RFM. Career: 2010

Clint McKay played for Yorkshire as an opening bowler but only in T20 matches. His best performance, four for 33, came on his debut, against Derbyshire at Headingley. For his native country he played in 66 matches, including 59 ODIs in which he took 97 wickets, and also appeared for Leicestershire and Victoria.

McHugh, Francis Prest

Born: 15/11/1925, Burmantofts, Leeds
RHB, RFM. Career: 1949

After a very short career with Yorkshire, Frank McHugh played in 92 matches in five seasons for Gloucestershire, taking 272 wickets as an opening bowler. His best performance was seven for 32 against Yorkshire at Huddersfield in 1955.

Marsh, Shaun Edward

Born: 09/07/1983, Narrogin, Western Australia
LHB, SLA. Career: 2017

Shaun Marsh came to Yorkshire part-way through his one season as an overseas T20 player but then replaced Peter Handscomb in the Championship side. An experienced international batsman with Australia he has represented his country in over 90 matches including 53 ODIs. He scored a century on his Test debut and is one of only three players to score over 1,000 runs in the BBL. He has had ten seasons in the IPL and his other major teams are Western Australia, Glamorgan, Kings XI Punjab and Perth Scorchers.

Marshall, Amos

Born: 10/07/1849, Yeadon, Leeds
Died: 03/08/1891, Yeadon, Leeds
RHB, LM. Career: 1874

Amos Marshall played in only two first-class matches, one for Yorkshire and one for the North at Lord's. He played for several clubs in Lancashire and the north-east and was also professional with Bradford for whom he took five for none against Dewsbury, who were all out for two, just two months before his death aged 42.

Martyn, Damien Richard

Born: 21/10/1971, Darwin, Australia
RHB, RM. Career: 2003

An attractive middle-order batsman, Damien Martyn played in 67 Tests and 208 ODIs for his native country. The highlight of his brief stay with Yorkshire was a brilliant career-best 238 from 159 balls against Gloucestershire at Headingley. He also played for Western Australia and Leicestershire.

Mason, Allan

Born: 02/05/1921, Addingham, Ilkley
Died: 22/03/2006, Silsden, Keighley
RHB, SLA. Career: 1947-50

Ten of Allan Mason's 18 games for Yorkshire came in 1949, when he displaced Johnny Wardle for a time, and resulted in a tally of 37 wickets. This period included his only five-for: five for 56 against Northamptonshire at Bradford. He played for five different clubs in the Bradford League, captaining Silsden, and also for Morecambe.

Maude, Emund

Born: 31/12/1839, Middleton, Leeds
Died: 02/07/1876, Headingley, Leeds
?HB. Career: 1866. Amateur

Edmund Maude made a considerable number of runs for Yorkshire Gentlemen during a career of about 15 years but achieved little with the county side. His other clubs included Leeds and Leeds Clarence.

Maxwell, Glenn James

Born: 14/10/1988, Kew, Melbourne, Australia
RHB, OB. Career: 2015

A specialist in the shorter formats, only four of Glenn Maxwell's 24 matches for Yorkshire were in first-class cricket. A brilliant hard-hitting batsman and very useful bowler he scored two centuries for the county and has played for several teams in the IPL and BBL as well as Hampshire and Victoria. He has made over 120 international appearances and in early 2017 became only the second player to hit centuries for Australia in all three formats.

Metcalfe, Ashley Anthony

Born: 25/12/1963, Horsforth, Leeds
RHB, OB. Career: 1983-95.
Cap No 128, 1986. Benefit: 1995

An attractive opening batsman with a wide range of strokes, Ashley Metcalfe formed, with Martyn Moxon, one of Yorkshire's most successful opening partnerships producing 21 first-wicket century stands in first-class cricket. Also successful in limited-overs cricket, their undefeated stand of 242 against Warwickshire at Headingley in 1990 is still a record for the county's first wicket.

After being in the first eleven at Bradford Grammar School for three years and playing for Farsley, Metcalfe burst into first-class cricket with 122 in his first match, against Nottinghamshire at Bradford. When he gained a regular place in the side in 1986 he scored over 1,800 first-class runs and in the following season scored over 1,000 runs in List A matches, still one of three Yorkshire players to achieve the feat. The leading run-scorer in Yorkshire's successful Benson & Hedges victory he won the match award in four of the seven games.

From 1996 Metcalfe had two seasons with Nottinghamshire and then eight with Cumberland and scored a further 16,000 runs for Farsley. After a brief period as Manager of Yorkshire's Cricket Centre, he became chief executive of British Weight Lifting in 2013.

Micklethwait, William Henry

Born: 13/12/1885, Whiston, Rotherham
Died: 07/10/1947, Broom Grange, Rotherham
LHB. Career: 1911. Amateur

Although he scored 44 in the only

innings of his first game for Yorkshire, William Micklethwait was never given another chance and that game remained his only first-class match. An attacking middle-order batsman, he played for Rotherham Town for several years and played in goal for the football team of the same name, also playing amateur international soccer for England.

Middlebrook, James Daniel

Born: 13/05/1977, Leeds
RHB, OB. Career: 1998-2015

Having been released by Yorkshire in 2001, James Middlebrook returned in 2015 aged 38 due to a lack of spinners. In his eight seasons with Essex and five with Northamptonshire he was used more as an allrounder opening the batting for the latter. Only one of his 45 first-class scores of 50-plus was for Yorkshire.

An adaptable cricketer, Middlebrook took to all three formats playing in well over 500 matches. He had four years in the Academy team and played club cricket for Ongar, Pudsey Congs and New Farnley. In 2017 he was on the reserve list of first-class umpires.

Middlebrook, Willie

Born: 23/05/1858, Middlethorpe, Morley, Leeds
Died: 26/04/1919, Morley, Leeds
RHB, RFM. Career: 1888-89

A debut performance of four for 68 against the Australians and a career-best five for 59 against Cambridge University a year later were stand-out performances for Willie Middlebrook. His results in county matches were less productive but he played successfully for several clubs including Preston, Morley and Bradford.

Midgley, Charles Augustus

Born: 13/11/1877, Wetherby
Died: 24/06/1942, Bradford
RHB, RFM. Career: 1906. Amateur

With a batting average over ten runs higher than that for his bowling it is surprising that Charles Midgley was not given more than four games, which were consecutive, for Yorkshire. He played no other first-class cricket but had begun with a half-century on debut.

Milburn, Stuart Mark

Born: 29/09/1972, Harrogate
RHB, RMF. Career: 1992-95

Although Stuart Milburn first played for Yorkshire while aged 19 his bowling did not develop as had been hoped. He played in both forms of the game but his List A games were all in 1995. After leaving Yorkshire he had two seasons with Hampshire where he gained much more opportunity and took 39 wickets in 21 first-class matches.

Miller, David Andrew

Born: 10/06/1989, Pietermaritzburg, South Africa
LHB, OB. Career: 2012

With 133 shorter-form international matches to his credit for South Africa but no Tests, David Miller is a white-ball specialist. He played in this role for Yorkshire and was the leading batsman in the Club's successful T20 season with almost 400 runs at an average of nearly 50. An effective middle-order batsman, he has appeared in three World Cups and several T20 tournaments.

At the start of the 2017/18 season he scored a century from only 35 balls against Bangladesh at Potchefstroom – ten balls faster than the previous world record for T20I cricket.

Milligan, Frank William

Born: 19/03/1870, Farnborough,
Hampshire
Died: 31/03/1900, Ramathlabama,
Mafeking, Transvaal, South Africa
RHB, RF. Career: 1894-98. Amateur.
Cap No 26.

An exciting cricketer, Frank Milligan's formative years were spent in Derbyshire. A hard-hitting but impatient batsman, he always wanted to score runs quickly but never made a century. An erratic bowler, his best analysis was seven for 61 for the Gentlemen against the Players at Scarborough in 1898. His peak came in 1897 when he scored 744 runs and took 43 wickets. He captained Yorkshire in three matches.

Milligan toured South Africa in 1898/99 and played in two Tests. He remained in the country to fight in the Boer War but fell while defending Mafeking. There is a memorial to him in Harold Park, Low Moor, Bradford.

Mitchell, Arthur

Born: 13/09/1902, Baildon Green,
Bradford
Died: 25/12/1976, Bradford
RHB, RS. Career: 1922-45.
Cap No 62, 1928. Benefit 1937

A player who epitomised the perceptive dourness of Yorkshire cricket, Arthur Mitchell played vital roles with the county for almost 50 years. He was part of Baildon Green's first team when aged only 15 before he moved to Tong Park and Saltaire prior to his county debut.

A batsman with a solid defensive technique, Mitchell was a natural upper-order player and eventually settled into the number three position after the retirement of Edgar Oldroyd. Dogged and determined, he occupied the crease so effectively that he was sometimes accused of being excessive in his cautionary approach. His leg-side strokes brought him many runs, however, but his first century for Yorkshire, 189 at Northampton in 1926, remained his highest score.

Mitchell was at his best in the 1930s, when Yorkshire won seven titles in nine years. His best season came in 1933 when he scored 2,300 runs, a total which included eight centuries, four of which came in consecutive innings. It was one of ten seasons in which he passed 1,000 runs and he was rewarded by touring India in the following winter. He played in all of the three Tests but the only half-centuries of his six-match career, spread over four years, were both in the Headingley Test of 1935 against South Africa.

It was as a brilliant close-to-the-wicket fielder for which Mitchell will also be remembered. He specialised in front of the wicket but also caught well in the slip cordon and was always an intimidating presence, especially when the spin bowlers were in operation. Nine times he took at least 30 catches in a season, his best being 47 in 1939.

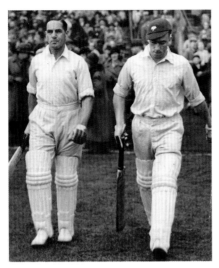

Arthur Mitchell (right) walks out to bat with Herbert Sutcliffe against Lancashire at Headingley in 1936.

After the Second World War Mitchell became Yorkshire's first full-time coach. His blunt and brusque manner was not to everyone's liking but he was a good judge of a player's potential and, during his 25-year tenure of office, did much to aid the development of those who became the fulcrum of the county teams. He continued to play and had professional engagements with Bowling Old Lane, Hunslet and Underhill before retiring in 1952. His final first-class match, for the North at Harrogate, had come in 1947.

Mitchell, Frank

Born: 13/08/1872, Market Weighton, Beverley
Died: 11/10/1935, Blackheath, Kent
RHB, RMF. Career: 1894-1904.
Amateur. Cap No 27

Frank Mitchell had two seasons in the first eleven at St Peter's School, York before captaining Cambridge University in the third of his four years there. The better of his two full seasons with Yorkshire, whom he captained in six matches, was 1901 when he scored 1,807 runs. His highest score, 194 at Leicester, had come two years earlier.

Mitchell was a sound batsman who drove well and played in two Tests in South Africa in 1898/99. He then served in the Boer War, settled there and captained two touring teams to England, playing in three Tests in 1912. He also played for England at rugby, Sussex at soccer and gained an athletics Blue, later becoming a sports journalist.

Monks, George Derek

Born: 03/09/1929, Sheffield
RHB, WK. Career: 1952.

Glasgow was the venue and Scotland the opposition for the only first-class match played by George Monks. The Sheffield United wicket-keeper, he was deputising for Don Brennan.

Moorhouse, Robert
Born: 07/09/1866, Berry Brow, Huddersfield
Died: 07/01/1921, Taylor Hill, Huddersfield
RHB, OB. Career: 1888-99.
Cap No 15. Grant: 1900

Bobby Moorhouse was a regular in the Yorkshire side for only four seasons. A middle-order batsman whose early cricket was with Armitage Bridge, he was a brilliant fielder at cover point, being regarded as one of the best of the era. Despite being short in stature he was a plucky batsman and stood firm against the faster bowlers, receiving many bruises when batting on unreliable surfaces. He did not have a sound technique but because of his bravery he sometimes scored runs when others found them hard to come by.

Moorhouse played in over 25 matches in each of the seasons from 1894 to 1897 but passed the 1,000-run mark only once. His highest score of 113 came at Taunton in 1896. Because of his undistinguished batting statistics it may be surmised that he could have often been selected ahead of others through his fielding. A good turn of speed and a safe pair of hands were characteristic of his prowess in this department. After his playing days he coached at Sedburgh School.

Morkel, Morné
Born: 06/10/1984, Vereeniging, Transvaal, South Africa
LHB, RFM. Career: 2008

One of the shortest playing careers in Yorkshire's history ended on the third day of what became his only match when Morné Morkel tore a hamstring in his 16th over. Tall, he had the ability to make the ball rise disconcertingly. His distinguished record for his native country of well over 200 games in all three formats includes 272 wickets in 78 Tests.

Morris, Alexander Corfield
Born: 04/10/1976, Barnsley
LHB, RMF. Career: 1995-97

Alex Morris showed considerable promise as an all-rounder in playing in 22 games for England U-19 and making his Yorkshire second eleven debut aged 16. He had a disappointing county career, however, but his six seasons with Hampshire were more productive, him twice taking 50 first-class wickets in a season. A tall bowler, he often used his height effectively. Later he tried his luck with Derbyshire and Nottinghamshire but played only in their second elevens. He played for Barnsley from 2006 and moved to Hoylandswaine five years later.

Mosley, Henry

Born: 08/03/1850, Kildwick, Skipton
Died: 29/11/1933, Crossland Moor, Huddersfield
RHB, LF. Career: 1881

A bowler with a good turn of speed, Henry Mosley spent most of his club career as professional with Saltaire. He also had the same status with Farsley and Great Horton.

Motley, Arthur

Born: 05/02/1858, Osmondthorpe Hall, Leeds
Died: 28/09/1897, Canning Town, Essex
RHB, RF. Career: 1879. Amateur

Neither of Arthur Motley's games for Yorkshire were county matches. He was reputed to have a very irregular action but this did not prevent him taking seven hat-tricks in club cricket, most of which was with Leeds Clarence, in 1879 alone. When he emigrated and played for Wellington, New Zealand it was only as a batsman!

Mounsey, Joseph Thomas

Born: 30/08/1871, Heeley, Sheffield
Died: 06/04/1949, Ockford Ridge, Godalming, Surrey
RHB, RRM/OB. Career: 1891-97. Cap No 23

A middle-order batsman, Joe Mounsey was involved with each of Yorkshire's first two official Championship wins but only played one full season – in 1894. Four of his seven half-centuries came that year but he never made a century. Occasionally sound in his batting, he worked hard and was given several opportunities.

Mounsey played for both Sheffield Heeley and Sheffield United and in 1899 became coach at Charterhouse School. He remained there for 48 years – as coach for 28 and then as groundsman for 11 before umpiring.

Moxon, Martyn Douglas

Born: 04/05/1960, Stairfoot, Barnsley
RHB, RMF. Career: 1980-97
Cap No 126, 1984. Benefit: 1993

Martyn Moxon as Yorkshire's Director of Cricket.

A batsman who was, technically, one of the best of his generation, Martyn Moxon made 74 in his first Test innings, in 1986, topped the batting averages in New Zealand 18 months later but his ten Tests were spread over six different series.

After early experience with Monk Bretton, Barnsley and Bowling Old Lane, Moxon made his debut for Yorkshire in List A cricket before scoring a century in his first first-class match in 1981, the first to do so for Yorkshire for 60 years. The following season saw him become only the third batsman to score 1,000 runs in a season for the second eleven.

An orthodox opening batsman whose drives on the off-side were his best strokes, Moxon had three

significant partners for Yorkshire – Geoff Boycott, Ashley Metcalfe and Michael Vaughan. Metcalfe was the longest-serving of these but he shared triple-century stands with each of the other two. His highest innings, of 274 not out, came at Worcester in 1994. His best season was in 1991 when he scored 1,669 first-class runs, him passing 1,000 runs in a season on eleven occasions. In successfully

adapting his game to the demands of List A cricket, his total of 7,380 runs is Yorkshire's third-highest.

A very good slip fielder in his early days, Moxon was also a useful bowler; he took five for 31 in a Benson & Hedges Cup quarter-final against Warwickshire at Headingley – the only five-for of his career in either format.

Appointed Yorkshire captain in

1990, Moxon held the post for six seasons but his team finished in the top half of the Championship table only once although there were three such placings in the Sunday leagues and two semi-finals in limited-overs matches. In 1997 he was appointed Yorkshire's director of coaching but left after four years to become first eleven coach with Durham. He was persuaded to return to the White Rose county in 2007 and, as Director of Cricket, has overseen a period of considerable success, including the two Championship victories of 2014 and 2015.

Myers, Hubert

Born: 02/01/1875, Yeadon, Bradford
Died: 12/06/1944, Hobart, Tasmania,
Australia
RHB, RMF/LBG. Career: 1901–10
Cap No 36. Grant: 1911

An all-rounder whose bowling was the superior skill, Hubert Myers established himself in the Yorkshire side in 1904 and played regularly for the rest of his career. He took almost 200 wickets in the three seasons from 1904 with his swing bowling but it deteriorated thereafter. His best year with the bat was in 1910 when he passed 900 runs before being dropped. He took a best of eight for 81 against Gloucestershire at Dewsbury in 1904 but never made a century. Useful enough to be considered for representative cricket, he played in five games for either the North or the Players.

Myers emigrated to Tasmania soon into the 20th century's second decade and played occasionally for the state side; he became coach for the Tasmanian Cricket Association and helped it achieve first-class status.

Myers, Matthew

Born: 12/04/1847, Yeadon, Leeds
Died: 08/12/1919, Yeadon, Leeds
RHB, RRMF/S. Career: 1876–78

A solid opening batsman, Matthew Myers played regularly for two seasons, coming third in the averages in his first year in the side. He also represented the North and Players of the North and played for several teams in club cricket on both sides of the Pennines. He had professional engagements with, notably, Yeadon, Bacup and Burnley.

Naved-ul-Hasan, Rana

Born: 28/02/1978, Sheikhupura,
Punjab, Pakistan
RHB, RFM. Career: 2008/09

A limited-overs specialist, Rana Naved-ul-Hasan played consistently in all three formats in his time with Yorkshire but his lively pace bowling never produced more than four wickets in an innings. Often used as a pinch-hitter in List A matches, he scored three half-centuries batting at number three. With his hard-hitting batting having been given more prominence he almost reached the status of that of an authentic all-rounder.

Rana Naved played in 74 ODIs but only nine Tests for Pakistan and his many teams included Sussex and Derbyshire.

Naylor, John Edward

Born: 11/12/1930, Thurcroft,
Rotherham
Died: 27/06/1996, Bramhall,
Stockport, Cheshire
RHB, SLA. Career: 1953

Having taken a mere five wickets in four matches for the second eleven, John Naylor was given a chance with the county side in the absence of Johnny Wardle but was even less successful. His league cricket was with Haworth Colliery and, as professional, for Doncaster.

Newstead, John Thomas

Born: 08/09/1877, Marton-in-
Cleveland, Middlesbrough
Died: 25/03/1952, Blackburn,
Lancashire
RHB, RM/OB. Career: 1903-13.
Cap No 38

John Newstead had such an outstanding season in 1908 – 927 runs and 140 wickets - that he was selected to play for the North and the Players. He also played a full season in the following year but with much less success. Consequently, 42 of his 109 first-class matches were spread over nine seasons.

On the Lord's ground staff for four years from 1904, Newstead developed into an accurate bowler and his seven for ten against Worcestershire at Bradford in 1907 provided the springboard for his brief success. His one century came at Trent Bridge in 1908 in a game in which he also took a five-for. He later

played for Rishton, Lidget Green, East Bierley, Church and Haslingden.

Nicholson, Anthony George

Born: 25/06/1938, Dewsbury
Died: 03/11/1985, Harrogate
RHB, RMF. Career: 1962-75
Cap No 110, 1963. Benefit: 1973

The best of Fred Trueman's many opening partners, Tony Nicholson was one of the unsung heroes of the 1960s Championship-winning sides. He made his debut relatively late having spent five years in Rhodesia (now Zimbabwe) but made up for lost time by taking 68 wickets in his first season.

At a livelier pace than first appearances gave, Nicholson bowled with control and variety, his strong physique enabling him to bowl for long spells into the wind. Although often overshadowed, his career-best figures of nine for 62 propelled Yorkshire to an important win at Eastbourne in 1967.

In taking 274 Championship wickets in the three seasons from 1966, Nicholson was Yorkshire's leading bowler in its hat-trick of titles, his best period coinciding with this feat. In all first-class cricket his best season, with 113 wickets, was 1966. The nearest he came to international honours was when he was selected for the 1964/65 tour of South Africa but had to withdraw through injury. Hanging Heaton was his first club but he was later coach and professional with Marske.

Nicholson, Neil George
Born: 17/10/1963, Danby, Whitby
LHB, RM. Career: 1988-89

A hard-hitting batsman, Neil Nicholson was a regular choice for the second eleven for a few seasons but played only one significant innings in his seven matches, in both formats, for the first team. He played club cricket for Marske and East Bierley.

Oates, William
Born: 01/01/1852, Coolattin,
Shillelagh, Wicklow, Ireland
Died: 09/12/1940, Clifton Park,
Rotherham
RHB, RRMF, WK. Career: 1874-75

An all-rounder in club cricket, Willie Oates deputised for George Pinder as wicket-keeper in his short Yorkshire career. Captain of Elsecar, for a time, he also played for Wentworth and Doncaster.

Oates, William Farrand
Born: 11/06/1929, Aston, Sheffield
Died: 15/05/2001, Port Moody,
Vancouver, Canada
RHB, RM/OB. Career: 1956

An attractive middle-order batsman, Billy Oates had a very short career with Yorkshire but played for Derbyshire for seven seasons from 1959, scoring over 4,500 runs in 121 matches. He played for several clubs, all in Yorkshire, including Aston Hall, Sheffield United, Golcar as professional, Paddock and Elland and captained the Huddersfield League side. He died very suddenly while on holiday.

Old, Christopher Middleton
Born: 22/12/1948, Middlesbrough
LHB, RFM. Career: 1966-82
Cap No 112, 1969. Benefit: 1979

One of England's best seam and swing bowlers of his era, Chris Old started with a wicketless first season, playing in just two games, but soon made rapid progress and first played for his country in 1970 in two matches against the Rest of the World.

Old played in a total of 46 Tests and took 143 wickets. His best performance was seven for 50 against Pakistan at Edgbaston in 1978 when he achieved the very rare feat of taking four wickets in five balls. His economical bowling was most valuable in List A cricket and he is the only bowler to take 300 wickets for Yorkshire. An extremely useful lower-order batsman, he scored over 7,500 runs, including six centuries, in first-class cricket to add to his 1,070 wickets.

Old was appointed Yorkshire captain for the 1981 season but was sacked by manager Ray Illingworth halfway through the 1982 campaign. Embittered, he moved to Warwickshire and in 1984 he took revenge on the county of his birth with match-figures of 11-99 and a half-century in a game at Headingley. After his three seasons in the midlands he played for Northumberland. His elder brother, Alan, was a brilliant rugby union stand-off who played 16 times for England.

Oldham, Stephen
Born: 26/07/1948, High Green, Sheffield
RHB, RMF. Career: 1974-89
Testimonial: 2003

A steady pace bowler, Steve Oldham was most effective for Yorkshire in limited-overs matches. Although he took over 50 wickets in 1978 he had his best years in the first-

class game with Derbyshire for whom he played for four seasons from 1980. His career-best seven for 78 came at Edgbaston in 1982 and his eventual career totals came to over 200 wickets in each format.

Oldham's early clubs included Elsecar and Barnsley where he started to make a name for himself as a coach. Shortly after his return to Yorkshire he took over the captaincy of the second eleven then held various posts on the staff including assistant coach and cricket manager; he had been bowling coach for eight years when he left at the end of 2011 following the county's relegation in the Championship.

Oldroyd, Edgar
Born: 01/10/1888, Healey, Batley
Died: 27/12/1964, Truro, Cornwall
RHB, RM/OB. Career: 1910-31
Cap No 57, 1921. Benefit: 1927

One of Yorkshire's best batsmen never to play Test cricket, Oldroyd made the number three spot all his own following Percy Holmes and Herbert Sutcliffe in the order. He made his first-class debut at the age of 21, having played for Staincliffe and Dewsbury, but did not establish himself in the Yorkshire side until 11 years later, partly because of the First World War. Once this had been achieved he then struck over 1,000 runs in each of the ten seasons from 1921.

One of the most reliable batsmen in the country, Oldroyd was particularly skilful on wet pitches, his strong defence and patience proving invaluable although he could also be a powerful stroke-maker. Sadly he was knocked unconscious by a ball from Ted McDonald in the 1926 Roses match at Old Trafford and he was never quite the same batsman thereafter but there was no long-term damage.

Following retirement he played for Pudsey St Lawrence, as professional, with Len Hutton and in 1933 became the first Bradford League player to score 1,000 runs in a season. Eleanor Oldroyd, the BBC sports presenter, is his great grand-daughter.

Oyston, Charles
Born: 12/05/1869, Armley, Leeds
Died: 15/07/1942, Leeds
LHB, SLA. Career: 1900-09

As only an occasional replacement for Wilfred Rhodes, Charles Oyston took no more than nine wickets in any one season. In each of the six years from 1901 he was the leading bowler for the second eleven either in terms of average or number of wickets. Most of his club cricket was for Leeds but he was also professional with Wortley and Bingley.

Padgett, Douglas Ernest Vernon
Born: 20/07/1934, Dirk Hill, Bradford
RHB, RM. Career: 1951-71
Cap No 101, 1958. Benefit: 1969
Testimonial: 1978

A loyal servant of Yorkshire CCC for almost 50 years, Doug Padgett was, at the time of his debut, the county's youngest-ever player, it coming 44 days before his 17th birthday. He had already played for Idle from the age of 13.

A classically correct batsman, Padgett was stylish and attractive and he always appeared neat at the crease. An adaptable player, he usually batted at number three but often opened the batting when required. Someone who always put the needs of his side first, he could be cautious but could score rapidly if necessary. This was epitomised most of all when he made 79 in a 61-minute partnership of 141 with Bryan Stott at Hove in 1959. Yorkshire scored 215 in 105 minutes to win the Championship in exhilarating style.

Doug Padgett in his time as Yorkshire coach.

That season brought Padgett 2,181 runs, including a career-best 161 not out at Oxford, and it remained the best of the 12 occasions when he passed the 1,000-run target. He was rewarded with two Test caps in 1960 against South Africa and a non-Test tour of New Zealand in the following winter but that was the end of his international experience. He continued to be an important

member of the Yorkshire side and by the time of his retirement he found himself with nine winners' medals - seven in the Championship and two in the Gillette Cup.

His playing days over, he turned his immediate attention to the development of Yorkshire's young players and fulfilled the role of coach for 28 years, for eight seasons combining this with being second eleven captain. An outstanding judge of good players, he famously spotted Michael Vaughan batting on the outfield during the lunch interval of a county game at Sheffield. Although the county won little in his time, he remained phlegmatic, his quiet and undemonstrative approach earning the respect of all.

Padgett, George Hubert
Born: 09/10/1931, Silkstone, Barnsley
RHB, RM. Career: 1952

Only two of Hubert Padgett's six matches were in the Championship. An all-rounder who batted in the middle-order, he also played for Barnsley.

Padgett, John
Born: 21/11/1860, Scarborough
Died: 02/08/1943, Withington, Manchester
RHB. Career: 1882-89

John Padgett played for Yorkshire only in 1882 and 1889. His first club was Scarborough but he later moved to Lancashire where he played for Leyland and Milnrow.

Parker, Bradley
Born: 23/06/1970, Mirfield, Wakefield
RHB, RM. Career: 1992-99

Not having gained a regular place in the Yorkshire side, Bradley Parker, in 1996, then broke the record for most runs – 1,481 – in a second eleven red-ball season. He followed this with his best season for the first team, scoring over 800 runs in first-class matches and over 300 in List A cricket. Having been released at the end of the following year he then spent ten seasons with Northumberland.

A middle-order batsman, Parker had shown promise when given a run in the side in 1994, scoring a century against Surrey at Scarborough, but lacked consistency. His highest innings came in 1997 at The Parks, Oxford.

Parkin, Cecil Harry
Born: 18/02/1886, Eaglescliffe, Durham
Died: 15/06/1943, Cheetham Hill, Manchester
RHB, OB/LB. Career: 1906

One who courted controversy, Cecil Parkin played for Yorkshire after success with Ossett, but it was then discovered that his birthplace was 20 yards over the border. He then played for Durham and in league cricket before, in 1914, making his debut for Lancashire for whom he took 901 wickets in 157 games in nine seasons. He also played in ten Tests.

Parratt, John
Born: 24/03/1859, Morley, Leeds
Died: 06/05/1905, Morley, Leeds
?HB. Career: 1888-90

John Parratt played in just two matches for Yorkshire but was a useful all-rounder in club cricket with various sides including Leeds St John's, Selkirk, Werneth and Morley.

Parton, John Wesley
Born: 31/01/1863, Wellington, Shropshire
Died: 30/01/1906, Rotherham
?HB. Career: 1889

John Parton had a very brief career with Yorkshire but also played for Shropshire as well as a few clubs including Worksop, Haslingden and Werneth where he was professional.

Patterson, Steven Andrew
Born: 03/10/1983, Beverley
RHB, RMF. Career: 2005-
Cap No 170, 2012. Testimonial: 2017

Steven Patterson bowling against Surrey at Headingley in 2016.

An indispensable member of the Yorkshire attack which helped to win two Championships in 2014 and 2015, it was Steve Patterson's role, as the third or fourth seamer, to keep things tight. This he did to an excellent degree and was the most economical of the five main pace bowlers in both campaigns. He also took useful wickets at times with his subtle movement off the seam and achieved the 50-wicket mark in two successive seasons from 2012.

It took Patterson some time to establish himself in the county side and he played in the Yorkshire Premier League from 2002 to 2009 with the Academy, sometime studying at Leeds University, and Driffield Town. A change of Yorkshire captain brought more opportunities and he was a regular from 2010. He repaid the faith shown in him many times over and produced career-best figures of six for 56 at Chester-le Street in 2016. Although not an automatic choice in white-ball cricket he has taken 150 wickets in the two formats combined. In his best season – 2010 – he took 36 wickets and these included a career-best of six for 32 against Derbyshire at Headingley in a Clydesdale Bank 40 game.

Pearson, Harry Eyre
Born: 07/08/1851, Attercliffe, Sheffield
Died: 08/07/1903, Nether Edge, Sheffield
RHB, RMF/RS. Career: 1878–80

Three of Harry Pearson's games for Yorkshire were at his local ground of Bramall Lane and all of his five career wickets were taken in his debut match. He also played for Sheffield and Pitsmoor and later became secretary of Sheffield Wednesday FC.

Pearson, John Henry
Born: 14/05/1915, Scarborough
Died: 13/05/2007, Scarborough
RHB. Career: 1934–36

'Jackie' Pearson played one match in each of three different seasons for Yorkshire as a middle-order batsman.

As a solid, bespectacled opening batsman in league cricket, he scored heavily in the north-east with Normanby Hall, Middlesbrough and Saltburn, later playing for Middleton.

Peate, Edmund
Born: 02/03/1855, Holbeck, Leeds
Died: 11/03/1900, Newlay,
Horsforth, Leeds
LHB, SLA. Career: 1879–87.
Cap No 6. Grant: 1900

The first of Yorkshire's long line of Test left-arm spinners, 'Ted' Peate's nine such games were all against Australia; in his best first-class season of 1882, 63 of his 214 wickets were in eight matches, including five for Yorkshire, against the tourists. The best of his two five-fors in Test cricket was six for 85 at Lord's in 1884.

Peate (registered Peat at birth) started his career as a fast bowler but when with Manningham, as professional, found that his control improved when he bowled more slowly. His variations of flight, length and speed were lethal on helpful pitches, none more so than when he achieved an astonishing career-best of eight for five against Surrey at Holbeck in 1883. Sadly, his heavy drinking led to a rapid deterioration in performance not to mention Lord Hawke's displeasure.

Peel, Robert

Born: 12/02/1857, Churwell, Morley, Leeds
Died: 12/08/1941, Morley, Leeds
LHB, SLA. Career: 1882-97.
Cap No 8. Benefit: 1894

The first bowler to take 100 wickets against Australia and the first Yorkshire bowler to take 100 Test wickets, Bobby Peel played in only 20 such matches. A match analysis of 11 for 68 (including his Test-best of seven for 31) came at Old Trafford in 1888.

Peel had match figures of nine for 129 on his Yorkshire debut and soon learnt to adapt his game to the quality of the pitch. His variations of flight and pace, together with his mastery of length made him virtually unplayable in helpful conditions and his captains could always rely on him to exercise control on good pitches.

In taking 100 wickets in each of eight seasons, Peel's best was 180 in 1895 this including a career-best nine for 22 against Somerset at Headingley. Though he usually batted in the lower order, his forcing style brought him over 12,000 full career runs and included a double century. He achieved the double in 1896 but the following year, sadly, his increasing bouts of drinking saw his dismissal. For many years a false story tended to be associated with Peel but he is now primarily recalled as being a great spin bowler.

Penny, Joshua Hudson

Born: 29/09/1856, Yeadon, Bradford
Died: 29/07/1902, Savile Town, Dewsbury
LHB, SLA. Career: 1891

Despite being much in demand in club cricket, Joshua Penny had the shortest possible career in the first-class game. His many clubs included Undercliffe, Guiseley, Ramsbottom, Dewsbury and Savile, Preston and Little Lever. A special match took place in September 1902 to raise funds for his memorial in Yeadon Cemetery.

Pickles, Christopher Stephen

Born: 30/01/1966, Mirfield, Wakefield
RHB, RM. Career: 1985-92

An attacking opening batsman in league cricket, Yorkshire tried to develop Chris Pickles into a bowling all-rounder but, after many opportunities (a total of 129 games in both formats), the experiment was abandoned and he was released. In List A cricket he was persevered with more, him having two seasons without a first-class appearance, but only once took four wickets in an innings.

The clubs for which Pickles played included Cleckheaton, Hanging Heaton and Spen Victoria. He also had three seasons with Northumberland from 1995.

Pickles, David

Born: 16/11/1935, Halifax
RHB, RF. Career: 1957-60

David Pickles burst on to the first-class scene by bowling sensationally fast and finished his first season in second place in Yorkshire's averages. This included seven for 61 at Taunton (12 in the match) but that remained his career-best as his effectiveness deteriorated thereafter.

Pickles played for Sowerby Bridge when aged 14 and was later professional with both Bowling Old Lane and Baildon. Having apparently claimed not to have originally been coached, the instruction he received with Yorkshire was said to have improved his faulty action but removed his natural flair.

Pinder, George

Born: 15/07/1841, Ecclesfield,
Sheffield
Died: 15/01/1903, Hickleton,
Doncaster
RHB, RLobs, WK. Career: 1867-80

The first of Yorkshire's longest-serving wicket-keepers, the correctly-named George Pinder Hattersley was the first choice in that role from 1870. He developed his technique so well with St Mary's and Sheffield Shrewsbury that his skill at standing up to fast bowling made him claim to be the first 'keeper to do so in first-class cricket.

Pinder stood at almost six feet and his long reach and good eyesight enabled him to take the ball with little apparent effort. However the rough pitches of the era in which he played seriously distorted some of his finger joints. As a hard-hitting lower-order batsman he occasionally made a valuable contribution and his highest score was 78 for North against South in 1873. In later life he was groundsman and storekeeper for Hickleton Main CC and colliery.

Platt, Robert Kenworthy

Born: 26/12/1932, Holmfirth
RHB, RMF. Career: 1955-63
Cap No 102, 1959

Bob Platt had only two full seasons in the Yorkshire side – 1959, when he took 89 wickets, and 1961. Although he was rather injury-prone, when fully-fit he was one of Fred Trueman's better opening partners. His career-best bowling figures came as soon as 1956 when he took seven for 40 at Bristol.

Leeds and Holmfirth were Platt's first clubs but he was often very successful for Halifax and Bradford. For the latter team he once took seven for none against Lidget Green (16 all out).

Platt played in two matches for Northamptonshire in 1964 but returned to Yorkshire and the county's second eleven for four seasons from 1968; he also served on Yorkshire's committee, including being chairman of the cricket committee, for several years until the re-organisation in 2001.

Plunkett, Liam Edward
Born: 06/04/1985, Middlesbrough
RHB, RFM. Career: 2013-
Cap No 174, 2013

Liam Plunkett began his county career with Durham at the age of 18 and two years later found himself playing for England in all three formats. After an initial 37 international appearances, including nine Tests, his career stalled somewhat, partly because of injury, but he also seemed to fall out of favour with Durham and played there in only two more full seasons.

Liam Plunkett bowling against Lancashire at Headingley in 2014.

His move to Yorkshire resurrected his career on both levels: he was involved in the Championship wins of 2014 and 2015 and took a Test-career best of five for 64 against Sri Lanka on his new home ground of Headingley. Soon regarded as a white-ball specialist, his hostile approach brought him much success with England, his 36 wickets in 2017's ODIs being the most for his country.

Pollard, David
Born: 07/08/1835, Cowmes, Huddersfield
Died: 26/03/1909, Lepton, Huddersfield
RHB, RRM. Career: 1865

David Pollard played in just two first-class matches, one for Yorkshire and one for England XI. His club cricket was with Lascelles Hall, Longsight, Yorkshire Gentlemen (as their first professional) and Constable Burton. He coached at St Peter's School, York, Cambridge University, Harrow and Winchester.

Pollitt, George
Born: 03/06/1874, Chickenley, Dewsbury
Died: 19/05/1942, Blackpool, Lancashire
?HB. Career: 1899

Batting at number nine, George Pollitt scored a half-century in his debut innings for Yorkshire but never played first-class cricket again. His early cricket was for Chickenley and he spent eight seasons with Bedfordshire as professional from 1900. After a brief spell with Ossett he had moved to Blackpool by time of the 1911 Census.

Prest, Charles Henry

Born: 09/12/1841, York
Died: 04/03/1875, Gateshead,
Durham
RHB. Career: 1864. Amateur

A fine batsman in club cricket, Charles Prest played in three county matches – two for Yorkshire and one for Middlesex in 1870. His clubs included Richmond (Surrey), Southgate, Wimbledon and Yorkshire Gentlemen. Multi-talented, he was also a noted sprinter, worked as a solicitor and a professional actor. His brother William played for 'Yorkshire' in its pre-official days.

Preston, Joseph Merritt

Born: 23/08/1864, Yeadon, Leeds
Died: 26/11/1890, Windhill,
Bradford
RHB, RMOB. Career: 1885–89.
Cap No 11

Joe Preston was an outstanding all-rounder who scored over 2,000 runs and took more than 200 wickets in his full, but short, first-class career. Originally a pace bowler, one of his deliveries instantly killed a batsman in club cricket when he was aged only 19.

A stylish batsman with a solid defence, Preston's bowling was his stronger suit, him taking 81 wickets

in 1888 including a career-best nine for 28 against MCC at Scarborough. He represented the North, the Players, toured Australia in 1887/88 and was England's twelfth man for one Test in 1886.

Tragically, he drank heavily, lost form and his place in the Yorkshire side. Two years later a cold turned into congestion of the lungs and, even more tragically, he passed away aged only 26.

Pride, Thomas

Born: 23/07/1864, York
Died: 16/02/1919, Canonbie,
Dumfries, Scotland
RHB, WK. Career: 1887

Thomas Pride made seven dismissals in his first match for Yorkshire, as deputy for Joe Hunter, but his move to Edinburgh meant that it remained his only first-class match. His first clubs were York and Constable Burton but he later played for Perthshire as well as Scotland.

Priestley, Iain Martin

Born: 25/09/1967, Horsforth, Leeds
RHB, RMF. Career: 1989

A well-built and tall bowler, Iain Priestley took four wickets in his debut first-class innings but they remained his career-total. He had played and coached in Auckland, New Zealand in the previous winter and later captained Manningham Mills, for whom he played mainly as a batsman, before he moved to Pudsey St Lawrence where he coached as well as played.

Pullan, Peter

Born: 29/03/1857, Guiseley, Leeds
Died: 03/03/1901, Menston, Ilkley
RHB, RS. Career: 1884

Despite his very short career with Yorkshire, Peter Pullan was a professional at several clubs. He had eight seasons at Golcar, three with Haslingden and others included Forfarshire, Bradford, Littleborough and Rastrick. He died in Menston Asylum but is buried in Guiseley.

Pujara, Cheteshwar Arvindbhai
Born: 25/01/1988, Rajkot, India
RHB, LB. Career: 2015

A specialist in the longer form of the game, Cheteshwar Pujara has scored over 4,000 runs in more than 50 Tests but played in only five ODIs. His four games for Yorkshire were all in the Championship. A solid number three, with a pleasing range of strokes, he has scored three triple-centuries. His other first-class teams are Saurashtra, for whom he made his debut aged 17, Derbyshire and Nottinghamshire.

Pyrah, Richard Michael
Born: 01/11/1982, Dewsbury
RHB, RM. Career: 2004-15
Cap No 167, 2010. Benefit: 2015

Richard Pyrah playing against Middlesex at Scarborough in 2014.

Rich Pyrah was the first Yorkshire player to be capped for his performances in limited-overs matches in which he was an outstanding all-rounder and brilliant fielder. Although his record in the County Championship was disappointing, he did play one famous innings: after Yorkshire had collapsed to 45 for eight against Lancashire at Headingley in 2011. His score of 117 played a vital part in a compelling game which the visitors won by only 23 runs.

The first Yorkshire bowler to take over 100 wickets in T20 cricket, Pyrah took his wickets through skilful use of swing and seam and also because his economy-rate often caused opposing batsmen to become careless and give their wickets away. His best performance in white-ball cricket was five for 16 in a T20 match against Durham at Scarborough in 2011. His best season in List A games had occurred the previous year when he took 41 wickets.

Pyrah moved seamlessly into coaching, firstly in 2015/16 with the Adelaide Strikers in the BBL and then with Yorkshire, assisting with the first eleven and being responsible for the Diamonds in its first season in the women's Kia Super League.

Radcliffe, Everard Joseph Reginald Henry
Born: 27/01/1884, Hensleigh, Tiverton, Devon
Died: 23/11/1969, St Trinians Hall, Richmond
RHB. Career: 1909-11. Amateur.
Cap No 49

Everard Radcliffe captained Yorkshire in his final season having deputised for Lord Hawke during the previous two years. The county finished in seventh place in 1911 – its lowest position between 1892 and 1947.

Radcliffe had led the first eleven at Downside School in the last two of his four years in the side and, though a negligible batsman at first-class level, he led Yorkshire in 56 of his 64 matches in the team. He also played for Yorkshire Gentlemen and became a knight in 1949 when he succeeded to his family title as its Fifth Baronet.

Ramage, Alan
Born: 29/11/1957, Guisborough
LHB, RFM. Career: 1975-83

An outstanding sportsman in his youth, Alan Ramage represented Yorkshire Schoolboys at the age of 12, the youngest ever to do so. He played for Marske when only 13 and made his Yorkshire debut aged 17 but did not appear in first-class cricket until four years later.

A lively fast bowler, Ramage disconcerted Surrey with his pace off the pitch when he took five for 65 at Harrogate in 1981. However, injuries and his soccer career with Middlesbrough and Derby County both contributed to him giving up the game when aged only 25.

Ramsden, Gary
Born: 02/03/1983, Dewsbury
RHB, RMF. Career: 2000

A promising bowler, Gary Ramsden played in just two matches for Yorkshire – one in each format. After leaving the county he tried his luck with Essex and then Derbyshire but got no further than their second elevens.

Randhawa, Gurman Singh
Born: 25/01/1992, Huddersfield
LHB, SLA. Career: 2011

Neither of Gurman Randhawa's two first-class matches – one for Yorkshire and one for Durham in 2016 – were in the Championship. He played for Rotherham Town, Chester-le-Street and Hoylandswaine after three years in the Academy team. An orthodox spin bowler, he also played for Shropshire, Northumberland and the second elevens of Derbyshire and Worcestershire.

Raper, James Rhodes Stanley
Born: 09/08/1909, Bradford
Died: 09/03/1997, Eastburn, Keighley
RHB, RMF. Career: 1936-47.
Amateur

Stanley Raper captained Yorkshire's second eleven from 1939 to 1948 and led the senior side in one match in 1947 having played in two games 11 years earlier. He had been in the first eleven at The Leys School for three years and played for several clubs including Bradford, Rawdon, Menston and Yeadon. He was on the Yorkshire committee for six years from 1956.

Rashid, Adil Usman

Born: 17/02/1988, Bradford
RHB, LBG. Career: 2006-
Cap No 164, 2008

A genuine all-rounder, Adil Rashid has four times scored a century and taken a five-for in the same match – a total exceeded for Yorkshire only by George Hirst and Wilfred Rhodes. He can also claim to be the county's best-ever leg-spinner.

Rashid first played for the Academy in 2004 and burst on to the first-class scene two years later with an analysis of six for 67 against Warwickshire at Scarborough in his first match. His England debut came in 2009 but he was then discarded for five years during which time he developed greater variety in his bowling. On his return he became a regular selection in white-ball cricket as well as making his Test debut, which he marked with five for 64 against Pakistan in Abu Dhabi. He has twice taken over 50 first-class wickets in a season, the most being 65 in 2008 when he also had career-best

figures of seven for 107 at the Rose Bowl.

With wristy attacking strokes, Rashid bats in the lower-middle order, his highest innings being 180 against Somerset at Headingley in 2013. All of his ten Tests have been in Asia and his total of international appearances numbers 88.

Rawlin, Eric Raymond

Born: 04/10/1897, Rotherham
Died: 11/01/1943, Greasborough, Rotherham
LHB, RFM. Career: 1927-36

Eric Rawlin played in five of his eight games for Yorkshire in 1935 by which time, as a pace bowler, his best days were behind him. He played for several clubs including Worksop, Sheffield United, Rotherham Town and Mexborough whom he later captained. His father also played for Yorkshire as well as Middlesex.

Rawlin, John Thomas

Born: 10/11/1856, Greasborough, Rotherham
Died: 19/01/1924, Greasborough, Rotherham
RHB, RFM. Career: 1880-85

During his career with Yorkshire John Rawlin also played for Rotherham, Elsecar and Leek but joined the Lord's groundstaff in 1887 and two years later began a long career with Middlesex. A hard-hitting batsman and good swing bowler he took eight for 29 at Bristol in 1893 and a year later took over 100 wickets in the season. In his 21-year career with Middlesex his 229 matches brought him over 5,500 runs and more than 600 wickets. He also represented the Players as well as the North and South!

Rawlinson, Elisha Barker

Born: 10/04/1837, Yeadon, Leeds
Died: 17/02/1892, Sydney, New
South Wales, Australia
RHB, RRMF. Career: 1867-75

Each of Elisha Rawlinson's first two games were both Roses matches – one for each county! He made his debut for Lancashire and the following week played for Yorkshire! He scored only two half-centuries in his 37 games for Yorkshire but his batting had a good reputation in club cricket especially with Burnley, Leeds Clarence, for whom he scored over 1,000 runs in 1874, and Malton, whom he captained from 1875 to 1882, his final season before emigrating.

Read, Jonathan

Born: 02/02/1998, Scarborough
RHB, WK. Career: 2016-

A promising wicket-keeper, Jonny Read was with the Academy side from 2015, made his first-class debut aged 18 and played in his first List A game a year later.

Redfearn, Joseph

Born: 13/05/1862, Lascelles Hall,
Huddersfield
Died: 14/01/1931, Lepton,
Huddersfield
LHB. Career: 1880

Registered at birth as Joah, Joe Redfearn had a very short career with Yorkshire but a longer one in club cricket. Amongst others, he played for Lascelles Hall, Padiham, Harrogate, where he was also groundsman, Rawtenstall, Bacup and Ramsbottom, often as a professional.

Render, George William Armitage

Born: 05/01/1887, Dewsbury
Died: 17/09/1922, Hanging Heaton,
Dewsbury
RHB, RMF. Career: 1919

George Render had a very short career with Yorkshire but played regularly in league cricket mainly for Batley and Dewsbury but also for Heckmondwike. Although used by the county only as a batsman, he was a good all-rounder.

Rhodes, Arthur Cecil

Born: 14/10/1906, Headingley, Leeds
Died: 21/05/1957, Headingley, Leeds
RHB, RMF/OB. Career: 1932-34
Cap No 71, 1932

Arthur Rhodes played regularly for Yorkshire in both 1932 and 1933 but in only one match in the following season. For the second eleven he had varied his bowling skilfully but the first team used him primarily as a pace bowler. He took five wickets in an innings five times, the best in the Championship being six for 48 at Tonbridge in 1932.

Rhodes played for Kirkstall Educational, Leeds and Spen Victoria before his first-class career and Royton, as professional, and Lidget Green afterwards.

Rhodes, Herbert Edward

Born: 11/01/1852, Hennerton Hall,
Henley-on-Thames, Berkshire
Died: 10/09/1889, Dover, Kent
RHB, WK. Career: 1878-83.
Amateur

Only ten of Herbert Rhodes' 25 first-class matches were for Yorkshire. He played in nine games for MCC and also represented the Gentlemen, later playing for Staffordshire and

Henley. He rowed for Cambridge in four Boat Races, was also a keen sailor and was tragically killed when he fell from his horse.

Rhodes, Steven John

Born: 17/06/1964, Dirk Hill,
Bradford
RHB, WK. Career: 1981-84

It was just 35 days after his 17th birthday when Steve Rhodes made his debut for Yorkshire but, as David Bairstow's deputy, he played in only three first-class and two List A matches. He then had a most distinguished 20-season career with Worcestershire before he went into coaching and eventually became its Director of Cricket. A big loss to Yorkshire, he also played in 11 Tests and nine ODIs.

Rhodes, Wilfred

Born: 29/10/1877, Kirkheaton,
Huddersfield
Died: 08/07/1973, Branksome Park,
Poole, Dorset
RHB, SLA. Career: 1898-1930.
Cap No 32 Benefit: 1911.
Testimonial: 1927

If anyone could lay claim to the title of being the best county cricketer of all-time then Wilfred Rhodes would be the leading contender in most people's eyes. He holds the records for taking most wickets in all first-class cricket (4,187), the double of 1000 runs and 100 wickets in a season most times (16), and the only player to pass both of the 30,000 runs and 3,000 wickets career-milestones.

Rhodes was a great left-arm spin bowler; in his youth he practised with considerable thoroughness and learnt the most important aspects of his trade, in particular the art of flight, imparting powerful spin and the vital component of being accurate in length. When he had learnt how to take advantage of batsmen's weaknesses he soon became the complete bowler taking 154 wickets in his first season including 13 for 45 at Bath on debut.

The first of his 58 Tests came in 1899 and, being the serious cricketer that he was, started to now work on his batting in earnest. The eventual outcome for one who batted at number 11 in his first Test series was that he became the first of Jack Hobbs' great opening partners and he remains the only England player to bat in all eleven places in the batting order.

After the First World War, Yorkshire had need of him to concentrate on his bowling again and so successful was he in reviving his skill and expertise that he was even recalled to Test cricket, after a gap of five years, and played a leading role in the regaining of the Ashes in 1926. He ended his career with two world

records for first-class cricket: the longest career (30 years, 315 days) and the oldest player (52 years, 165 days).

Rhodes took 200 wickets in three seasons – the Championship-winning seasons of 1900-02, his best being 261 in 1900. Twice he scored over 2,000 runs in a season, his best being 2,261 in 1911.

Many of Yorkshire's amateur captains relied on his knowledge and understanding of the game as well as his ability to read the pitch and match situation in conjunction with each other. This was so much so that when one such skipper was putting on his pads in readiness to bat he was told not to bother as Wilfred had just declared!

Rhodes, William

Born: 04/03/1883, Bradford
Died: 05/08/1941, Bradford
RHB, RFM. Career: 1911

William Rhodes' only first-class match was against the Indians. He also played for Bankfoot and Mexborough.

Rhodes, William Michael Harry

Born: 02/03/1995, Nottingham
LHB, RMF. Career: 2013-17

Will Rhodes first played for the Academy in 2011 and was later with Stamford Bridge. He played in 22 ODIs for England U19 and captained it in the 2014 World Cup. In his first season with Yorkshire he played in both forms of white-ball cricket and his first-class debut followed two years later. As a promising batsman he opened in that format and his bowling proved most useful in the shorter forms. A loan spell with Essex in 2016 gave him greater experience in the County Championship but further lack of opportunity with Yorkshire led him to join Warwickshire for the 2018 season.

Richardson, John Allan
Born: 04/08/1908, Sleights, Whitby
Died: 02/04/1985, Scarborough
RHB, OB. Career: 1936–47. Amateur

John Richardson made his first-class debut in 1934 for the Gentlemen and appeared in four different seasons for Yorkshire, playing in the Championship only in 1937. A talented batsman who was tall and powerful, he played for Scarborough for 32 years, captaining it in 24 and scoring almost 19,000 runs including six consecutive centuries in 1938.

Richardson, Richard Benjamin
Born: 12/01/1962, Five Islands Village, Antigua, West Indies
RHB, RM. Career: 1993–94.
Cap No 137, 1993

When Richie Richardson came to Yorkshire as its second official overseas player he had already been leading West Indies for 18 months. An attractive middle-order batsman, his first-class form for Yorkshire was disappointing but he was more productive in List A cricket.

Sadly Richardson became ill during his second season with the county and had to return home early. His main first-class team was the Leeward Islands and he played for

West Indies in over 300 matches including 86 Tests. In 2016 he became an ICC referee.

Richardson, Scott Andrew
Born: 05/09/1977, Oldham, Lancashire
RHB, RM. Career: 2000–03

A product of Manchester Grammar School and Saddleworth, Scott Richardson represented Lancashire in age-group teams before playing for Leicestershire and Worcestershire second elevens and then Yorkshire. A tall, solid opening batsman, seven of his 12 Championship matches were in the title-winning season of 2001. He had three seasons with Cumberland from 2004 and later played for New Farnley and Woodlands.

Riley, Harry
Born: 17/08/1875, Thackley, Bradford
Died: 06/11/1922, Bradford
?HB, LFM. Career: 1895–1900

Three of Harry Riley's four first-class matches came in the Championship-winning season of 1900 but he took only one wicket. He had six seasons in the Lancashire League with Colne and Rishton.

Riley, Martin

Born: 05/04/1851, Liversedge,
Cleckheaton
Died: 01/06/1899, Harrogate
RHB, RRFM. Career: 1878-82.
Amateur

Martin Riley played in 17 games for Yorkshire and 11 of these were in 1880 but only six were county matches. A free-scoring batsman, he also appeared once for an England XI. He played for several clubs captaining both Heckmondwike and Harrogate, other main ones including Scarborough, Yeadon and Malton.

Ringrose, William

Born: 02/09/1871, Ganton,
Scarborough
Died: 14/09/1943, Manston, Cross
Gates, Leeds
LHB, RFM. Career: 1901-06.
Cap No 37

The Championship-winning campaign of 1905 was the only year when Billy Ringrose played regularly for Yorkshire, him taking 73 wickets in his full first-class season of 20 matches. His best performance in a county match was figures of seven for 51 against Leicestershire at Sheffield but against the Australians at Bradford he took nine for 76, both in 1905.

Prior to his county career, Ringrose played for Sheffield United, Liverpool and Oxton. He suffered from ill-health in his final year with Yorkshire but then played for Forfarshire for seven seasons; he also represented Scotland in four first-class matches including three against Test-playing tourists. From 1923 to 1939 he served as Yorkshire's scorer.

Robinson, Arthur Leslie

Born: 17/08/1946, Brompton,
Northallerton
LHB, LMF. Career: 1971-77
Cap No 118, 1976

After playing for Harlsey and Northallerton, Arthur Robinson had two years with Leeds at the start of his county career. Tall and strongly-built, he was a whole-hearted bowler who led the attack in a weak Yorkshire side recovering from the retirement of Fred Trueman.

Robinson's best season was in 1974 when he took 43 first-class wickets and 28 in List A matches. His career-best performances in the two formats came on consecutive days in that same season and both at The Oval - six for 61 in the Championship and four for 25 in a John Player League match. He made his highest score of 30 not out when sharing a tenth-wicket stand of 144 with Arnie Sidebottom at Cardiff in 1977. After leaving Yorkshire he returned to Northallerton and later became its groundsman.

Robinson, Benjamin Lawrence Herbert

Born: 12/05/1858, Holbeck, Leeds
Died: 14/12/1909, Holbeck, Leeds
?HB. Career: 1879

Previously known as 'Henry', Herbert Robinson's one first-class match is his only recorded game other than one for Batley, also in 1879.

Robinson, Edward

Born: 27/12/1862, Honley, Huddersfield
Died: 03/09/1942, Clifton, Bristol
RHB. Career: 1887. Amateur

Edward Robinson's only first-class match was at Lord's against Middlesex. He also played for Honley but shortly after playing for Yorkshire he moved to Bristol where he became prominent in sport in Gloucestershire.

Robinson, Ellis Pembroke

Born: 10/08/1911, Denaby, Doncaster
Died: 10/11/1998, Conisbrough, Doncaster
LHB, OB. Career: 1934-49.
Cap No 78, 1937. Testimonial: 1949

The best two seasons of Ellis Robinson's career were 1939 and, especially so, 1946 when he took a career-best 167 wickets, the Second World War robbing him of some very productive years. These seasons were two of the five in which he took over 100 wickets and brought him selection for three representative teams in 1946.

As a boy, Robinson kept wicket for Denaby Main but began bowling leg-spin before a move to Barnsley. At Headingley coach George Hirst noticed his long fingers, advised him to try off-spin and he duly became a regular for the county in 1937. Tall, he spun the ball so much that he frequently had to bowl round the wicket to nullify the turn.

The 1939 season brought Robinson his best performance – eight for 35 in the Roses match at Headingley. Also a brilliant close fielder, the six catches he took in an innings at Bradford against Leicestershire in 1938 are still a Yorkshire record.

Following his release he had three seasons with Somerset where his 256 wickets took his total first-class tally satisfyingly over the 1,000-mark.

Robinson, Emmott

Born: 16/11/1883, Keighley
Died: 17/11/1969, Hinckley,
Leicestershire
RHB, RFM. Career: 1919–31
Cap No 55, 1920. Benefit: 1930

A very effective all-rounder, it is extraordinary to think that Emmott Robinson did not make his first-class debut until the age of 35. He first appeared for the second eleven in 1904 but from 1908 he was professional with Ramsbottom for six seasons before returning to play for Keighley and then Pudsey St Lawrence.

In many ways it is how Robinson played the game that he will be remembered for, rather than his impressive combined totals of runs and wickets. Cricket was a serious matter to him and he relished a tough battle in which he could perform with an uncompromising approach. This was typified mostly in his batting in which his cautious and determined mind-set ensured that bowlers always had to work hard for his wicket. His neglect of the cut-shot exemplified his risk-free attitude. He passed the 500-run mark in 11 successive seasons, twice scoring more than 1,000. His best season was in 1921 when he also played his highest innings – 135 not out at Leicester.

In his bowling Robinson tried to be as miserly as possible and delivered his out-swingers regularly on a good length. Only in his first season did he not take over 50 wickets, passing the 100-mark just once – in 1928. His best performance was in the Roses match at Bradford in 1920 when his figures were nine for 26. Despite his age, he was an excellent fielder both close to the wicket and in the covers, his agility and smartness earning genuine plaudits.

Emmott Robinson (left) with Maurice Leyland.

Following his county career, during which he experienced six Championship victories, Robinson played as professional for Benwell Hill, taking 115 wickets in a season at the age of 50, and then Sunderland. He also took up umpiring, standing in first-class cricket from 1937 to 1951, including the First Ashes Test of 1938. His first coaching experience was at a school in the Morecambe area but he later assisted with Yorkshire and his final post was as Leicestershire's official coach. He passed away the day after his 86th birthday.

Robinson, Mark Andrew

Born: 23/11/1966, Hull
RHB, RFM. Career: 1991–95
Cap No 136, 1992

From 1987 Mark Robinson had four seasons with Northamptonshire and one winter with Canterbury in New Zealand. An economical bowler, on his return to Yorkshire he acted as a foil for the faster bowlers and his nine for 37 against his first county at Harrogate in 1993 remained the best figures of his entire career. A negligible batsman, his 12 successive scoreless innings in 1990 set a new world record.

A year of absence from the first-class game was followed by playing for Sussex from 1997. In 2003 he became its coach and oversaw the most successful period in the county's history with seven trophies in as many seasons including its first three Championships. He later became cricket manager but in late-2015 was appointed head coach of the England Women's team and guided them to victory in the 2017 World Cup. Following this came opportunity to be involved with England's men's Test team.

Robinson, Oliver Edward
Born: 01/12/1993, Margate, Kent
RHB, RM. Career: 2013-14

Oliver Robinson played in only white-ball cricket for Yorkshire, and also Hampshire in 2014. A move to Sussex in 2015 gave him a fresh start and saw an improvement in both batting and bowling but he played in only six matches in 2017.

Robinson, Philip Edward
Born: 03/08/1963, Keighley
RHB, LM. Career: 1984-91
Cap No 132, 1988

Phil Robinson had only four years as a regular for Yorkshire, from 1988, and he was released at the end of the season in which he had made his highest first-class score – 189 in the Roses match at Scarborough.

Robinson played for Long Lee at the age of 13, Keighley two years later and Yorkshire's second eleven at the age of 17. He began well with the first team, playing 15 first-class matches in 1984 and finishing second in the averages but for three years he was then used mostly in List A cricket.

A stocky but attractive player, Robinson was a middle-order batsman who usually scored quickly. He passed the 1000-run mark in first-class matches in three seasons, including his final one, and his best was 1,402 in 1990.

Robinson played for both Cumberland and Leicestershire in 1992. With the midland county he had his best season in List A matches scoring 595 runs and making his only century in that format. He retired in 1999 having brought his full career totals up to over 7,500 first-class runs and more than 4,000 in the shorter format.

Robinson, Walter
Born: 29/11/1851, Greetland, Halifax
Died: 14/08/1919, Liverpool
RHB, RRM. Career: 1876-77

After scoring one half-century in seven games for Yorkshire, Walter Robinson moved to Lancashire. He played professionally for Haslingden, Littleborough, Bacup and Colne and, for nine seasons from 1880, for the county side. His 115 matches for Lancashire brought him over 3,500 runs and in 1883 he also played for the Players, the North and The Rest. His death certificate shows him as a 'cricket groundsman' living in Huyton.

Roebuck, Charles George
Born: 14/08/1991, Huddersfield
RHB, RM. Career: 2010

Despite being with the Academy and/or the second eleven from 2007 to 2013, Charlie Roebuck, an opening or middle-order batsman, played only once for the full Yorkshire side – a first-class match against India A. His two other such matches were for Leeds/Bradford MCCU and he also played for Kirkburton, Lightcliffe and Treeton.

Root, Joseph Edward
Born: 30/12/1990, Sheffield
RHB, OB. Career: 2009-
Cap No 171, 2012

Joe Root made such astonishingly rapid progress that by the age of 23 he was regarded as one of the best four batsmen in the world – the ICC rankings demonstrated this in all three formats and continued to do so.

He first played for Yorkshire in limited-overs cricket and made his first-class debut in the following season. A most attractive batsman, he has scored prolifically in all three formats and made double-centuries for both Yorkshire and England.

Root's Test debut came in late-2012 and his ODI debut early in 2013. It took some time for the management to find his best position in the order – he originally opened the batting for Yorkshire and also did so for England - but he eventually settled into the pivotal number three position in white-ball cricket and number four in Tests. However the international demands made on him were such that in the three seasons from 2013 he appeared in only nine games for Yorkshire.

Root's early captaincy experience included him leading the Yorkshire side when the county clinched the Championship at Trent Bridge in 2014. He was appointed England's 80th Test captain in 2017 and emerged victorious in each of that summer's series against South Africa and West Indies.

Roper, Edward
Born: 08/04/1851, Richmond
Died: 27/04/1921, Toxteth, Liverpool
RHB. Career: 1878-80. Amateur

'Teddy' Roper made his first-class debut in 1876 – for Lancashire to whom he returned after his brief time with Yorkshire. The highest innings of his full 36-match career was 68 on his Yorkshire debut. He played for several clubs, the main ones being Sefton and Liverpool, him holding secretarial posts with both. He was Lancashire Chairman for 13 years from 1899.

Joe Root batting against Middlesex at Lord's in 2014.

Rothery, James William

Born: 05/09/1876, Staincliffe, Batley
Died: 02/06/1919, Beckett's Park, Leeds
RHB. Career: 1903-10. Cap No 39
Grant: 1911

Jimmy Rothery was a regular in five of his eight years with Yorkshire but never scored more than 836 runs in a season, this being his total for 1906. The highest of his three centuries was 161 at Dover in 1908 but he also scored a century before lunch at Bournemouth in 1905. When in good form he was attractive to watch and possessed a pleasing off-drive. Unfortunately, his temperament let him down too often, him reputed to have been nervous when at the crease.

Rothery played for Harrogate for several years as well as Scarborough; while with Wearmouth in Durham he also played for the county. Sadly, he died in hospital at the age of 42 as a consequence of wounds suffered in the First World War.

Rowbotham, Joseph

Born: 08/07/1831, Highfield, Sheffield
Died: 22/12/1899, Morecambe, Lancashire
RHB, RRS/Lobs, WK.
Career: 1863-76

Yorkshire's captain in 1873 and 1875, Joe Rowbotham led his team to 13 wins and seven defeats - a creditable performance in an era when Gloucestershire and Nottinghamshire were the dominant forces.

A free-flowing batsman, Rowbotham played in the first match at Bramall Lane and played for 'Yorkshire' in the two seasons prior to it becoming an official club. His best season was in 1874 when he scored over 500 runs, his highest score of 113 having been at The Oval in the previous season. He played several times for the North and the Players and also in seven games for the All England XI; his main club side was Sheffield.

Rudolph, Jacobus Andries

Born: 04/05/1981, Springs, Transvaal, South Africa
LHB, LBG. Career: 2007-11
Cap No 159, 2007

Jacques Rudolph was a very successful Kolpak player in his four full seasons with Yorkshire and a few games at the end of the 2011 season. A fluent and stylish player, he batted in the upper order in all three formats.

In a career which included spells with Northerns, Eagles, Titans and Surrey, Rudolph played in

international cricket for South Africa from 2003, appearing in 94 such matches including 48 Tests. When with Yorkshire he passed 1,000 first-class runs in each of his four main seasons, his best being 2010 when he scored 1,375 including a career-best of 228 not out against Durham at Headingley. His form in that season's limited-overs matches was even more outstanding: in scoring 861 runs in 13 games he smashed the Yorkshire record for a List A league season. He joined Glamorgan in 2014 and became its captain a year later, retiring from the game at the end of the 2017 season.

Rudston, Horace
Born: 22/11/1878, Hessle, Hull
Died: 14/04/1962, Hessle, Hull
RHB. Career: 1902-07

In four of his 11 seasons in Yorkshire's second eleven Horace Rudston was the leading run-scorer. Unfortunately, except on rare occasions, he was unable to replicate this form when with the first team. Ten of his 21 games for the county

came in 1906 but he scored more runs in only five games in 1904, 233 of his 310 coming in one match when he struck a career-best 164 at Leicester. His club sides were Hessle, Hopton Mills and, where he played professionally for several years, Hull.

Ryan, Melville
Born: 23/06/1933, Huddersfield
Died: 16/11/2015, Dalton,
Huddersfield
RHB, RFM. Career 1954-65
Cap No 107, 1962

One of the best of Fred Trueman's opening partners, Mel Ryan was at his most effective in the early 1960s. Having had to wait until 1960 before claiming a regular place in the team he then had five successful seasons, his best being in 1962 when he took 81 wickets, and was a crucial member of three Championship-winning squads.

Ryan's early cricket was with Bradley Mills and he was a member of the David Brown Tractors team which won the Yorkshire Council in 1959 and 1960. With a long run-up and good action he was a hard-working pace bowler. All his first-class cricket was for Yorkshire and he later served on the county's committee for a time as well as being being on the board of directors of Huddersfield Town.

Ryder, Louis

Born: 28/08/1900, Thirsk
Died: 24/01/1955, Summerbridge,
Harrogate
RHB, RMF. Career: 1924

Lou Ryder had a very short career with Yorkshire but took wickets regularly in league cricket. He played for Thirsk, Leeds and, as professional for five seasons, Bowling Old Lane

Sadler, John Leonard

Born: 19/11/1981, Dewsbury
LHB, LBG. Career: 2002

John Sadler's only appearance for Yorkshire was in a List A match against West Indies A. In eight seasons from 2003 with Leicestershire and Derbyshire he scored over 3,000 runs in 66 first-class matches and also played in the other formats. After brief spells with Suffolk and Hoylandswaine he spent three years on Derbyshire's coaching staff before re-joining Leicestershire in the same capacity.

Sanderson, Ben William

Born: 03/01/1989, Sheffield
RHB, RMF. Career: 2008-11

Ben Sanderson made his debut for Yorkshire in first-class cricket but waited two more years before appearing in white-ball matches. A useful bowler, he had four seasons with the Academy before joining Rotherham Town. After three years with Shropshire he joined Northamptonshire in 2015 and took 55 first-class wickets in 2016 including a career-best eight for 73 against Gloucestershire at Northampton. In 2017 he conceded 77 runs in four overs against Yorkshire at Headingley - the record for a T20 match in England.

Sarfraz Ahmed

Born: 22/05/1987, Karachi, Pakistan
RHB, OB, WK. Career: 2017

Sarfraz Ahmed signed for Yorkshire as a replacement for Peter Handscomb and played only in the latter part of the T20 competition. Having played for Pakistan since 2007/08 he was appointed captain in 2017 in all three formats and led his team to victory in the Champions Trophy of that year. He has played in over 140 international matches, more than half of them being ODIs.

Savile, George

Born: 26/04/1847, Methley, Leeds
Died: 04/09/1904, Tetbury,
Gloucestershire
RHB. Career: 1867-74. Amateur

After captaining the first eleven at Rossall School George Savile had two seasons in the Cambridge University team, gaining a Blue in 1868. His top score for Yorkshire of 65 at Holbeck in 1868 was more than Lancashire managed in its two innings added together! His other main first-class team was Canterbury, New Zealand for whom he played in 1871/72.

Sayers, Joseph John

Born: 05/11/1983, Leeds
LHB, OB. Career: 2003-13.
Cap No 161, 2007

Joe Sayers made his first-class debuts for Oxford University in 2002 and Yorkshire two years later. A very correct and solid opening batsman, he was dogged by ill-luck and left the game at the age of 29.

As captain at Oxford, Sayers had high hopes held of him and his three early Championship centuries, including a career-best 187 at

Tunbridge Wells, in 2007 looked like a breakthrough. After the interjection of T20 cricket, he lost form and this setback was succeeded in 2008 by a serious illness.

In the following season Sayers was appointed vice-captain and, with 1,150 first-class runs, had his best season. He led Yorkshire in six matches, his teams being unbeaten in the competitive games. Later in his career he suffered from inconsistency in selection. His *Rose-Tinted Summer* was an honest and revealing account of Yorkshire's 150th anniversary season.

Schofield, Christopher John
Born: 21/03/1976, Barnsley
RHB. Career: 1996

Chris Schofield had one season with the Academy before playing in 17 games for England U-19, including eight 'Tests'. His one match for Yorkshire was in a non-Championship Roses fixture.

Schofield, Dennis
Born: 09/10/1947, Holmfirth
RHB, RMF. Career: 1970-74

Dennis Schofield played in three games in each format for Yorkshire. All of his first-class wickets were taken when he had figures of five for 42 at Worksop in 1974. Of strong build, most of his career as a club cricketer was with Broad Oak but he also played for Holmbridge, Holmfirth and Lightcliffe.

Scott, Emanuel
Born: 06/07/1834, Birkenshaw, Bradford
Died: 03/12/1898, Birkenshaw, Bradford
RHB, RRM. Career: 1864

Emanuel Scott had a very brief first-class career but played in several matches for club teams against the touring 'England' XIs. These were in various parts of the county but he also played as professional for both Birkenshaw Mills and Gildersome.

Sedgwick, Herbert Amos
Born: 08/04/1883, Richmond
Died: 28/12/1957, Stoke-on-Trent
RHB, RF. Career: 1906

A 'nine-day wonder' is a most apt description of Herbert Sedgwick's experience in first-class cricket. In three successive matches he took a total of 16 wickets including five for eight against Worcestershire at Hull and then a hat-trick in the second innings. After his time with Yorkshire he had lengthy spells with Rawtenstall and then Staffordshire in which county he also played for Knypersley as professional.

Sellers, Arthur

Born: 31/05/1870, Keighley
Died: 25/09/1941, Keighley
RHB. Career: 1890-99.
Amateur. Cap No 21

Better known now as the father of Brian, Arthur Sellers was an aggressive batsman and brave close-in fielder. He played for Keighley before his time in first-class cricket which included appearances for the Gentlemen and the North. For Yorkshire 38 of his 51 matches came in 1892 and 1893, the latter being his best season when he scored both of his centuries, the better being 105 against Middlesex at Lord's. He also played for Leeds and Yorkshire Gentlemen, served on one of Yorkshire's committees and later became a vice-president.

Sellers, Arthur Brian

Born: 05/03/1907, Keighley
Died: 20/02/1981, Eldwick, Bingley
RHB, OB, WK.
Career: 1932-48. Amateur
Cap No 70, 1932

The most brilliant captain in Yorkshire's history, Brian Sellers led his teams to six County Championships in his nine seasons in charge from 1933. Whether measured by most matches won or fewest games lost, Sellers comes out top of those captains who led the county for at least four seasons.

Sellers experienced captaincy at St Peter's School, York aged 16 and with Keighley. In deputising for Frank Greenwood in 1932 he led Yorkshire in 20 of its 28 Championship matches, won the title and the county swept almost all before it through the rest of the decade.

A determined lower-middle-order batsman, he three times scored over 1,000 runs in a season, his best being 1,143 in 1938. Although he scored only four centuries, one was a double – 204 at Fenner's in 1936.

Brian Sellers as Yorkshire's Cricket Committee Chairman.

A Test selector at various times from 1938 to 1955, he was awarded the MBE. An autocratic disciplinarian, Sellers took these qualities with him into Yorkshire's committee-work. As chairman of the cricket committee, he was responsible for the county losing Ray Illingworth and the sacking of Brian Close – two decisions which he came to regret and which took some of the gloss from his earlier great achievements.

Shackleton, William Allan

Born: 09/03/1908, Keighley
Died: 16/11/1971, Bridlington
RHB, LB/RM. Career: 1928-34

Allan Shackleton appeared for Yorkshire in only three seasons but was a very prolific all-rounder in league cricket. He played for Leeds and Pudsey St Lawrence but more for Keighley, partly as professional, Bowling Old Lane, for whom he scored about 5,000 runs and took over 400 wickets, and Brighouse, whom he captained for five seasons. He was also a noted coach.

Shahzad, Ajmal
Born: 27/07/1985, Huddersfield
RHB, RFM. Career: 2004-12
Cap No 165, 2010

The first Yorkshire-born player of Asian descent to represent the county, Ajmal Shahzad was aged 18 when he first did so and made his first-class debut two years later. With 41 first-class wickets in 2009 he made his international debut in the succeeding winter but his 15 games in two years included only one Test.

A strongly-built cricketer, Shahzad always looked to attack the batsman. His best performance came at Chester-le-Street in 2010 when he took five for 51 – still his career-best. A powerful striker in the lower-order, he often made useful runs.

Less effective in the shorter formats, Shahzad left Yorkshire after a disagreement, had one season with Lancashire, two with Nottinghamshire and joined Sussex in 2015 only to leave in mid-season two years later and sign for Leicestershire.

Sharp, Kevin
Born: 06/04/1959, Leeds
LHB, RM/OB. Career: 1975-91
Cap No 124, 1982. Benefit: 1991

Kevin Sharp came to early notice when, as captain of England U-19, he scored 260 not out at Worcester in a 'Test' against West Indies in 1978. His first Yorkshire game had been in List A cricket, his first-class debut coming one year later.

Sharp struggled to establish himself in the side, suffered from stress and loss of form but scored his first century in 1980. Three winters spent with Griqualand West in South Africa were followed by him scoring 1,445 runs – the one time he passed 1,000 – in 1984.

An attractive player in both formats, Sharp played some important innings such as his 181 against Gloucestershire at Harrogate. His highest score in List A matches was 114 at Chelmsford in 1985. With 633 runs, that was his best season in the shorter form and he was part of two trophy-winning teams, notably having the second-highest aggregate in the John Player League in 1983.

Sharp had five seasons with Shropshire from 1993 before becoming its coach. He served as Yorkshire's batting coach in 2002-11 developing the generation which included Joe Root and in 2012 took up the same role with Worcestershire in combination with being its second eleven coach. He has also spent some time helping England's batsmen.

Sharpe, Charles Molesworth
Born: 06/09/1851, Codicote,
Hertfordshire
Died: 25/06/1935, Ilkley
RHB, RRS. Career: 1875. Amateur

All of Charles Sharpe's nine first-class matches came in 1875, including seven games for Cambridge University, in which he took 69 wickets. These included nine five-fors, his best being seven for 43 at The Oval. He also gained a Blue in soccer. Having been Yorkshire's first southern-born player he later worked as a member of the clergy in Sheffield, Huddersfield and Elsecar.

Sharpe, Philip John
Born: 27/12/1936, Shipley, Bradford
Died: 19/05/2014, Harrogate
RHB, OB. Career: 1958-74
Cap No 105, 1960. Benefit: 1971

When Phil Sharpe made his Test debut in 1963 his sheer brilliance as a slip-fielder was a major factor in his selection. He had scored 2,252 runs and snaffled 71 catches during the previous season and had been very unlucky not to have toured Australia on the back of totals which, surprisingly, he never again achieved.

At Worksop College Sharpe had captained the first eleven in his final season and played in a variety of other sports as well. His first club was

Pudsey St Lawrence and he later played for Bradford. His first-class debut came in 1956 and was for the Combined Services.

Stockily-built, Sharpe passed 1,000 runs for the first of 12 seasons in 1960. He played well off the back-foot, his cuts, hooks and pulls all being effective, as well as him possessing a fine cover-drive. His 12 Test appearances were spread over five different series but he was an ever-present in the six Tests of 1969; his one century came against New Zealand that year but three of his four half-centuries were scored against the might of West Indies in 1963 and his final Test career average of 46.23 compared highly favourably with that of his contemporaries. A utility batsman, he was just as prolific in the middle-order as when he opened the innings. This adaptability enabled him to play an important role in seven Championship-winning teams.

But it is as a cricketer who spent so much of his time fielding in the slips that he will mostly be remembered. His powers of concentration were immense and his stillness enabled

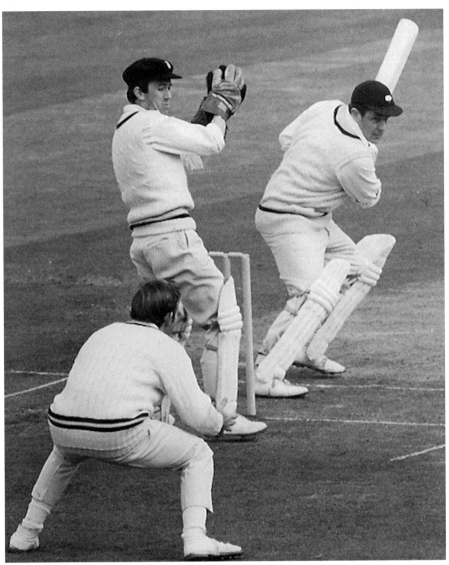

Phil Sharpe batting for Yorkshire against MCC at Lord's in 1969. The wicket-keeper is Bob Taylor.

him to delay catching the ball until the very last millisecond, it almost appearing as though the ball was going to go past him. Often standing between Jimmy Binks and Brian Close, batsmen who edged the ball into that particular cordon knew that they were highly unlikely to get away with a missed chance.

Following his time with Yorkshire, Sharpe had two seasons with Derbyshire during which he made a career-best 228 at The Parks. Six seasons with Norfolk came next and he also spent some of his retirement running a travel company specialising in cricket tours. His continuing interest in Yorkshire was as a committee-member for several years up until the re-organisation in 2001.

Shaw, Christopher

Born: 17/02/1964, Hemsworth, Wakefield
RHB, RFM. Career: 1984-88

When Chris Shaw took five for 41 at Bournemouth in only his second List A match, expectations were high. However, four years later he had just established himself in the Yorkshire team in both formats when he succumbed to a puzzling neck injury and this ended his senior career at the age of 24. Tall, he bowled very straight and had taken a total of 72 wickets, including 46 in first-class cricket, in what became his final season. He continued in league cricket with Undercliffe, Adel and Mirfield but had lost pace and effectiveness. He saved his best performance in first-class cricket for the Roses match at Headingley in 1987 when he took six for 64.

Shaw, James

Born: 12/03/1865, Linthwaite, Huddersfield
Died: 22/01/1921, Armley, Leeds
RHB, SLA. Career: 1896-97

'Jimmy' Shaw had only a brief career with Yorkshire although he took four wickets in the first innings in which he bowled. He played club cricket for Wakefield, as professional, and Scarborough.

Shaw, Joshua

Born: 03/01/1996, Wakefield
RHB, RMF. Career: 2015-

Son of Chris, Josh Shaw first played for Yorkshire in a T20 match aged 19 and he made his first-class debut a year later. Having been with the Academy side for four years, he played in four 'Tests' and 16 ODIs for England U-19. A most promising bowler, he was on loan to Gloucestershire for much of 2016 and 2017 when he took 47 wickets in 17 first-class matches, including five for 79 against Sussex at Bristol.

Sheepshanks, Ernest Richard

Born: 22/03/1910, Arthington, Otley
Died: 31/12/1937, Caudiel, Alto Palancia, Castellón, Spain
RHB. Career: 1929. Amateur

Dick Sheepshanks captained the Eton College first eleven in the second of his two seasons in the team but had only one innings in first-class cricket. He was killed in the Spanish Civil War working as a Reuters correspondent.

Shepherd, Donald Arthur

Born: 10/03/1916, Whitkirk, Leeds
Died: 29/05/1998, Norbiton, Surrey
RHB, OB. Career: 1938. Amateur

Donald Shepherd was captain at Leeds Grammar School for the final three years of his five in the first eleven. He was drafted late into the Yorkshire side against Oxford while studying at the University but made a duck in his only first-class innings. He was later awarded the OBE for his work as a civil servant in the Colonial Service.

Shotton, William

Born: 01/12/1840, Lascelles Hall, Huddersfield
Died: 26/05/1909, Kirkheaton, Huddersfield
RHB, RRM. Career: 1865-74

William Shotton's two games for Yorkshire were separated by a gap of nine years. He batted in the middle order but was a good opening batsman in club cricket, in which he played for a considerable number of teams; the main one was Lascelles Hall but he also played for Ravenscourt in Middlesex and coached at a school in Edinburgh.

Sidebottom, Arnold

Born: 01/04/1954, Barnsley
RHB, RFM. Career: 1973-91
Cap No 121, 1980. Benefit: 1988

One of England's 'one-Test wonders', Arnie Sidebottom had his time of glory in the Ashes series of 1985 when he took one wicket before injury curtailed the experience. He had first played for Yorkshire at the age of 19 and was a whole-hearted bowler, his best years being in the 1980s when he four times took over 60 first-class wickets in a season. His best performance of eight for 72 came in 1986 against Leicestershire at Middlesbrough.

In limited-overs matches, Sidebottom could usually be relied upon to bowl an economical spell. Although he was injured for much of the successful John Player League season of 1983, he played a full part in the Benson & Hedges Cup triumph of 1987, coming top of Yorkshire's bowling averages and being the only pace bowler to concede fewer than three runs per over.

After retirement Sidebottom remained on the county staff, was the bowling coach until 2002 and later worked as cricket professional at Woodhouse Grove School. A noted footballer, he played for Manchester United, Huddersfield Town and Halifax Town.

Ryan Sidebottom bowling against Gloucestershire in a
CGU National League match at Cheltenham in 1999.

Sidebottom, Ryan Jay

Born: 15/01/1978, Huddersfield
LHB, LFM. Career: 1997-2017
Cap No 150, 2000. Testimonial: 2017

One of the best swing bowlers of his generation, Ryan Sidebottom, son of Arnie, played in 65 international matches. His 79 wickets in 22 Tests included a hat-trick at Hamilton and a best performance of seven for 47 at Napier, both in New Zealand in 2007/08. He was also an important member of the team which won the World T20 in 2010. Most of his England appearances were during the period 2004-10 while he was playing for Nottinghamshire and collecting two Championship-winners medals.

The only player to take part in Yorkshire's three Championship-winning seasons of the 21st century, Sidebottom led the attack by both taking wickets and bowling economically, results achieved through his angle of delivery and his ability to move the ball both ways. Having given up playing in List A matches after 2013 and T20 cricket a year later he was able, latterly, to concentrate on the longer form of the game and consequently stayed very fit. Four times he took 50 or more first-class wickets in a season, his best being in 2011 when his 62 victims included a career-best seven for 37 against Somerset at Headingley. By the time of his retirement at the end of the 2017 season he had taken 762 wickets in his full first-class career of 230 matches.

Sidgwick, Robert

Born: 07/08/1851, Embsay Kirk, Skipton
Died: 23/10/1933, Mandeville, Manchester, Jamaica
RHB. Career: 1882. Amateur

Robert Sidgwick kept his place in the Yorkshire side, despite a batting

average of below five and a top score of 17, because of his brilliant fielding in the covers. He also played for Skipton, Keighley and Harrogate and emigrated in the late-1880s, playing one match for Jamaica in 1895.

Silverwood, Christopher Eric Wilfred

Born: 05/03/1975, Pontefract
RHB, RFM. Career: 1993-2005
Cap No 143, 1996. Benefit: 2004

One of the best of several seam bowlers which Yorkshire produced in the 1990s, Chris Silverwood was a player who gave his all for both county and country. He played in six Tests and seven ODIs, the former being spread over a period of six

Chris Silverwood bowling at Lord's in the Benson & Hedges Super Cup final against Gloucestershire in 1999.

years. Four Tests came on the tour of South Africa in 1999/2000 during which he took his Test-best of five for 91 at Cape Town.

Silverwood's energetic approach and action produced hostile deliveries and effective seam movement. Three times he took over 50 wickets in a first-class season, his best being 63 in 2006 by which time he had moved to Middlesex with whom he spent four seasons. His best season for Yorkshire was in 1999 when he took 59 wickets; a best performance had come two years earlier with seven for 93 against Kent at Headingley. He topped the averages in Yorkshire's title-winning season of 2001.

In 2010 Silverwood became bowling coach with Essex and in the autumn of 2015 was appointed Head Coach. His first two seasons in charge saw the county win promotion to the Championship's first division and then win the title.

He left Essex to take up an appointment as England's bowling coach from the start of 2018.

Silvester, Stephen

Born: 12/03/1951, Hull
RHB, RF. Career: 1976-77

Stephen Silvester's short career with Yorkshire came only after he had already played for the second elevens of both Warwickshire and Derbyshire. He also played for Northumberland, in 1979, and his several clubs included Hull, Harrogate, Bowling Old Lane, Undercliffe and Bingley.

Simpson, Edward Thornhill Beckett

Born: 05/03/1867, Crofton, Wakefield
Died: 20/03/1944, Walton, Wakefield
RHB. Career: 1889. Amateur

Edward Simpson's first-class debut was for Oxford University against the Australians in 1888. A solid opening or middle-order batsman, his only half-century in 19 innings was also for Oxford. He played for the family firm of Hodgson's and Simpson's, for eight seasons, and Yorkshire Gentlemen.

Sims, Herbert Marsh

Born: 15/03/1853, Mount Tavy, Tavistock, Devon
Died: 05/10/1885, Thorpe, Whitby
RHB, RRF. Career: 1875-77.
Amateur

Herbert Sims was in the first eleven at St Peter's School, York in 1871 and had three years in the Cambridge team. He played in 18 first-class matches for the University scoring 375 runs and taking 65 wickets. An attacking batsman and erratic bowler, only two of his five games for Yorkshire were county matches. He entered the church in 1876 but suddenly died at the age of 32 after catching a chill.

Slinn, William

Born: 13/12/1826, Sheffield
Died: 19/06/1888, Wortley, Sheffield
RHB, RRF. Career: 1863-64

One of Yorkshire's first outstanding bowlers, William Slinn also played for the county for two years prior to the Club being formed, taking 46 wickets in only six matches.

With Ikey Hodgson he formed the White Rose's first great bowling partnership even though it was short-lived. Although fast, Slinn had a graceful action and made the ball hurry off the pitch. He twice played for England elevens and for a host of clubs, mostly Sheffield.

Smailes, Thomas Francis

Born: 27/03/1910, Ripley, Harrogate
Died: 01/12/1970, Harrogate
LHB, RFM/OB. Career: 1932-48
Cap No 73, 1934. Benefit: 1948

As a very useful all-rounder, Frank Smailes was an integral member of the Yorkshire side in the 1930s and was a member of seven Championship-winning teams. His first clubs were Ilkley, Harrogate, then both Forfarshire and Brighouse as professional. By 1934 he was established in the Yorkshire team and his aggressive, hard-hitting batting often gave the innings the required impetus. He opened the bowling, making the ball move in either direction, then changed to spin later. The 1938 season was Smailes' best; he took ten wickets in the match against the Australians, made his highest score – 117 against Glamorgan at Cardiff - and completed the double. The following season he became only the third Yorkshire bowler to take all ten wickets in an innings when he achieved figures of ten for 47 against Derbyshire at Sheffield.

Belatedly, Smailes gained a Test cap against India at Lord's in 1946. By now he was unfortunately suffering from varicose veins - a result of the War; he struggled on for two more seasons and ended his career with five years for Walsall.

Smales, Kenneth

Born: 15/09/1927, Horsforth, Leeds
Died: 10/03/2015, Torpoint,
Cornwall
RHB, OB. Career: 1948-50

After club cricket with Horsforth, Keighley and Bradford, Ken Smales played in nine Championship matches in his first season with Yorkshire but no more thereafter. However, from 1951 he had eight seasons with Nottinghamshire taking 367 wickets in 148 matches. He remains that county's only bowler to take all ten wickets in an innings – for 66 against Gloucestershire at Stroud in 1956.

He spent 30 years as secretary of Nottingham Forest FC including its great years under Brian Clough.

Smith, Alfred Farrer

Born: 07/03/1847, Birstall, Leeds
Died: 06/01/1915, Ossett, Wakefield
RHB, RRMF. Career: 1868-74

An amateur in his first year, Alfred Smith played in only four seasons for Yorkshire. He had a regular place in the side through each of 1873 and 1874 but then gave up the game at the age of 27. A steady and reliable batsman, he was strong on the leg-side. His highest innings was 99 for Players of the North against Players of the South at Prince's, London in what was his only other first-class match. He umpired in first-class cricket for ten seasons from 1892.

Smith, Ernest

Born: 19/10/1869, Morley, Leeds
Died: 09/04/1945, Eastbourne, Sussex
RHB, RFM. Career: 1888-1907.
Amateur. Cap No 13

A very useful all-rounder, Ernest Smith's appearances were often restricted to August when he was free from teaching duties. He led Yorkshire on 16 occasions when Lord Hawke was unavailable.

Smith was in the first eleven at Clifton College for two years; his first-class debut was for Oxford University - in the same year as his county debut - and he won his Blue in 1890 and 1891. An attacking batsman and effective swing bowler he contributed to seven Championship-winning teams but seemed to save his best form for the festivals of Scarborough and Eastbourne, where he was later a prep-school head teacher, and where he made his final first-class appearance in 1928. He regularly represented the Gentlemen and the North, scored over 7,500 runs and took more than 450 wickets in his overall total of 242 first-class matches.

Smith, Ernest

Born: 11/07/1888, Barnsley
Died: 02/01/1972, Blackburn, Lancashire
RHB, LMS. Career: 1914-26

Ernest Smith played in only three seasons for Yorkshire, 11 of his 16 games coming in 1919. An accurate spinner, his best analysis was six for 40 at Bradford in 1914. He began his club career with Barnsley and Ossett but mostly played as a professional in Lancashire, his teams there including Colne and Rawtenstall, him having four seasons with each.

Smith, Fred

Born: 18/12/1879, Yeadon, Leeds
Died: 20/10/1905, Nelson, Lancashire
LHB. Career: 1903

Fred Smith was given an extended run in the Yorkshire side in June and July of his only year in the team but made only two half-centuries. He also played for Yeadon and moved to Nelson in an attempt to qualify for Lancashire. His death at the age of 25 was from pneumonia, him having worn wet clothes after playing rugby.

Smith, Fred

Born: 26/12/1885, Idle, Bradford
Died: unknown
?HB. Career: 1911

Fred Smith's one first-class match was against the Indians at Hull and he also played for Idle and Keighley.

Smith, George

Born: 19/01/1875, Thorp Arch, Wetherby
Died: 16/01/1929, Thorp Arch, Wetherby
?HB. Career: 1901-06

George Smith's two first-class matches were separated by a gap of five years and only one was in the Championship – a game in which he neither batted nor bowled.

Smith, John

Born: 23/03/1833, Yeadon, Leeds
Died: 12/02/1909, Worcester
LHB, LRFM. Career: 1865

John Smith played for both Lancashire and Yorkshire in 1865 but then just the former in 1866 and 1869, his full record being 181 runs and 18 wickets in eight matches. He also played for several clubs in Lancashire, Scotland and Yorkshire, his longest spell being at Batley. Groundsman at Marlborough College from 1874, he fulfilled the same role at Worcester from 1883 until his death.

Smith, Neil

Born: 01/04/1949, Ossett, Wakefield
Died: 04/03/2003, Wakefield
RHB, WK. Career: 1970-71

Neil Smith succeeded Jimmy Binks as Yorkshire's wicket-keeper but, after 14 matches, seven in each format, he was replaced by David Bairstow. Although he returned for one match in 1971 he moved two years later to Essex where he spent nine seasons. His original clubs were Readicut, Lascelles Hall and Bradford but he also had three seasons with Cheshire from 1987.

Smith, Rodney

Born: 06/04/1944, Batley
RHB, SLA. Career: 1969-70

A successful, solid opening batsman in club cricket, Rodney Smith batted in the lower middle-order in his short career for Yorkshire.

His league cricket was with Hartshead Moor as professional, Liversedge and Heckmondwike whom he captained to six trophies in 11 seasons.

Smith, Walter

Born: 19/08/1845, Horton, Bradford
Died: 02/06/1926, Thornbury, Bradford
RHB. Career: 1874

A strong off-side player, Walter Smith was given a brief run in the Yorkshire side but after only one half-century in five games was discarded. Most of his other cricket was for Bradford. The above records are believed to be correct but there is ongoing research into this player who was erroneously known as Walker Smith from 1983 to 2017 and given his details.

Smith, William

Born: 01/11/1839, Darlington, Durham
Died: 19/04/1897, South Bank, Middlesbrough
RHB. Career: 1865-74

William Smith played in only four seasons for Yorkshire, both of his half-centuries coming in 1867. A tall and strongly-built batsman, he scored 90 at Middlesbrough in Yorkshire's first official home Roses match when no other batsman made more than 33. Most of his club cricket was for Middlesbrough and Bradford.

Smithson, Gerald Arthur

Born: 01/11/1926, Spofforth, Harrogate
Died: 06/09/1970, Abingdon, Berkshire
LHB, RM. Career: 1946-50.
Cap No 84, 1947

An attractive batsman, Gerald Smithson had a brilliant run of form in 1947 and this led to two Test appearances on the West Indies tour of the following winter. This came about only after the issue of him being released from National Service as a 'Bevin Boy' in the mines was raised in Parliament. Unfortunately, an injury to a shoulder forced him to miss the whole of the 1948 season and he was never quite the same again.

Following his release he had six seasons with Leicestershire from 1951 in which he scored over 5,000 runs in 154 matches. He played for Hertfordshire while coach at Caterham School and finished his career as coach and groundsman at Abingdon School. He died suddenly at the age of 43 but his name now lives on in this latter school's Gerald Smithson Cricket Day – a T20 tournament instituted in 2009.

Smurthwaite, James

Born: 17/10/1916, North Ormesby, Middlesbrough
Died: 20/10/1989, Middlesbrough
RHB, RM/OB. Career: 1938-39

An in-swing bowler when not bowling his spinners, Jim Smurthwaite took five for seven against Derbyshire at Sheffield in 1939 but the onset of war prevented further opportunities. Most of his league cricket was with Guisborough but he also played for Billingham, Saltburn and, as professional, Sheffield United.

Sowden, Abram

Born: 01/12/1853, Great Horton, Bradford
Died: 05/07/1921, Heaton, Bradford
RHB, RRFM. Career: 1878-87

Abram Sowden appeared in only five seasons for Yorkshire and his final first-class match was for an England XI in 1902. A successful batsman in other cricket, he played for a few clubs, staying with Bingley and Bradford the longest. An excellent coach, his death certificate showed him as Abraham but Abram was on his birth certificate.

Squire, Dick

Born: 31/12/1864, Cleckheaton, Dewsbury
Died: 28/04/1922, Scholes, Cleckheaton, Dewsbury
RHB, SLA. Career: 1893

In his only game for Yorkshire Dick Squire made a pair and took no wickets or catches. Professional at Brighouse for several years, he was registered as Squires at birth.

Squires, Peter John

Born: 04/08/1951, Ripon
RHB, LB. Career: 1971-76

An attractive middle-order batsman and excellent out-fielder, Peter Squires first played for Yorkshire in the John Player League and made his first-class debut a year later. He never gained a regular place in the team, him scoring only seven half-centuries in his 105 games in both formats.

After two years in the first eleven at Ripon Grammar School he played for Ripon and Harrogate before his first-class career, and Billingham and Manningham Mills, both as professional, afterwards.

Squires is better known for his exploits in rugby union. A brilliant winger firstly for Ripon, Harrogate and Yorkshire, he played 29 times for England and also represented the British Lions in New Zealand in 1977. Having trained at St John's College, York, he taught PE at Harrogate Grammar School in the 1970s.

Stanley, Harry Cecil

Born: 16/02/1888, Rotherham
Died: 18/05/1934, Scarborough
RHB. Career: 1911-13. Amateur

Of Harry Stanley's eight games for Yorkshire seven came in 1913 but he never scored a half-century. Tall, he was a good close-in fielder but played in only a little club cricket, mostly for Sheffield United and York.

Stanyforth, Ronald Thomas

Born: 30/05/1892, Chelsea, London
Died: 20/02/1964, Kirk Hammerton, York
RHB, WK. Career: 1928. Amateur

In that he captained England – on the Test tour of South Africa in 1927/28 – without having played for a county, Ronald Stanyforth holds a unique place in the history of English cricket. Most of his 61 first-class matches were for MCC (38) or the Army (10) but his debut was for Oxford University in 1914.

Stanyforth was awarded the Military Cross in the First World War and was later promoted to the rank of major. In retirement he was a trustee of MCC, a patron of Yorkshire CCC and wrote a book on wicket-keeping.

Starc, Mitchell Aaron

Born: 30/01/1990, Baulkham Hills, Sydney, Australia
LHB, LFM. Career: 2012

Having first played for New South Wales at the age of 19 Mitchell Starc made his international debut 18 months before his time with Yorkshire for whom he played in all three formats. He was particularly outstanding in the successful T20 campaign being the best bowler in terms of wicket-aggregate, average and economy rate. He has now played over 120 times for Australia, having taken 148 wickets in his 36 Tests.

Stead, Barry

Born: 21/06/1939, Leeds
Died: 15/04/1980, Drighlington, Batley
LHB, LMF. Career: 1959

A stocky bowler, Barry Stead took seven for 76 on his debut for Yorkshire but that was in what became his penultimate game for the county. From 1962 he played for Nottinghamshire for 15 seasons taking over 600 first-class wickets and more than 200 in List A cricket. He returned to Yorkshire and captained Morley but died of cancer aged 40.

Stemp, Richard David

Born: 11/12/1967, Erdington, Birmingham
RHB, SLA. Career: 1993-98
Cap No 142, 1996

One of the very first cricketers to

benefit from the rescinding of the only-Yorkshire-born policy, Richard Stemp arrived after three years with Worcestershire and in five of his six seasons with the White Rose county took over 40 first-class wickets. His best aggregate was 49 in 1994 when he also had the best figures of his career – six for 37 at Durham. Although Yorkshire tended to use him less in List A matches, he took over 30 wickets in each of the 1996 and 1997 seasons.

After leaving Yorkshire Stemp had four more years in the first-class game – three with Nottinghamshire and one with Leicestershire. He was close to international honours in the mid-1990s when he was chosen in a twelve for a home Test match and also went on two tours with England A.

Stephenson, Edwin

Born: 05/06/1832, Sheffield
Died: 05/07/1898, Tue Brook,
Liverpool
RHB, RRF, WK. Career: 1863-73

Prior to the formation of the official Club, 'Ned' Stephenson had been playing for the county for two years. His first-class debut had come in 1854 and he had also played for the North and 'England' in the pre-1863 part of his career.

A frequent opening batsman, he scored English cricket's first run in Australia as a member of the first (non-Test) touring party to visit there in 1861/62. The leading wicket-keeper/batsman of his day, he scored almost 2,000 runs and made over 100 catches and stumpings in his full first-class career.

Stephenson, John Stewart

Born: 10/11/1903, Brough, Hull
Died: 07/10/1975, Horsham, Sussex
RHB, RM. Career: 1923-26.
Amateur

In leading Yorkshire for one match (his second!), John Stephenson remains, at the age of 19, the county's youngest-ever captain. He led the first eleven at Shrewsbury School in the last of his four years in the side. His career at Oxford University, where he won Blues in each of his last two years, ran concurrently with his county career. He won four soccer Blues and his son was Col JR Stephenson who was in secretarial positions at Lord's from 1979 to 1993.

Stevenson, Graham Barry

Born: 16/12/1955, Ackworth,
Pontefract
Died: 21/01/2014, Pontefract
RHB, RMF. Career: 1973-86
Cap No 119, 1978

An exciting all-rounder, Graham Stevenson had a very short international career but it included a match-winning performance in an ODI at Sydney in 1979/80. Figures of four for 33 (at the time England's best in an ODI debut) were followed by an innings of 28 not out when England were 129 for eight; despite having to chase 164 he helped see his country home by two wickets.

Stevenson first played for Barnsley at the age of 16 and made his Yorkshire debut one year later. An attacking lower-order batsman, he compiled his highest innings in 1982 when he batted at number 11 against Warwickshire at Edgbaston. With the scoreboard showing 143 for nine he smote 115 not out in the company of Geoff Boycott and their stand of 149 remains the record for Yorkshire's tenth wicket. An energetic bowler, his best performance was eight for 57 against Northamptonshire at Headingley in 1980 – his best first-class season with both bat and ball.

Injury-prone, Stevenson also appeared to lack confidence in his own ability despite an outward enthusiasm. He moved to Northamptonshire in 1987 but left the game after one season. Having later suffered much from ill-health he died at the early age of 58.

Stott, William Bryan

Born: 18/07/1934, Yeadon, Leeds
LHB, RM. Career: 1952-63
Cap No 98, 1957

Bryan Stott first played for Yorkshire when 23 days short of his 18th birthday. When he established himself in the county side in 1957 he formed an opening partnership with Ken Taylor which saw many an innings begin with some fast scoring. The briskness was built on firm foundations and the pair had a really good understanding when running between the wickets.

Stott passed the 1,000-runs-in-a-season mark five times, his best year being 1959 when he scored 2,034

runs. This included 96 in 86 minutes in the final game at Hove when the winning runs brought Yorkshire its first Championship for 13 years. The following year he made his highest score – 186 at Edgbaston.

Having left the playing side of the game at an early age, Stott was on the Yorkshire committee for over ten years and did much to establish the cricket school at Headingley and the Academy.

Stringer, Peter Michael
Born: 23/02/1943, Gipton, Leeds
LHB, RFM. Career: 1967-69

Peter Stringer took four wickets in each of his first two innings in first-class cricket but failed to take further opportunities given by Yorkshire. Strongly-built, he played for Colton, East Bierley, Bradford and Pudsey St Lawrence before spending three years with Leicestershire from 1970. His first season there was his best and included his only five-for – against Yorkshire at Sheffield.

Having obtained a coaching position with the Wanderers, Johannesburg, he emigrated to South Africa but returned in 1980 and again played for Colton.

Stuchbury, Stephen
Born: 22/06/1954, Sheffield
LHB, LMF. Career: 1978-82

Although used by Yorkshire predominantly as a List A player, Stephen Stuchbury played in limited-overs matches in only three seasons and in first-class cricket in only two. His best performance was five for 16 in a John Player League match at Leicester in 1982. He played club cricket for Sheffield United, Holmfirth and Sheffield Collegiate.

Sugg, Frank Howe
Born: 11/01/1862, Ilkeston, Derbyshire
Died: 29/05/1933, Waterloo, Liverpool
RHB. Career: 1883

Frank Sugg had a very distinguished career after his time with Yorkshire. From 1884 he had three seasons with Derbyshire but then played for Lancashire until 1899. He played in two Test matches in 1888 and frequently represented the North and the Players. An attacking batsman, he scored 9,546 runs in his 234 games for Lancashire and later had two seasons as a first-class umpire. A multi-talented sportsman, he played for six football clubs, three of which - Sheffield Wednesday, Derby County and Burnley - he captained.

Sugg, Walter
Born: 21/05/1860, Ilkeston, Derbyshire
Died: 21/05/1933, Dore, Derbyshire
RHB, RM. Career: 1881

An attractive batsman, Walter Sugg had a very brief career with Yorkshire but played for Derbyshire from 1884 to 1902 scoring 3,460 runs in 128 matches. He was also a useful bowler and very good fielder in the covers. With his brother, Frank, he ran two stores of sports outfitters in Liverpool. He died on his birthday in a suburb of Sheffield which became part of Yorkshire in 1934.

Sullivan, Joseph Hubert Baron
Born: 21/09/1890, York
Died: 08/02/1932, Parkgate, Chester, Cheshire
RHB, RMF. Career: 1912. Amateur

In a spasmodic first-class career, Joseph Sullivan played in four games in 1912 and one in each of four seasons for the Europeans in India in the early-1920s. A stylish batsman, he had two years in the first eleven at St Peter's School, York and played twice for Cambridge University but did not gain a Blue.

Sutcliffe, Herbert

Born: 24/11/1894, Summerbridge, Harrogate
Died: 22/01/1978, Cross Hills, Keighley
RHB, RM. Career: 1919-45.
Cap No 53, 1919. Benefit: 1929.
Testimonial: 1935

The only batsman from any county to score over 1,000 runs in every one of the 21 seasons between the two world wars, Herbert Sutcliffe made 1,839 in his first campaign – a record for a debutant. Prior to his county career he played for a handful of clubs including West of Scotland but mainly for Pudsey St Lawrence.

Herbert Sutcliffe (on left) walks out to bat with Percy Holmes.

The 1922 season saw him pass 2,000 runs for the first of 14 consecutive years – a record which still stands. Two years later he played in the first of his 54 Tests and began an opening partnership with Surrey's Jack Hobbs in which he developed a similar understanding as he had already done with his regular Yorkshire partner, Percy Holmes. In Australia in 1924/25 he became the first England player to score two centuries in the same Test and passed the 1,000-run mark in only 12 innings – still a record for his country.

Sutcliffe had an impeccable technique and an imperturbable temperament. The more difficult the pitch, the greater were his powers of concentration. A seven-hour innings of 161 in the final Test of 1926 after an overnight thunderstorm was the major contribution to the Ashes being regained. When conditions were in the batsman's favour he demonstrated strokes all round the wicket and could score very quickly. He was strong off either foot and had an outstanding judgement of line, length and pace.

Sutcliffe was at his best in the five seasons from 1928. He passed 3,000 runs in three of these and topped the national averages in each of the three from 1930. His partnership with Hobbs, however, ended in 1930, them having averaged 87.81 - another world Test record which still stands. After averaging 96.96 in 1931 he scored his only triple-century – against Essex at Leyton in the world record stand of 555 with Holmes - in his best season of 3,336 runs a year later. His highest Test score of 194 came at Sydney on the bodyline tour in the succeeding winter. He

Herbert Sutcliffe.

eventually ended his Test career with an average of 66.85 against Australia and an overall average of 60.73 - both still records for England. In his final full season of 1939 he became the oldest player to carry his bat and ended his career with over 50,000 first class runs and 151 centuries.

A Test selector for three years from 1959, the Sutcliffe Gates were later erected at Headingley – 'in honour of a great Yorkshire and England cricketer'.

Sutcliffe, William Herbert Hobbs

Born: 10/10/1926, Pudsey
Died: 16/09/1998, Collingham,
Wetherby
RHB, LB. Career: 1948-57. Amateur Cap No 95, 1952

Captain of Yorkshire in the 1956 and 1957 seasons, Billy Sutcliffe led a talented side but one which suffered from disunity and he left the first-class game after the experience despite being aged only 30. The team finished in seventh and third places, respectively.

Sutcliffe captained Rydal School's first eleven in the last of his four years in the team and then joined Leeds. He first represented the Gentlemen in 1951 and his highest innings for Yorkshire − 181 at Canterbury − came a year later. In 1955 he scored over 1,000 runs for the only time and went to Pakistan on the MCC (non-Test) tour the following winter. Thereafter his form deserted him − another factor in his decision to retire.

Back with Leeds he became, in 1959, the first batsman to score 1,000 runs in the Yorkshire League and later played for Harrogate. His father was the legendary Herbert.

Swallow, Ian Geoffrey
Born: 18/12/1962, Barnsley
RHB, OB. Career: 1983-89

Very much a specialist in the first-class game, only eight of Ian Swallow's 69 games for Yorkshire were limited-overs matches. However, he never gained a regular place in the side and took only one

five-for − seven for 95 at Trent Bridge in 1987. Ironically, he was given most opportunities in what turned out to be his final season with Yorkshire.

Economical rather than penetrative, Swallow often performed a holding role and he was also a useful lower-order batsman. He played for Somerset for two seasons from 1990 and his league cricket was with Elsecar, Barnsley and Sheffield United.

Swanepoel, Pieter Johannes
Born: 30/03/1977, Paarl,
Cape Province, South Africa
RHB, RMF. Career: 2003

Although Pieter Swanepoel represented Yorkshire in all three formats, he played in only seven matches, taking nine wickets. This was after List A appearances for YCB and before he played for Cambridgeshire in 2004-06. In league cricket he had seven seasons with Woodlands and also played for Sheffield United and Whitley Hall.

Tait, Thomas
Born: 07/10/1872, Langley Moor,
Durham
Died: 06/09/1954, Brierley,
Pontefract
RHB. Career: 1898-99

A prolific run-scorer in club cricket, particularly for Barnsley, Thomas Tait received little opportunity with Yorkshire.

Tasker, John
Born: 04/02/1887, South Kirkby,
Pontefract
Died: 24/08/1975,
Greenham Common, Berkshire
RHB. Career: 1912-13. Amateur.
Cap No 51

John Tasker played in 23 games for Yorkshire in his first season but scored only three half-centuries. Despite this he was given eight more matches in 1913 but then gave up the game although he played in two first-class matches for the forces in 1919. He played club cricket for Pontefract and Wakefield and also represented the Civil Service.

Tattersall, Geoffrey
Born: 21/04/1882, Ripon
Died: 29/06/1972, Harrogate
RHB. Career: 1905. Amateur

A talented sportsman, Geoffrey Tattersall had a very brief career for Yorkshire but captained Harrogate in three of his ten seasons with it. He also played for Harrogate at rugby union, representing Yorkshire 25 times and playing in an England trial in 1903. In addition, he was captain of Harrogate Golf Club.

Tattersall, Jonathan Andrew
Born: 15/12/1994, Harrogate
RHB, LB. Career: 2013-

A highly promising opening batsman and brilliant out-fielder, Jonny Tattersall had three years in the Academy team and was vice-captain of England U-19 in the World Cup in 2014. He played for Yorkshire in two List A matches separated by four years. Between these appearances he tried his luck with the second elevens of Durham and Derbyshire. He joined Lincolnshire in 2016 and continued to score prolifically for his club Harrogate.

Taylor, Christopher Robert
Born: 21/02/1981, Leeds
RHB, RFM. Career: 2001-08

An upper-order batsman, Chris Taylor played irregularly for Yorkshire but was a success in 2006 for Derbyshire. That season – the first of two with that county - he scored the only five centuries of his career, including one against Yorkshire, in two formats. He returned north in 2008 but was released again, after one more season. He had one year with Staffordshire and most of his league cricket has been with Lightcliffe, whom he captained for two seasons, but he also played for Spondon. He went into coaching and formed All Rounder Cricket Ltd.

Taylor, Harry
Born: 18/12/1900, Idle, Bradford
Died: 28/10/1988, Bradford
RHB, RM. Career: 1924-25

Harry Taylor, a middle-order batsman, played for Bowling Old Lane before his short county career. From 1928 he had 14 seasons with Lightcliffe during which he scored almost 10,000 runs and later became its professional coach. He also had one year with Undercliffe.

Taylor, Henry Storm
Born: 11/12/1856, Scarborough
Died: 16/11/1896, Great Lever, Lancashire
RHB, RM. Career: 1879

An opening batsman, Henry Taylor had a very brief career with Yorkshire but played successfully for club teams in the east of the county including Scarborough and Malton. He died from typhoid fever at the age of 39.

Taylor, John
Born: 02/04/1850, Pudsey
Died: 27/05/1924, Boston Spa, Wetherby
RHB, RRM. Career: 1880-81

Jack Taylor played for the North in 1875 but that was his only first-class match other than his appearances for Yorkshire. A middle-order batsman, light on his feet, his clubs were Batley, whom he also captained, and Armley.

Taylor, Kenneth

Born: 21/08/1935, Huddersfield
RHB, RM, LB. Career: 1953-68
Cap No 99, 1957. Benefit: 1968

A man with three outstanding talents, Ken Taylor made his debut for Yorkshire at the age of 17 and gradually developed as a dashing opening batsman and brilliant fielder in the covers. His speed was also a feature of his running between the wickets and his straight driving and late cutting were trademark strokes.

Ken Taylor in his third career as an art teacher.

Taylor's best season was in 1961 when he scored 1,494 runs including his only double century, at Edgbaston. Three Tests came in 1959 (two) and 1964. His useful, accurate and - usually - medium pace bowling brought him one five-for, a significant six for 75 in the Roses match of 1961 at Old Trafford. He later coached in

South Africa and New Zealand and had three seasons with Norfolk.

From 1953 Taylor played centre half for Huddersfield Town and, later, Bradford City but his career as a full-time professional ended in 1966 when he began teaching art in a Huddersfield school. He had qualified ten years earlier at Slade School of Fine Arts, London and later became Head of Art at Gresham's School, Norfolk. His portraits of former team-mates are on display at Headingley.

Taylor, Nicholas Simon

Born: 02/06/1963, Holmfirth, Huddersfield
RHB, RFM. Career: 1982-83

Nick Taylor had four seasons in the first eleven at Gresham's School then made his first-class debut while still aged 18. A strong bowler, he played in four games in each of his two seasons with Yorkshire, his best bowling being five for 49 against Sussex at Headingley. After his release, he spent two seasons with Surrey and one with Somerset who gave him more opportunities in List A cricket.

Taylor, Tom Launcelot

Born: 25/05/1878, Headingley, Leeds
Died: 16/03/1960, Chapel Allerton, Leeds
RHB, WK. Career: 1899-1906.
Amateur. Cap No 33

A natural leader, Tom Taylor captained both Uppingham School's first eleven, for two of the three seasons he was in the team, and Cambridge University in 1900. This was his fourth year in the side and he gained a Blue three times.

An attacking batsman who scored

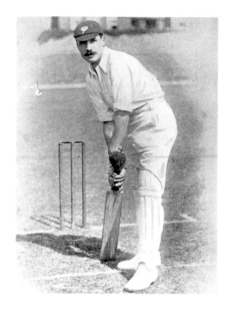

over 1,000 runs in each of the three Championship-winning seasons of 1900-02, his best being 1,517 in 1902, Taylor could also play in a solid manner especially on a pitch which favoured the spinner. His highest innings was 156 against Hampshire at Harrogate in 1901. Although a good wicket-keeper, he rarely played in that role for Yorkshire. Given his

captaincy experience, it was widely thought that he would eventually take over from Lord Hawke but he gave up full-time cricket at the age of 24.

At hockey Taylor gained a Blue and later played for England and he was also a Yorkshire doubles champion at tennis. He was President of Yorkshire CCC from 1956 until his death.

Tendulkar, Sachin Ramesh
Born: 24/04/1973, Mumbai, India
RHB, LB, OB, RM. Career: 1992
Cap No 134, 1992

Six days after his 19th birthday but already a veteran of 16 Tests and 39 ODIs for India, Sachin Tendulkar made his debut for Yorkshire as the county's first-ever official overseas player. He scored over 1,000 runs in the Championship, is still the

Tom Taylor as Yorkshire President.

youngest to do so for Yorkshire, and topped the limited-overs averages, scoring a century in each format.

By the time of his retirement at the age of 40 Tendulkar held the world records for most runs, centuries and appearances in both Tests and ODIs. A beautiful stroke-player, he was worshipped in his homeland and admired throughout the rest of the world.

Thewlis, Herbert
Born: 31/08/1865, Lascelles Hall, Huddersfield
Died: 30/11/1920, Lascelles Hall, Huddersfield
RHB. Career: 1888

Herbert Thewlis had a very short and unproductive career for Yorkshire. In club cricket he was especially successful with Lascelles Hall and also played for Holbeck, Eagley and Todmorden.

Thewlis, John (Sen.)
Born: 11/03/1828, Kirkheaton, Huddersfield
Died: 29/12/1899, Lascelles Hall, Huddersfield
RHB, RRM. Career: 1863-75

In scoring 108 at The Oval in 1868, John Thewlis had the honour of making Yorkshire's first century. He

was the only cricketer to play in every match in the county's first three seasons, also having played for 'Yorkshire' one year prior to the Club's official formation.

A solid opening batsman, Thewlis played for several representative sides including 'England' as well as the North and the Players. He played for a host of different clubs including Accrington, Enfield and Glossop as professional but spent most of his time with Lascelles Hall. As an umpire in first-class cricket from 1869 to 1887 he stood on an irregular basis.

As a boy Thewlis refused to attend school for fear of being teased over his white hair. Late in life he fell on very hard times but as a result of a hard-hitting piece in the Yorkshire Evening Post in late 1897 he was given employment as groundsman at Greenfield.

Thewlis, John (Jun.)
Born: 21/09/1850, Lascelles Hall, Huddersfield
Died: 09/08/1901, Lascelles Hall, Huddersfield
RHB, RRM. Career: 1879

John Thewlis was one of the nephews of John Thewlis, Sen but had a much less illustrious career. Yorkshire utilised him only as a batsman but as an all-rounder he played for several clubs, mostly Lascelles Hall and Yorkshire United.

Thornicroft, Nicholas David
Born: 23/01/1985, York
LHB, RFM. Career: 2002-07

The youngest player to make his first-class debut in a Roses match, Nick Thornicroft played in a total of only five Championship games for Yorkshire, none being after 2004, and spent part of 2005 on loan to Essex. A product of Easingwold School, Sheriff Hutton and the Academy, he possessed a good action and was prone to be erratic but took five for 42 against Gloucestershire at Headingley in a National League match. He later played in Scotland and for Easingwold.

Thornton, Arthur

Born: 20/07/1854, Silsden, Keighley
Died: 18/04/1915, Saltaire, Shipley, Bradford
RHB. Career: 1881

Arthur Thornton had a short and unsuccessful career with Yorkshire. One game for Saltaire and two for Yorkshire Colts are the only other games in which he is recorded as having played.

Thornton, George

Born: 24/12/1867, Skipton
Died: 31/01/1939, Kensington, London
LHB, LMS. Career: 1891. Amateur

Dr George Thornton's first notable teams were Edinburgh, for whom he played while studying at the University, and Scotland. After his short career with Yorkshire, which began with a pair, he had seven seasons with Middlesex, scoring over 1,000 runs in 33 matches with one century and also taking one five-for, while also appearing for Hampstead. In 1902/03, when with Transvaal, he played in one Test for South Africa but nine years later represented Ceylon (now Sri Lanka)!

Thorpe, George

Born: 20/02/1834, Sheffield
Died: 02/03/1899, Lowfield, Sheffield
RHB. Career: 1864

A very short (5ft 3in) man, George Thorpe played for several clubs in the Sheffield area as well as some further afield such as Wakefield, Buxton and Richmond. In addition to his one game for Yorkshire he played in one match in 1862 for the unofficial county team.

Threapleton, Joseph Williamson

Born: 20/07/1857, Crimbles, Pudsey
Died: 30/07/1918, Lowtown, Pudsey
RHB, WK. Career: 1881

As the regular Yorkshire second eleven wicket-keeper, Joseph Threapleton was able to deputise for Joseph Hunter but did so in only one match. He also played for Bradford and Harrogate

Tinsley, Henry James

Born: 20/02/1865, Welham, Malton
Died: 10/12/1938, Heworth, York
RHB, RMF. Career: 1890-91

Eight of Henry Tinsley's nine games for Yorkshire were in his first season, during which he took all of his career total of four wickets. He batted high in the order to start with but was demoted when his performances did not justify this. Having already played for Leyland, he moved over the Pennines for more regular cricket and was with Enfield and then Church. From 1894 he also played for Lancashire in four matches in three seasons but again without success.

Townsley, Richard Andrew John

Born: 24/06/1952, Castleford
LHB, RM. Career: 1974-75

As a middle-order batsman,

Andrew Townsley played in just one first-class match in each of his two seasons with Yorkshire in addition to five John Player League games in 1975. His very successful club career included Castleford, Bradford, Lidget Green, Birstall, for whom he did the double in 1978, and Heckmondwike. A solid batsman and effective seam bowler, he also had one season with Oxfordshire in 1980.

Towse, Anthony David
Born: 22/04/1968, Bridlington
LHB, RFM. Career: 1988

David Towse's one first-class match was not in the Championship. He also played for Middlesex second eleven in 1988. In 1996 he was with Lincolnshire and then had eight seasons with Wales Minor Counties for whom he appeared in 11 List A matches scoring 114 runs and taking 18 wickets. He later played for Guisborough, Driffield Town and Thirsk.

Trueman, Frederick Sewards
Born: 06/02/1931, Stainton, Maltby, Rotherham
Died: 01/07/2006, Steeton, Keighley
RHB, RF. Career: 1949-68
Cap No 93, 1951. Benefit: 1962

The smooth acceleration followed by the pure and high action were the hallmarks of Fred Trueman's delivery, the results of which elevated him to the status of being regarded as Yorkshire's, and probably England's, greatest fast bowler.

Roche Abbey was Trueman's first club and he joined Sheffield United in the year before his first-class debut at the age of 18. In his early matches he was undeniably fast but also erratic and tended to be expensive but by 1951 he was a fixture in the Yorkshire team. That season saw the first of his four hat-tricks, which equalled the Yorkshire record.

During 1952 Trueman made his Test debut – in spectacular style. At Headingley three very early wickets

Fred Trueman leads England off the field during The Oval Test against Australia in 1964 after taking his 300th Test wicket. On the left is skipper Ted Dexter and on the right are Jim Parks, Ken Barrington and Tom Cartwright.

reduced India to none for four. In the Old Trafford Test of the same series he took eight for 31 and this remained his best performance for England. Eventually, in 1964, he became the first bowler from any country to take 300 Test wickets. Between these two peaks, though, came disappointments through being overlooked for tours as well as home Tests for what appeared to be no good reason other than his plain-speaking. Nevertheless it was still almost 20 years until an England bowler was able to pass his record.

As Trueman matured so did his bowling; the pace from his youth merged with outstanding control of seam and swing. He used the yorker and bouncer occasionally and his legendary strength and stamina kept him going through hot days and long seasons with hardly ever an injury. On 12 occasions he took at least 100 wickets in a season, his best being 175 in 1960. His best figures of eight for 28 had come at Dover in 1954.

An attacking tail-end batsman, this part of Trueman's game also matured enough for him to score three centuries late in his career. His immense contribution to the Yorkshire team, for whom he was the leading wicket-taker in the seven Championship victories in which he took part, was his close-in fielding, him taking many catches, especially at short leg. He also led the county in 21 matches; he took particular pleasure from defeating the 1968 Australians.

In retirement he remained involved with the game as commentator and was eventually awarded the OBE in 1989 - a late but just reward for one of the greatest personalities the game has ever seen.

Tunnicliffe, John

Born: 26/08/1866, Low Town, Pudsey
Died: 11/07/1948, Westbury Park, Bristol
RHB, RS, WK. Career: 1891-1907
Cap No 24. Benefit: 1903

John Tunnicliffe was an outstanding opening batsman and slip fielder. He played for Pudsey Britannia from the age of 16 and made his first century two years later. As a vital member of the Yorkshire side, he was involved in all of the county's first seven Championship titles. In retirement he was coach at Clifton College, a post he held for 15 years, one of his pupils being Wally Hammond. He later joined the Gloucestershire committee and his son acted as that county's secretary from 1921 to 1935.

Tunnicliffe gained his nickname of 'Long John' from his considerable height (6 ft 2 in) and he used this to bat in an aggressive manner. As he became more mature he took on the sheet-anchor role forming a formidable opening partnership with Jack Brown. The pair became, in 1896 at Lord's against Middlesex, only the second in all first-class cricket to record century stands in each innings of a match. Two years later they broke the world record for any wicket with a colossal 554 (Tunnicliffe 243, the highest innings of his career) against Derbyshire at Chesterfield. This was in the best season of his career when he scored 1,804 runs as part of a sequence during which he passed the 1,000-run mark in every season from 1895 to 1907 except 1903.

It is possible that Tunnicliffe was the best slip fielder which Yorkshire have ever had. He stood very still then would suddenly lunge out when the ball came in his direction. Not only did he take more catches than any other player, four times he took over 50 in a season and in 1901 took 70 – a Yorkshire record which has been equalled only once. In 1897 against Leicestershire at Headingley he created another Yorkshire record by taking seven catches in the match, equalling the feat against the same opponents three years later at Leicester. Three fielders have since also taken seven catches in a match but none have done so twice.

As a Methodist lay preacher and teetotaller, Tunnicliffe was much admired by Lord Hawke who regarded him as someone he could ask advice from or confide in. Despite being a professional he had the honour of leading Yorkshire in ten matches. A clear feather in the cap of a successful and respected cricketer.

Turner, Alban
Born: 02/09/1885, Darton, Barnsley
Died: 29/08/1951, Goldthorpe, Rotherham
RHB, OB. Career: 1910–11

Alban Turner played in a similarly small number of matches in each of his two seasons in the Yorkshire team but with limited success as a middle-order batsman. A very good opening batsman in club cricket and useful bowler (he did not bowl in first-class cricket), he played for Barnsley and Rotherham as well as two other teams whom he captained – Bolton-on-Dearne and Hickleton Main.

Turner, Brian
Born: 25/07/1938, Sheffield
Died: 27/12/2015, Wath-on-Dearne, Rotherham
LHB, RMF. Career: 1960-61

Son of Cyril, Brian Turner played in just one match in each of his two seasons and then left the professional game. He was with Sheffield United from the age of 15 and topped the Yorkshire League bowling averages in 1964 and 1965. As professional with Golcar from 1968, he took over 1,000 wickets but varicose veins caused his retirement.

Turner, Cyril
Born: 11/01/1902, Wombwell, Barnsley
Died: 19/11/1968, Wath-on-Dearne, Rotherham
LHB, RM. Career: 1925-46
Cap No 74, 1934. Testimonial: 1946

Associated with Sheffield United from 1924 to 1953, Turner later took up coaching and also occasionally scored for Yorkshire in the period 1952-59.

Turner, Francis Irving

Born: 03/09/1894, Barnsley
Died: 18/10/1954, Killearn,
Stirlingshire, Scotland
RHB, RM. Career: 1924

'Irvine' Turner, elder brother of Cyril, topped the Yorkshire second eleven batting averages in both 1922 and 1923 but failed to do himself justice at first-class level. On moving to Scotland he played for Uddingston for several seasons including five as professional.

Tyson, Cecil Thomas

Born: 24/01/1889, Brompton-by-
Sawdon, Scarborough
Died: 03/04/1940, Leeds
LHB, RFM. Career: 1921

The first Yorkshire player to score a century on his first-class debut, Cec Tyson scored 100 not out and 80 not out at Southampton. Unfortunately terms could not be agreed for his continuing engagement and he earned more by working, and playing professionally for Scarborough and later Castleford. In 1926 he played twice for Glamorgan while with Gowerton. A class batsman was then lost to the county game.

Ullathorne, Charles Edward

Born: 11/04/1845, Hull
Died: 02/05/1904, Cheetham Hill,
Manchester
RHB, RRMF. Career: 1868-75

Never a regular in the Yorkshire side, Charles Ullathorne, a defensive middle-order batsman, did not score a half-century in first-class cricket. He was, however, a brilliant fielder at cover-point and played three times for the United North of England XI. He played for several clubs, mostly Hornsea and Hull teams, but later took up coaching and was engaged for two years in Geneva before laying the turf at Eccles and taking up a post as that club's first groundsman and coach.

Ulyett, George

Born: 21/10/1851, Crabtree,
Pitsmoor, Sheffield
Died: 18/06/1898, Pitsmoor, Sheffield
RHB, RF. Career: 1873-93.
Cap No 4

The first Yorkshire batsman to score 10,000 runs for the county, George Ulyett also made England's first Test century in Australia and took part in the first century opening stand in Test cricket, each of these being in 1881/82.

Ulyett played the game in a most positive manner and earned the nickname 'Happy Jack' with good reason. Tall and strong, he was renowned for his powerful hitting, in complete contrast to Louis Hall, his dour Yorkshire opening partner. He carried his bat only once but that was to the tune of 199 not out – the highest score of his career - against Derbyshire at Sheffield in 1887. This came four years after his best season when he scored 1,562 runs.

A good enough bowler to take 50 Test wickets, Ulyett always wanted to bowl at speed but had a useful in-swinger as part of his armoury. Six times he took as many as seven wickets in an innings, the best being seven for 30 against Surrey at Sheffield in 1878. An excellent fielder in any position, his first-class total of 368 catches, which, with his 653 wickets and over 20,000 runs all added up to a genuine all-rounder. He was the only player to play in both Australia's first Test as well as South Africa's – two of his 25 such games.

Ulyett umpired in the County Championship in both the 1894 and 1895 seasons but a few years later caught a chill while watching cricket and this developed into pneumonia. A tragically early death for a popular and whole-hearted man and cricketer.

Usher, John
Born: 26/02/1859, Templemore, Tipperary, Ireland
Died: 09/08/1905, Haslingden, Lancashire
LHB, SLA. Career: 1888

After his very short career with Yorkshire and spells with Heckmondwike, Holbeck, Holmfirth and Wortley, John Usher took his quality spin bowling into Lancashire. There he played for several clubs including four as professional – Bacup, Rishton, Whalley, for whom he three times took 100 wickets in a season, and Haslingden. Sadly, he drowned himself following serious financial problems.

van Geloven, Jack
Born: 04/01/1934, Guiseley, Leeds
Died: 21/08/2003, Edinburgh
RHB, RM. Career: 1955

Jack Geloven (as registered at birth) had a very short career with Yorkshire after being with Guiseley and Lidget Green. He then had ten seasons with Leicestershire as a very useful all-rounder scoring over 7,000 runs and taking almost 500 wickets in 244 first-class matches until 1965. He then had eight seasons with Northumberland and umpired in first-class cricket for seven years from 1977.

Vaughan, Michael Paul
Born: 29/10/1974, Salford, Manchester
RHB, OB. Career: 1993-2009
Cap No 141, 1995. Benefit: 2005

The first British-born cricketer to benefit from the relaxation of the Yorkshire-born-only policy, Michael Vaughan joined the Academy after playing for Sheffield Collegiate. He was inconsistent in his early years

with Yorkshire although he passed 1,000 first-class runs in four of his first six full seasons. He made his Test debut in Johannesburg in 1999/2000 and was soon promoted to opening the batting, a role he had fulfilled with Yorkshire from his very first innings.

The most elegant batsman of his generation, Vaughan had a wide range of attacking strokes, especially the drive and pull and these, allied to his excellent defensive technique, enabled him to play several long innings. Some of these came in the Test series of 2002 and 2002/03 when he scored over 1,500 runs in 12

games and his performances in Australia promoted him to the top of the world rankings.

Elevated to the England Test captaincy in 2003, Vaughan led the team to victory in five consecutive series in 2004 and 2005. The sequence concluded and reached its climax with a series of nail-biting games against Australia which culminated in tumultuous scenes as the Ashes were regained for the first time for 18 years. He was awarded the OBE in the succeeding New Year's Day honours.

Dogged thereafter by a knee injury,

Vaughan's career gradually spiralled downwards and he resigned the England captaincy in 2008 after a record-breaking 26 wins in 51 Tests. He had also been ODI skipper but neither his batting nor captaincy produced the same kind of results as in Test cricket.

A very useful off-spinner, Vaughan could have bowled more than he did but took four wickets in an innings on a few occasions. He remained in the game to become a forthright member of the media and also spent one year on the Board of Yorkshire CCC.

Verelst, Harry William

Born: 02/07/1846, Claughton, Birkenhead, Cheshire
Died: 05/04/1918, Aston-cum-Aughton, Rotherham
RHB, WK. Career: 1868-69.
Amateur

Only three of Harry Verelst's 11 first-class matches were for Yorkshire. His other teams, such as MCC and Gentlemen, were associated with his status. He played for Yorkshire only as a middle-order batsman but occasionally kept wicket for other teams.

Verity, Hedley

Born: 18/05/1905, Headingley, Leeds
Died: 31/07/1943, Caserta, Italy
RHB, SLA. Career: 1930-39
Cap No 69, 1931.
Benefit: 1945 (Memorial Fund)

Possibly the greatest of Yorkshire's long line of left-arm spin bowlers, Hedley Verity was in the top three in the national County Championship averages in all of his ten seasons in the first-class game and dismissed Don Bradman more times in Tests than any other bowler. He also holds one world record which is likely never to be beaten.

Verity's early cricket was with Yeadon, Horsforth Hall Park and Accrington prior to him being rejected by Warwickshire. After taking 64 wickets in 12 matches in his debut first-class season, he took almost three times as many in 1931. These included ten for 36 against Warwickshire at Headingley, him becoming only the second Yorkshire bowler to take all ten wickets in an innings. In only a year's time this would almost pale into insignificance as Nottinghamshire's batsman, also at Headingley, succumbed to the best analysis of all-time – ten for ten. The wickets were taken in 52 balls, the last seven falling in 15 deliveries, the innings ending with a hat-trick.

Verity had all of the skills associated with great spin bowlers: he varied his flight, length and speed of delivery; his control of spin was outstanding; tall, he was able to achieve extra bounce from responsive pitches. On wetter pitches he bowled more slowly and gave the ball more flight but still surprised the batsman with a faster in-swing or yorker. In

Waddington, Abraham

Born: 04/02/1893, Clayton, Bradford
Died: 28/10/1959, Throxenby,
Scarborough
RHB, LMF. Career: 1919-27
Cap No 54, 1919. Grant: 1928

Known as Abram and usually shortened to Abe, Waddington had had to wait for the First World War to finish before he could make his first-class debut. Having developed into a mature bowler with Crossley Hall, Sandy Lane, Lidget Green and Laisterdyke he took exactly 100 wickets in his first season with Yorkshire. A total of 141 wickets came in the following year – this remaining his best - and this led to his two Test appearances in Australia in the succeeding winter.

In the early part of his career, Waddington had good pace and his curved run-up gave him a flowing action. He bowled a good length, could make the ball rear awkwardly

the nine seasons in which he passed the 100-wicket mark, none of the totals were fewer than 150 and three were above 200 – the best being 216 in 1936. The high point of his Test career came in 1934 when he took eight for 43 at Lord's against Australia; 14 of his 15 wickets in the match all came on one day!

Tragically, Verity was wounded in battle on Sicily and died soon after on the mainland. Much-mourned, he was always admired for his calm and modest demeanour as well as his most skilful bowling.

as well as move off the pitch. A career-best of eight for 34 against Northamptonshire at Headingley came when he was at his peak in 1922. A year later he sustained an arm injury and persistent shoulder trouble probably brought forward his retirement.

Waddington's sporting prowess also extended to him playing golf for Yorkshire as well as keeping goal for Bradford City and Halifax Town.

Wade, Saul
Born: 08/02/1858, Farsley, Bradford
Died: 05/11/1931, Oldham,
Lancashire
RHB, OB. Career: 1886-90.
Cap No 12

A useful all-rounder, Saul Wade's best season came in 1887 when he scored almost 600 runs and took 45 wickets. However, he was a regular in the Yorkshire side for only three seasons and never made a century. His best bowling figures of seven for 28 were at Cheltenham in 1886.

Although an opening batsman in club cricket, Wade batted in the lower-middle-order for Yorkshire and bowled his off-spin very slowly. Having started out in Leeds he played for Saddleworth and then as professional for Church and Accrington. He umpired a full season of first-class cricket in 1905.

Wainman, James Charles
Born: 25/01/1993, Harrogate
RHB, LM. Career: 2014-16

A product of The Grammar School at Leeds, James Wainman was in the Academy team for four seasons before playing for Barnsley and later Farsley. His three Yorkshire matches were all in the shorter formats.

Wainwright, David James
Born: 21/03/1985, Pontefract
LHB, SLA. Career: 2004-11
Cap No 166, 2010

Regarded as a very promising all-rounder, David Wainwright toured with England Lions to UAE in 2009/10 and put in some very useful performances for Yorkshire in his time in the side.

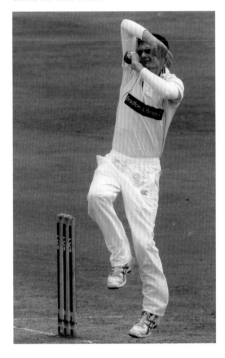

After three seasons in the Academy team, Wainwright was at Loughborough University, for whom he played in five first-class matches, before playing for Yorkshire in all three formats. In 2007 he was very effective in the T20 season and will also be remembered for his two first-class centuries, the higher of which – 104 not out at Hove - helped save the county from relegation in 2008. After four seasons with Derbyshire he had one game for Hampshire and joined Shropshire and Castleford whom he captained.

Wainwright, Edward

Born: 08/04/1865, Tinsley, Sheffield
Died: 28/10/1919, Park, Sheffield
RHB, OB. Career: 1888-1902.
Cap No 16. Benefit: 1898

A valuable all-rounder who played in six Championship-winning seasons, Ted Wainwright scored over 1,000 runs in each of three seasons and passed the 100-wicket mark in five, completing the double in 1897 when his 1,610 runs represented his best year with the bat. His best season as a bowler had been three years earlier when he took 166 wickets including a career-best of nine for 66 against Middlesex at Sheffield.

Wainwright's early cricket was with Tinsley but after his first-class career played in Nottinghamshire for Wiseton and then Worksop. He spun the ball appreciably on responsive pitches but was less effective in dryer conditions. In Australia in 1897/98, when he played in four of his five Tests, he was given only 12 overs. As a batsman he had a sound defence and often scored valuable runs at a speed which suited the team. His cuts and off-drives were his best attacking strokes and his highest innings was 228 at The Oval in 1899.

On retirement, Wainwright became coach at Shrewsbury School where he remained for many years.

Wainwright, Walker

Born: 21/01/1882, Rotherham
Died: 31/12/1961, Winchester, Hampshire
LHB, SLA/LM. Career: 1903-05

Younger brother of Ted, Walker Wainwright was on the Lord's ground-staff and played for Sheffield Collegiate before his county career. He played well in his first season, taking six for 49 against MCC on his debut, but that remained his only five-for. He occasionally umpired in first-class cricket between 1910 and 1939, including a Test match, but never stood in the County Championship. He coached at Winchester for several years.

Waite, Matthew James

Born: 24/12/1995, Leeds
RHB, RFM. Career: 2014-

A promising all-rounder, Matthew Waite had four seasons in the Academy team and later played for York. He originally played for Yorkshire only in white-ball cricket but made his first-class debut in 2017. His best contribution was figures of four for 65 against Worcestershire in the Royal London Cup in 2017.

Wake, William Robert

Born: 21/05/1852, Sheffield
Died: 14/03/1896, Norwood, Sheffield
RHB, RS. Career: 1881. Amateur

William Wake, nephew of Bernard (see Appendix 1) had a very short career with Yorkshire, his only first-class team. His main club was Pitsmoor where he later became president.

Walker, Ashley

Born: 22/06/1844, Bowling, Bradford
Died: 26/05/1927, Harrold,
Bedfordshire
RHB, RRS/Lobs. Career: 1863-70.
Amateur

Ashley Walker was in the first eleven at Westminster School for three seasons and gained a Blue in each of his three years at Cambridge from 1864. He represented the North but was not a regular member of the Yorkshire side. His many clubs included Bradford, Dewsbury and South Wales. He worked in Ceylon (now Sri Lanka) for 25 years and did much for cricket there.

Walker, Clifford

Born: 27/06/1919, Golcar,
Huddersfield
Died: 03/12/1992, Lindley,
Huddersfield
RHB, RM. Career: 1947-48

In four games in his first season Cliff Walker's batting average was well over 40 but he was given only one further opportunity and so moved to Hampshire. There he scored almost 5,000 runs in 126 matches in six seasons from 1949, the highest of his eight centuries being 150 not out at Bristol. Originally with Slaithwaite, and both Golcar and Littleborough as professional, he later played for Brighouse, Windhill and David Brown Tractors.

Walker, Thomas

Born: 03/04/1854, Mill Green,
Holbeck, Leeds
Died: 28/08/1925, Roundhay, Leeds
RHB, RS. Career: 1879-80

Tom Walker played in his first three games for Yorkshire as an amateur. A much more prolific batsman in club cricket, he founded Leeds Leamington, being captain for several years, winning the Emsley Cup three years running and he also played for Holbeck and Elland. A good coach, he helped Bobby Peel.

Waller, George

Born: 03/12/1864, Pitsmoor, Sheffield
Died: 11/12/1937, Ecclesfield,
Sheffield
RHB, RM. Career: 1893-94

Occasionally captain of the second eleven, George Waller had a very short career with Yorkshire but played as a successful all-rounder for Sheffield United as professional, Middlesbrough, Wrexham and Burnley. A good footballer, he played for both Sheffield clubs and Middlesbrough and was a trainer until 1930.

Wallgate, Lamplough

Born: 12/11/1849, Norton, Malton
Died: 09/05/1887, Harrogate
RHB, RRMF. Career: 1875-78.
Amateur

Only one of Lamplough Wallgate's three matches for Yorkshire was a county match. An opening batsman and good all-rounder, he played for Malton before spending 15 years with Hull Town including spells as captain and treasurer.

Ward, Albert

Born: 21/11/1865, Waterloo, Stourton,
Leeds
Died: 06/01/1939, Heaton, Bolton,
Lancashire
RHB, LB. Career: 1886

Albert Ward's early cricket was with Hunslet but from 1889 to 1904 he played for Lancashire, scoring over 15,000 runs in 329 matches. He also played in seven Tests scoring 419 runs in five of them in Australia in 1894/95 but was never chosen again. An opening batsman with a very solid defence who drove hard he later ran a sports outfitters shop in Bolton.

Ward, Frederick

Born: 31/08/1881, Heckmondwike, Batley
Died: 28/02/1948, Dewsbury
LHB, SLA. Career: 1903

Despite playing for Yorkshire's second eleven at the age of 19 he left the county after his one game for the first team. Most of his club cricket was for Heckmondwike and Dewsbury.

Ward, Humphrey Plowden

Born: 20/01/1899, Amotherby, Malton
Died: 16/12/1946, Thornton-le-Dale, Pickering
RHB, WK. Career: 1920. Amateur

Only one of Humphrey Ward's 66 first-class matches was for Yorkshire, for whom he played only as a batsman. He spent three years in the first eleven at Shrewsbury School and three years in the Oxford University team from 1919, twice gaining a Blue. His work in the Indian Civil Service enabled him to play for Europeans and Madras. In his full career he scored over 3,500 runs and made 85 dismissals. He represented Great Britain at soccer in the 1920 Olympics.

Wardall, Thomas Arthur

Born: 19/04/1862, Eston Junction, Middlesbrough
Died: 20/12/1932, Burnley, Lancashire
RHB, RS. Career: 1884-94. Cap No 10

In only one of Tom Wardall's six seasons with Yorkshire was he a regular member of the team. A solid batsman, two of his three centuries came against Gloucestershire and his donkey-drops were responsible for a five-for against Surrey at Sheffield. Although starting out with Middlesbrough, for whom he was professional for seven seasons, most of his club cricket was in Lancashire for Colne, Burnley, Bacup and Accrington.

Wardlaw, Iain

Born: 29/06/1985, Dewsbury
RHB, RMF. Career: 2011-13

Only four of Iain Wardlaw's 31 games for Yorkshire were in first-class cricket and 26 of his 28 appearances for Scotland (2013-15) were in white-ball cricket. These included 22 ODIs, five of which were in the 2015 World Cup. A lively bowler, he spent seven seasons with Cleckheaton and moved to Hoylandswain in 2016.

Wardle, John Henry

Born: 08/01/1923, Ardsley, Barnsley
Died: 23/07/1985, Fishponds, Hatfield, Doncaster
LHB, SLA/C. Career: 1946-58
Cap No 85, 1947. Benefit: 1957

After the death of Hedley Verity in the Second World War, Johnny Wardle became the latest standard-bearer for Yorkshire's tradition of producing world-class left-arm spinners. Traditional in style he was certainly not, however, and bowled the chinaman and googly not only just as well as his more orthodox deliveries but also on a regular basis.

Such was Wardle's early progress with Yorkshire that his Test debut came only 18 months after his first county game. He took over 100 wickets in a season ten times, his best being 195 in 1955. One year earlier he had taken nine for 25 in the Old Trafford Roses match and this remained his career-best. His best return in his 28 Tests was seven for 36 at Cape Town in 1956/57; his 26 wickets in the four Tests on that South African tour represented his best series but, because of his rivalry with Tony Lock, he was never an England regular.

Johnny Wardle wearing his 1954/55 Australia and New Zealand tour blazer.

Wardle's career ended in very unfortunate circumstances; after writing criticism in the press of Ronnie Burnett, Yorkshire's captain, not only was he sacked by his county but also de-selected to tour Australia. Club cricket for Rishton and Nelson as well as seven seasons with Cambridgeshire from 1963 followed and he was a considerable help to Geoff Cope in the remodelling of his action after he had been banned.

Waring, John Shaw
Born: 01/10/1942, Ripon
RHB, RFM. Career: 1963-66

John Waring tended to play for Yorkshire only when others were unavailable but featured in nine Championship matches in his best season of 1966. This included him taking seven for 40 (ten for 63 in the

match) in the Headingley Roses match. A tall, strong pace bowler, he started out with Dishforth, Thirsk and Ripon, and was with Leeds, Harrogate and Scarborough during his county career. In 1967 he tried his luck with Surrey, Nottinghamshire and Warwickshire and had four seasons with Cumberland from 1970. His later clubs were Bingley and Darlington whom he also captained.

Waring, Seth
Born: 04/11/1838, Billingley, Dearne, Rotherham
Died: 17/04/1919, Keighley
RHB, RRMF. Career: 1870. Amateur

Seth Waring's very brief career with Yorkshire came during his long association with Keighley which included 12 seasons as captain and five years as secretary. Other clubs made him fruitless overtures of professional terms.

Warren, Adam Craig
Born: 02/07/1975, Hobart, Tasmania, Australia
RHB, RMF. Career: 2005

Adam Warren played in three white-ball games for Yorkshire in mid-season and took five wickets. He also tried his luck with three other counties and was with several clubs, mainly Randwick in Australia and Bootle in Lancashire.

Washington, William Arthur Irving
Born: 11/12/1879, Wombwell, Barnsley
Died: 20/10/1927, Wombwell, Barnsley
LHB. Career: 1900-02. Cap No 35

Irving Washington played half a season for Yorkshire in 1900 and a full campaign two years later but not at all in 1901. His club cricket was for Mitchell Main, whom he later captained, and Barnsley, him playing for each of these teams both before and after his county career. An attractive batsman, he scored over 1,000 runs in 1902, this including his only century which came against Surrey at Headingley. Sadly, he then contracted tuberculosis. Part of his convalescence was in South Africa where he played in a first-class match for Griqualand West. Two of his nephews were the Kilner brothers.

Watson, Haworth

Born: 26/09/1880, Barnoldswick
Died: 24/11/1951, Doncaster
RHB, WK. Career: 1908-14

Haworth Watson deputised for David Hunter as wicket-keeper, playing in as many as ten games in 1910 but on Hunter's retirement the county chose Arthur Dolphin instead. Watson's 29 matches were spread over six seasons, him also playing once for the North. He never scored a half-century but his highest score of 41 came in his final game. The clubs for which he played included Skipton and Bradford. He umpired in first-class cricket for just one season, in 1931.

Watson, Willie

Born: 07/03/1920, Bolton-on-Dearne, Rotherham
Died: 24/04/2004, Johannesburg, South Africa
LHB, RM. Career: 1939-57
Cap No 82, 1947. Benefit: 1956

In his seventh Test match Willie Watson came to the wicket at Lord's with the score on 12 for three. Not only did he proceed to score his maiden Test century but, in the company of Trevor Bailey, took part in a four-hour partnership which ultimately denied victory for Australia. Watson's 109 was compiled in almost six hours and remained the most celebrated feat in his entire career. Despite this outstanding success, Watson never really established himself in the England side and batted in every position in the top six in his 23 Tests in nine series.

Watson's early cricket was with Royds Hall Grammar School, where he captained the first eleven, and Paddock. He began his career for Yorkshire as a 19-year-old and eventually played his first full season in 1947. This marked the first of 14 occasions when he scored over 1,000 runs. A fluent stroke-maker, he batted very stylishly but could adapt his game to the needs of the team.

After leaving Yorkshire Watson played for Leicestershire, captaining the county in four seasons from 1958, and scored over 7,700 runs in 117 matches. As a double-international he played four times for England at soccer, including in the 1950 World Cup. He later took up coaching in South Africa.

Waud, Brian Wilkes

Born: 04/06/1837, Chester Court, Selby
Died: 31/05/1889, Toronto, Canada
RHB, WK. Career: 1863-64.
Amateur

Brian Waud played in one match for 'Yorkshire' in 1862 and was a member of the official Club's very first eleven a year later. He was in the first team at Eton and played for Oxford University for four years from 1857. He kept wicket at Oxford but not for Yorkshire and played for Canada v USA in 1881.

Willie Watson batting for the Players against the Gentlemen at Lord's in 1955. The wicket-keeper is Australia's Ben Barnett.

Webster, Charles

Born: 09/06/1838, Ecclesall, Sheffield
Died: 06/01/1881, Sheffield
RHB. Career: 1868

In his three games for Yorkshire Charles Webster batted either in the top three or the bottom two! Small in stature (5 ft, 3 in) he played once for 'Yorkshire' in 1861 as well as regularly for some Sheffield teams.

Webster, Henry Haywood

Born: 08/05/1844, Handsworth, Sheffield
Died: 05/03/1915, Port Elizabeth, South Africa
RHB, RRM. Career: 1868

Harry Webster, whose second name was registered as Hayward on his death, had a very brief career with Yorkshire. He also played for Sheffield, Birmingham and Staffordshire. He emigrated in 1881 to play professionally for Port Elizabeth as well as coach.

Weekes, Lesroy Charlesworth

Born: 19/07/1971, Plymouth, Montserrat
RHB, RFM. Career: 1994-2000

A very lively bowler, neither of Lesroy Weekes' two first-class matches for Yorkshire, which were separated by six years, were in the Championship. Of his 24 such matches 20 were for Leeward Islands. He also played for Northamptonshire as well as YCB and Lincolnshire in List A cricket. His main club sides were Elsecar and Wath-on-Dearne and his brief time with Doncaster Town saw him break the Yorkshire League record for most wickets in a season. He later became Head of Cricket at Mount St Mary's College, Chesterfield.

West, John

Born: 16/10/1844, Little Sheffield, Sheffield
Died: 27/01/1890, Little Sheffield, Sheffield
LHB, LRMF. Career: 1868-76

John West played regularly for Yorkshire in the period 1871-73 but only 13 wickets in eight matches in 1872 represented his best season. He took three five-fors, his best being five for three against Surrey at Sheffield in 1870. On the Lord's ground-staff for 20 years, he played in several matches for MCC. His umpiring in first-class cricket from 1872 to 1889 included one Test in 1886 against Australia, but only rarely did he stand in county matches.

Wharf, Alexander George

Born: 04/06/1975, Bradford
RHB, RMF. Career: 1994-97

Alex Wharf played in only 13 matches in the two formats for Yorkshire and had two succeeding seasons with Nottinghamshire. In his ten years with Glamorgan, however, he developed into such a good all-rounder that he played for England in 13 ODIs. For the Welsh county he scored almost 3,000 runs and took over 200 wickets in first-class cricket, his figures in List A matches being over 1,000 runs and almost 150 wickets. In 2014 he was appointed a first-class umpire, after three years on the reserve list, and has since been a regular on the county circuit.

Whatmough, Francis John

Born: 04/12/1856, Wilsden, Bradford
Died: 03/06/1904, Rastrick, Huddersfield
RHB, RF. Career: 1878-82

Frank Whatmough, who was registered as Whatmuff at birth, played in just three seasons for Yorkshire. He was a good bowler in club cricket, being professional at Scarborough and was also with Haslingden, Burnley and Bingley, amongst others.

Wheater, Charles Henry

Born: 04/03/1860, Hunmanby, Filey
Died: 11/05/1885, Scarborough
RHB, RM. Career: 1880. Amateur

A top-order batsman, Charles Wheater's two Yorkshire matches were both in the Scarborough Festival. They were his only games in first-class cricket and his other teams included Cambridge University Nomads, Scarborough and Sunderland. He suffered from complex health problems.

White, Archibald Woollaston

Born: 14/10/1877, Tickhill, Doncaster
Died: 16/12/1945, Torhousemuir, Wigtown, Scotland
RHB, RM. Career: 1908-20.
Amateur. Cap No 47

Archibald White played in only one match for Yorkshire prior to 1911 but then captained the county in ten matches before being appointed to the post in 1912. He led Yorkshire to the County Championship in his first season in charge and two more top-four finishes before handing over the reins after the First World War.

White was in the first eleven at Wellington College for three years before going up to Cambridge (no first-class matches) and eventually becoming a lieutenant-colonel in the army. He succeeded to a hereditary knighthood when he became his Scottish family's Fourth Baronet. White's clubs included Yorkshire Gentlemen and captaincy of Tickhill, where he later became president, and Worksop.

White, Craig
Born: 16/12/1969, Morley
RHB, RFM/OB. Career: 1990–2008
Cap No 138, 1993. Benefit: 2002

Yorkshire's best all-rounder of his era, Craig White was particularly effective in limited-overs matches and is the county's only player to have scored over 3,000 runs and taken over 200 wickets in this format.

White emigrated with his parents to Australia at the age of seven and was brought up in Victoria. He eventually played for Australia U-19 but came to England in 1990 on a cricket scholarship and joined Yorkshire's Academy. So rapid was his progress that he made his debut for both second and first elevens in that first season.

A multi-talented player, White was at this stage an off-spin bowler, who also kept wicket, and a forcing right-handed batsman who could adapt his game to be able to bat in any position in the order. Having scored over 850 runs in first-class cricket in each of the 1992 and 1993 seasons as well as having converted his bowling style, he made his Test debut in 1994. Although he did not become a regular in the England team until 2000 he was then an automatic selection for over three years and became the first Yorkshire player to be credited with both a century and a five-for in Test cricket since Wilfred Rhodes. He played in 30 Tests and 51 ODIs.

Appointed county captain in 2004, White led the first eleven to promotion from the Championship's second division in the second of his three seasons in charge. From 2009 he was the first team's assistant coach and took up the same post with Hampshire in 2012 being promoted to be head coach in late 2016.

Whitehead, John Parkin
Born: 03/09/1925, Uppermill, Saddleworth
Died: 15/08/2000, Southampton, Hampshire
RHB, RFM. Career: 1946–51

John Whitehead's first club was Oldham and this brought him to the attention of Lancashire for whom he played briefly in non-first-class cricket in 1945. A useful pace bowler, he never gained a regular place in the Yorkshire side but played for both Lascelles Hall and Littleborough as professional as well as Pudsey St Lawrence. He spent three years with Worcestershire from 1953 then took up a lectureship at Southampton University.

Whitehead, Lees
Born: 14/03/1864, Birchen Bank, Friarmere
Died: 22/11/1913, West Hartlepool, Durham
RHB, RMF. Career: 1889-1904
Cap No 19. Grant: 1905

Despite his long career with Yorkshire, Lees Whitehead's only full season with the county was in 1889 although he played in over 20 matches in the Championship-winning season of 1901. A useful all-rounder, he was a very good fielder and one who executed twelfth-man duties impeccably.

Early club cricket with Friarmere was followed by spells at Rawtenstall and Denton before him becoming professional at West Hartlepool for six seasons from 1899. While on the ground-staff at Lord's, he played in 15 first-class matches for MCC. Two of his three five-fors came in the Scarborough Festival, the other, five for 26, was at Gloucester in 1889.

Having settled in the north-east, Whitehead became a director of Hartlepools United and died from pneumonia after having caught a chill watching soccer.

Whitehead, Luther
Born: 25/06/1869, Hull
Died: 17/01/1931, Buenos Aires, Argentina
RHB. Career: 1893

Luther Whitehead had a very short career for Yorkshire but was successful with Leeds Leamington and Ossett with whom he was professional. He died whilst on a business trip.

Whiteley, John Peter
Born: 28/02/1955, Otley
RHB, OB. Career: 1978-82

Peter Whiteley made his debut for the Yorkshire second eleven at the age of 17 and played for Gloucestershire's two years later while studying at Bristol University. He took seven wickets in his first Championship match, against Glamorgan at Sheffield (AP), but failed to gain a regular place. His best season was in 1981 when he played in 17 of the 22 Championship matches and made his only List A appearances. For the second eleven he was the leading wicket-taker for three consecutive seasons from 1978. He had a long career with Harrogate.

Whiting, Charles Percival
Born: 18/04/1888, Dringhoe, Skipsea, Hornsea
Died: 14/01/1959, Driffield
RHB, RF. Career: 1914-20

But for the First World War, Charles Whiting would have undoubtedly played more for Yorkshire than his four games in 1914 and two six years later. He surprised the Essex batsmen with his high speed to take five for 46 at Headingley in 1914. Other than having two seasons with Leeds as a professional, all his club cricket was for Driffield.

Whitwell, Joseph Fry

Born: 22/02/1869,
Saltburn-by-the-Sea, Middlesbrough
Died: 06/11/1932, Langbaurgh Hall,
Great Ayton, Middlesbrough
RHB, RM. Career: 1890. Amateur

Joseph Whitwell spent five years in the first eleven at Uppingham School, captaining the side in his final season. He had a very brief career with Yorkshire but had seven seasons with Durham including four as captain and led it to the Minor Counties Championship title in 1901.

Whitwell, William Fry

Born: 12/12/1867, Stockton-on-Tees,
Durham
Died: 12/04/1942, Leazes Park,
Newcastle-upon-Tyne
RHB, RFM. Career: 1890. Amateur

Elder brother of Joseph, William Whitwell captained Uppingham School's first eleven in the last of his four years there and Durham CCC for four seasons from 1893. A hard-hitting batsman in club cricket with Redcar, Norton-on-Tees and Saltburn, his bowling earned him two five-fors in first-class matches – one for Yorkshire at Lord's and one in 1894 in North America.

Widdup, Simon

Born: 10/11/1977, Doncaster
RHB, OB. Career: 2000-01

An opening batsman, 13 of Simon Widdup's 15 games for Yorkshire, in both formats, came in his first season. After four years with the Academy side he topped the county's second eleven limited-overs averages in three consecutive seasons. He also played for the YCB in List A matches in 2002 and spent several years playing for Doncaster Town and Barnsley before having one season with Welbeck.

Wigley, David Harry

Born: 26/10/1981, Bradford
RHB, RFM. Career: 2002

A lively bowler, David Wigley spent time with the Academy before his very brief experience with Yorkshire. He then played for Loughborough UCCE before furthering his first-class career with Worcestershire, Gloucestershire and, mostly, Northamptonshire. Although he played in all three formats he was better suited to the first-class game in which, overall, he took 136 wickets in 50 matches. His father was chaplain to Yorkshire CCC.

Wilkinson, Anthony John Anstruther

Born: 28/05/1835, Mount Oswald,
Durham
Died: 11/12/1905, Anerley, Bromley,
Kent
RHB, RS. Career: 1865-68. Amateur

In the loose regulations of the time, Anthony Wilkinson divided his time between Yorkshire and Middlesex (19 games) even playing for both in the same season. He scored over 1,000 runs and took over 50 wickets in his overall total of 61 matches which also included appearances for MCC (17) and various Gentlemen teams. He chaired the meeting which formed Durham CCC in 1874 and played for it in its first two seasons. His son, Cyril, captained Surrey in 1914-20.

Wilkinson, Frank

Born: 23/05/1914, Hull
Died: 26/03/1984, Hull
RHB, RMF. Career: 1937-39

Frank Wilkinson played for Hull Town for many years from the age of 16 and joined Yorkshire as an amateur. A total of 12 of his 14 games for the county came in the 1938 season, before which he had turned professional. His only five-for - seven for 68 at Bournemouth – also occurred in 1938.

Wilkinson, Henry

Born: 11/12/1877, Hillhouse, Huddersfield
Died: 15/04/1967, Simonstown, Cape Province, South Africa
RHB. Career: 1903-05. Amateur. Cap No 40

Henry Wilkinson had just one full season for Yorkshire, this being in 1904 when he scored his only century – against MCC in the Scarborough Festival. In that he could open the innings or bat in the middle order he was a useful player. He was stylish and had a sound defence.

Most of Wilkinson's club cricket was with Harrogate; he captained the team for 11 of his 17 seasons there and scored over 5,000 runs. He also played for East Stirlingshire and represented Yorkshire at rugby.

Wilkinson, Richard

Born: 11/11/1977, Barnsley
RHB, OB. Career: 1998

Richard Wilkinson's one game for Yorkshire was first-class but not in the Championship. All of his four games in List A cricket were for YCB in 2001-02. Having played for the Academy as a 16-year-old effective all-rounder he returned to captain the team in 2007 and 2008. He played for Northumberland in 2009 and his club cricket was with Barnsley, Hoylandswaine and Whitley Hall.

Wilkinson, William Herbert

Born: 12/03/1881, Thorpe Hesley, Rotherham
Died: 04/06/1961, Winson Green, Birmingham
LHB, SLA. Career: 1903-10. Cap No 41

William Wilkinson's one full season for Yorkshire was the Championship-winning one of 1908 when he passed the 1,000-run mark for the only time in his career. A hard-hitting batsman with some powerful strokes but a poor fielder, his one century came in the following year against Sussex at Sheffield.

On leaving Yorkshire he moved to the midlands where he played in the Birmingham League with Mitchells and Butlers, as professional, until 1953 but also had three seasons with Walsall. A good soccer player, he had eight seasons as a defender with Sheffield United FC.

Willey, David Jonathan

Born: 28/02/1990, Northampton
LHB, LFM. Career: 2016-
Cap No 181, 2016

A talented all-rounder, David Willey made his debut for Northamptonshire at the age of 19 in all three formats. He has been particularly effective in white-ball cricket and made his ODI and T20I debuts in 2015 since when, as an opening bowler, he has been ever-present in all of England's short-form squads. His 118 in a T20 match against Worcestershire at Headingley was Yorkshire's highest innings in the format but his record lasted only 25 days. His father, Peter, played for Northamptonshire, Leicestershire and England and was an outstanding umpire.

Williams Ambrose Causer

Born: 01/03/1887, Middlewood, Darfield, Barnsley
Died: 01/06/1966, Morecambe, Lancashire
RHB, RF. Career: 1911-19

'Billy' Williams played his early cricket with Darfield, Mitchell Main and Barnsley. Nine of his 12 matches for Yorkshire came in 1919 when ten of his 25 wickets were against Hampshire at Dewsbury, including his career-best nine for 29. He returned to club cricket and played for at least nine such sides including Haslingden, Todmorden, Darlington and Mexborough Athletic.

Williamson, Kane Stuart

Born: 08/08/1990, Tauranga, Bay of Plenty, New Zealand
RHB, OB. Career: 2013-
Cap No 175, 2013

One of the best batsmen in the world in all three formats, Kane Williamson made both his first-class and List A debuts at the age of 17. A very correct, stylish batsman and useful bowler, he played for Yorkshire in 41 games in all three formats but not in 2015, making over 600 runs in nine matches in the Championship-winning season of 2014.

Kane Williamson batting against Middlesex at Scarborough in 2016.

Williamson has played in over 200 international matches, scoring over 5,000 runs in more than 60 Tests, and became New Zealand's full-time captain in 2016. He also played first-class cricket for Northern Districts and Gloucestershire.

Wilson, Benjamin Birdsall

Born: 11/12/1879, Scarborough
Died: 14/09/1957, Harrogate
RHB, RFM. Career: 1906-14.
Cap No 43. Grant: 1919

As an opening batsman, Ben Wilson became an important member of the Yorkshire team. However, he played in only ten games in his first three seasons but had a regular place in five of the next six years scoring over 1,000 runs in each of them. His final season, when he scored 1,605 runs, was his best and also included his highest innings of 208 against Sussex at Bradford.

Scarborough was Wilson's first club side and he joined it as a bowler but later became a very reliable batsman. Unfortunately he often played in a dour manner and scored slowly although he had a strong physique and struck the ball hard when attacking.

Wilson went into coaching after the First World War, spending 11 years at Harrow School before working at St Peter's School, York, in New Zealand and finishing at Harrogate. His son, Ben, played in one match for Warwickshire.

Wilson, Clement Eustace Macro

Born: 15/05/1875, Bolsterstone, Sheffield
Died: 08/02/1944, Calverhall, Whitchurch, Shropshire
RHB, RMF/SLA. Career: 1896-99.
Amateur. Cap No 30

A very useful all-rounder, Clem Wilson's career total of 52 matches in which he scored 1,665 runs and took 125 wickets, included 33 for Cambridge University and two Tests on the tour of South Africa in 1898/99. He captained Cambridge, as he had Uppingham School, in the last of his three years (1895-97) in the first eleven. Having given up first-class cricket in 1899 to enter the church, he was vicar of Sand Hutton,

York and finished up at Lichfield Cathedral. Very knowledgeable on the history of the game, he had a large collection of books and cricketana. Rockley Wilson was one of his brothers and his grandfather was RC Thorp (see appendix 1).

Wilson, Donald

Born: 07/08/1937, Settle
Died: 21/07/2012, York
LHB, SLA. Career: 1957-74
Cap No 106, 1960. Benefit: 1972

One of the stalwarts of Yorkshire's team who won seven Championships in the 1959-68 period, Don Wilson was the last of the county's famous line of left-arm spin bowlers to play for England. Five of his Tests came in India in 1963/64 but only one more seven years later.

Tall (6 ft 3 in), Wilson used his height to flight the ball intelligently, always maintained a good length and bowled in an attacking manner. On five occasions he took over 100 wickets in a season, his best of 109 coming in 1968 one year after he had produced his best bowling figures in the Championship with seven for 21 against Warwickshire at Middlesbrough. In 1966 he became only the third Yorkshire bowler to take two hat-tricks in a season.

A hard-hitting tail-end batsman and good fielder, especially at short leg, Wilson played the game with a great deal of enthusiasm. After three years with Lincolnshire and coaching in South Africa he took this infectious approach into being head coach for MCC at Lord's for 13 years from 1977. He returned to Yorkshire and concluded his career by being Director of Sport at Ampleforth College.

Don Wilson in his later career at Ampleforth College.

Wilson, Evelyn Rockley

Born: 25/03/1879, Bolsterstone,
Sheffield
Died: 21/07/1957, Winchester,
Hampshire
RHB, RS. Career: 1899-1923.
Amateur. Cap No 34

Rockley Wilson's career is in two distinct halves. After captaining the first eleven at Rugby School, where he was coached by Tom Emmett, in the last of his three years in the first eleven, he went up to Cambridge and played for the University for four years from 1899, leading the side in 1902. The following year he took up a teaching appointment at Winchester College and did not re-appear in the county game until 1913. In both parts of his career his commitment to Yorkshire was always restricted to the time after the end of the summer term – while at both Cambridge and Winchester.

A very effective all-rounder, Wilson, as a batsman, liked to attack but also had a solid technique. He bowled with a low action but spun the ball both ways from an immaculate line and length. In his career total of 136 matches, which included 38 for Cambridge, he scored over 3,500 runs and took more than 450 wickets. He toured Australia in 1920/21 as vice-captain and played in his one Test match aged 41. He continued at Winchester, being in charge of cricket until 1929 and eventually retired in 1945. He was a noted authority on the history of cricket and had a large library on the game. One of his brothers was Clem and he was grandson of RC Thorp (see appendix 1).

Wilson, Geoffrey
Born: 21/08/1895, Potternewton, Leeds
Died: 29/11/1960, Southsea, Hampshire
RHB, RM. Career: 1919-24.
Amateur. Cap No 58, 1922

Captain of Yorkshire from 1922 to 1924, Geoffrey Wilson had an outstanding record in leading the county to the Championship title in all three seasons. He also led Harrow School's first eleven in the last of his

three seasons in it but had a moderate record at Cambridge University, gaining only one Blue. A poor batsman at county level, he made only one half-century after his debut season but was a brilliant cover-point. He resigned the captaincy after a problem in a match with Middlesex.

Wilson, George Arthur
Born: 02/02/1916, Harehills, Leeds
Died: 24/09/2002, Oxford, Oxfordshire
RHB, SLA. Career: 1936-39.
Amateur

Seven of George Wilson's 15 matches for Yorkshire came in 1938 when he made both of his half-centuries. He played for Whitkirk in his youth and then Saltaire and Windhill after his county career was over.

Wilson, John
Born: 30/06/1857, Hoyland, Barnsley
Died: 11/11/1931, Millhouses, Sheffield
RHB, RU/SLobs. Career: 1887-88.
Amateur

John Wilson played in two games in each of his two seasons and achieved some success with his unusual bowling style. In his successful club career he was with Elsecar, Pitsmoor, Sheffield Wednesday, Barnsley, whom he captained, and Millhouses. He was president of the Sheffield Cricket Association.

Wilson, John Philip
Born: 03/04/1889, Gilling East, Malton
Died: 03/10/1959, Tickton, Beverley
RHB, RS. Career: 1911-12. Amateur

John Wilson was not successful in first-class cricket but, as a jockey, rode over 200 winners including Double

Chance in the 1925 Grand National. He was awarded both the DFC and DSC in the First World War and the AFC in the New Year Honours in 1917. He served in the Royal Naval Air Service and rose to the rank of major.

Wilson, John Victor

Born: 17/01/1921, Scampston, Malton
Died: 05/06/2008, Yedingham, Malton
LHB, RM. Career: 1946-64
Cap No 89, 1948. Benefit: 1958

One of Yorkshire's most successful captains, Vic Wilson was the first beneficiary of the county's important policy-change in 1960. From 1883 to 1959 all of the appointed skippers had been amateurs but after the resignation of Ronnie Burnett, Wilson was the obvious candidate to replace him. His status had always been that of a professional so it was very much a ground-breaking appointment.

Wilson's first club was Malton but he also played for Undercliffe, Bingley and Bowling Old Lane before starting his first-class career at the age of 25 in the first season after the end of the Second World War. By 1948 he had established himself at

Vic Wilson (left) with Fred Trueman.

number three in Yorkshire's very strong line-up and played as the fulcrum of the innings for several years. That season was the first of 14 occasions when he scored 1,000 runs and his best year came in 1951 when he made 2,027 runs. One year later saw his highest innings of 230 against Derbyshire at Sheffield.

Very strong, Wilson possessed some very powerful strokes and used his height to play his attacking shots in a very ebullient manner. Straight drives and strokes through point were the best part of his armoury and his consistent performances came from a solid temperament. At his best against the quicker bowlers, his relative lack of footwork against the spinners occasionally let him down. Nevertheless he scored a total of over 21,000 runs in all first-class cricket.

A brilliant fielder, especially at short-leg, Wilson took over 50 catches in a season four times with a

best of 62 in 1955. This succeeded a winter spent in Australia where he was made 12th man in each of the five Tests but, despite several matches for MCC, the Players and the North, that was the sum of his experience in representative cricket.

Wilson's three seasons as Yorkshire's captain saw the side finish in first, second and first places in the County Championship. Although very much an orthodox leader, he welded a group of talented individuals into a consistently winning unit.

Wood, Arthur
Born: 25/08/1898, Fagley, Bradford
Died: 01/04/1973, Middleton, Ilkley
RHB, WK. Career: 1927-46
Cap No 65, 1929. Benefit: 1939

When Yorkshire won eight County Championship titles in the ten seasons from 1931 to 1946 it had as its wicket-keeper one of the most enthusiastic cricketers ever to play for the county. Even on the rare days when the side was up against it Arthur Wood would encourage his team-mates with his own brand of humour and lively personality.

Wood first kept wicket when with Bradford and on joining Yorkshire played in 225 consecutive first-class

matches (222 in the Championship) before missing a game. Taking the ball from the bowling of such great players as George Macaulay, Bill Bowes and Hedley Verity meant that he always had to be on the top of his game not only in terms of the quality of the bowling but also the variety of styles.

Although Wood was stockily built he was very agile and moved rapidly into position to take the ball being particularly brilliant on the leg side. His best season was 1934 when he snared a total of 93 victims. He had to compete for a Test place with Les Ames and George Duckworth and did not play for England until 1938 when he made his debut five days before his 40th birthday. Despite scoring a half-century in his first innings four Tests was the sum total of his experience at that level.

In 1935 Wood became the first Yorkshire 'keeper to score over 1,000 runs in a season. His 1,249 runs also included the only century of his career – 123 not out against Worcestershire at Sheffield. He could play in both an attacking and defensive mode and always batted according to the needs of his team.

Wood's final cricket was with Undercliffe with whom he had ten seasons and also captained.

Wood, Barry
Born: 26/12/1942, Ossett, Wakefield
RHB, RM. Career: 1964

Barry Wood played for Hanging Heaton, Mirfield and Barnsley before embarking on a distinguished career with Lancashire (1966-79). As an opening or middle-order batsman and very useful bowler he played important roles in the Red Rose county's several limited-overs trophy successes and appeared in 12 Tests and 13 ODIs. From 1980 he had four seasons with Derbyshire, captaining it in the last three.

Wood, Christopher Harland
Born: 23/07/1934, Manningham, Bradford
Died: 28/06/2006, Cookridge, Leeds
RHB, RMF. Career: 1959

Chris Wood took four wickets in the first innings of his debut match but that remained his best performance. He was professional with Pudsey St Lawrence and also played for Tong Park.

Wood, George William
Born: 18/11/1862, Huddersfield
Died: 04/12/1948, Mold Green, Huddersfield
?HB, WK. Career: 1895

In his very short career for Yorkshire George Wood acted as deputy for wicket-keeper David Hunter. Both of his matches were in the Championship.

Wood, Gregory Luke
Born: 02/12/1988, Dewsbury
LHB, WK. Career: 2007

Greg Wood had five seasons with the Academy team and also played in 24 games for England U-19, including two 'Tests'. His one appearance for Yorkshire was as a batsman in a non-competitive List A match.

Wood, Hugh
Born: 22/03/1855, Ecclesall, Sheffield
Died: 31/07/1941, Whitchurch, Aylesbury, Buckinghamshire
RHB, SLA. Career: 1879-80.
Amateur

Hugh Wood played in six county matches in 1879 but his four games in the following season were all in the Scarborough Festival. He gained a Blue in the second of his two years in the Cambridge University team, for whom he took 51 wickets in ten games, including five five-fors, the best being seven for 41 at The Oval. He was ordained after a short teaching career and died in the vicarage he had occupied for 33 years.

Wood, J H
?HB. Career: 1881. Amateur

Both of JH Wood's two games for Yorkshire were against Surrey. In the first match he opened the batting but was 'absent hurt' in the second. He also played for Sowerby Bridge. There is ongoing research into details of this player.

Wood, Matthew James

Born: 06/04/1977, Huddersfield
RHB, OB. Career: 1997-2007
Cap No 151, 2001

Matthew Wood batting against
Derbyshire at Headingley in 2005.

In a remarkably inconsistent start to his first-class career with Yorkshire, Matthew Wood averaged, with the bat, either over 45 or less than 20 in his first six full seasons (1998-2003). As an opener, he was, however, a very important member of the Championship-winning side of 2001. The best of his four 1,000-run seasons was in 2003 when he scored 1,432; this included the highest of his three double centuries – 207 at Taunton.

A very stylish batsman with strokes all round the wicket, Wood had a well-founded technique; he was better suited to the longer form of the game but did play in both white-ball formats and made some high scores in each. Appointed vice-captain in 2003, he led Yorkshire in 44 matches over two seasons including 15 in the Championship and the county's first-ever T20 game.

Wood played in three U-19 'Tests' and also toured Bangladesh with the MCC in 1999/2000. He was one of the first entrants into the National Academy at Loughborough in 2000/01 and finished his career by spending the 2008 season with Glamorgan. He later took up a post as personal development manager for the PCA in the north of England.

Wood, Ronald

Born: 03/06/1929, Ossett, Wakefield
Died: 22/05/1990, Stanley, Wakefield
RHB, SLA. Career: 1952-56

Ronald Wood regularly deputised for Johnny Wardle and he was an accurate bowler. Over half of his eventual total of wickets for Yorkshire came in his first season including eight for 45 in Glasgow and one of his two other five-fors. Elder brother of Barry, he played for several clubs including Lidget Green and Walsden where he was professional.

Woodford, John Douglas

Born: 09/09/1943, Little Horton,
Bradford
RHB, RM. Career: 1968-73

John Woodford played in both formats for Yorkshire but gained a regular place in the team only in List A matches in 1972. During that year his bowling kept him in the side. Able to bat in any position in the top of the order and capable of scoring quickly, he was utilised mostly as an opener in first-class cricket but he scored only one century – 101 against Warwickshire at Middlesbrough in 1971.

Having captained the first eleven at Colton Grammar School as well as English Schools, Woodford played for Bradford and Bowling Old Lane before his county career. He had five seasons with Northumberland from 1975 and his later clubs included

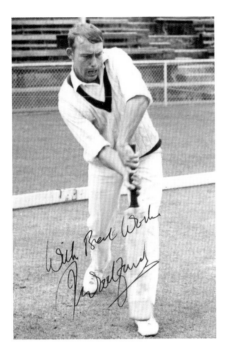

Guisborough, as professional, Middlesbrough, Marske and Liversedge. He went into the manufacturing of sports goods.

Woodhead, Frank Ellis

Born: 29/05/1868, Woodthorpe, Huddersfield
Died: 25/08/1943, Marsh, Huddersfield
RHB, RRMF. Career: 1893-94. Amateur

Frank Woodhead captained the first eleven at Loretto School but played in only one first-class match for Cambridge University. Only one of his four games for Yorkshire was in the Championship but he twice won the Huddersfield league batting prize. At golf he was Yorkshire amateur champion in 1894.

Woodhouse, William Henry

Born: 16/04/1856, Bradford
Died: 04/03/1938, Bradford
RHB. Career: 1884-85. Amateur

William Woodhouse scored a half-century in his debut innings but he made only one more in his nine-match career for Yorkshire. Most of his club cricket was for Manningham but he also played for Bradford and Skipton.

Wormald, Alfred

Born: 10/05/1855, Morley, Leeds
Died: 06/02/1940, Gomersal, Batley
RHB, WK. Career: 1885-91

Alfred Wormald made a few appearances for Yorkshire in just four seasons and although he was a good wicket-keeper the preference was for Joe Hunter. He played club cricket for Gomersal and Hunslet.

Worsley, William Arthington

Born: 05/04/1890, Hovingham, Malton
Died: 04/12/1973, Hovingham, Malton
RHB. Career: 1928-29. Amateur
Cap No 61, 1928

With Herbert Sutcliffe having declined the offer of the Yorkshire captaincy, the post went to Captain William Worsley who led the side under his army rank's title. He had never previously played first-class cricket and every one of his games for the county was as skipper – a unique record in Yorkshire's history.

Worsley was born into a cricketing tradition at Hovingham Hall, a ground having been laid in front of the main building. A hard-hitting batsman, he was in the first eleven at Eton but then played no important cricket for ten years. In his two seasons in charge Yorkshire finished in fourth and second places in the Championship but lost only one game under his leadership.

Worsley joined the Yorkshire committee in 1931 and held the post

Sir William Worsley as Yorkshire President.

of president from 1961 until his death and was MCC president in 1961/62. In 1936 he had succeeded to his family's title as the Fourth Baronet, becoming Sir William in the process.

Wrathmell, Lewis Franklin

Born: 22/01/1855, Houses Hill, Kirkheaton, Huddersfield
Died: 16/09/1928, Upper Hopton, Dewsbury
RHB. Career: 1886

Lewis Wrathmell's only first-class cricket was a university match. His clubs were Lascelles Hall, Blackburn, Golcar and Mirfield.

Wright, Robert

Born: 19/07/1852, Adwalton, Drighlington, Leeds
Died: 02/01/1891, Oldham, Lancashire
RHB, RRS. Career: 1877

Robert Wright, whose real name was Robert Wright Ward, made his first-class debut for Colts of the North at Lord's in 1875 but this and his two games for Yorkshire were his only such experiences. A middle-order batsman and useful bowler, he had two seasons with Friarmere and also made occasional appearances for Harrogate and Batley.

Wright, Thomas John

Born: 05/03/1900, North Ormesby, Middlesbrough
Died: 07/05/1962, Aberystwyth, Cardiganshire, Wales
?HB. Career: 1919. Amateur

A brilliant all-rounder at St Peter's School, York where he captained the first eleven, Thomas Wright's one match for Yorkshire was a university game.

Yardley, Norman Walter Dransfield

Born: 19/03/1915, Gawber, Barnsley
Died: 03/10/1989, Nether Edge, Sheffield
RHB, RM. Career: 1936-55.
Amateur. Cap No 79, 1937

One of Yorkshire's longest-serving captains, Norman Yardley led the county for eight seasons from 1948 until his retirement. Under his leadership the county were joint-champions in 1949, were runners-up four times and was only once not in the top four.

Yardley's experience of captaincy began at St Peter's School, York where he led the first eleven for two seasons, continued at Cambridge University – captain in 1938 – and culminated in his appointment to lead England's Test team in 1947. He captained his country in 14 of his 20 Tests but in only four games was his team victorious, him coming up against the all-conquering 1948 Australians.

A hard-hitting batsman who was particularly strong on the leg-side, Yardley passed the 1,000-run mark eight times, his best being in 1947 when he scored 1,906 runs. His highest score was 183 not out against Hampshire at Headingley in 1951. His deceptive bowling was often useful; he captured Don Bradman's

wicket in three consecutive Test innings in 1946/47 and would often bowl when others found it tough.

A shrewd and well-respected captain, Yardley was a good judge of how to set a field for a particular batsman or bowler as well as the timing of a declaration. A Test selector for four years from 1951, he was Yorkshire's president from 1981 but resigned after three years because of the Club's in-fighting. A talented all-round sportsman, he gained a hockey Blue and was North of England squash champion six times.

Yeadon, James

Born: 10/12/1861, Yeadon, Leeds
Died: 30/05/1914, Yeadon, Leeds
RHB, WK. Career: 1888

As a wicket-keeper, James Yeadon deputised for Joe Hunter in his brief career with Yorkshire. He played club cricket for Penny Hill, Yeadon and Colne but his career ended when a leg was crushed in a mix-up over a run-out. He umpired in the County Championship in 1898.

Younus Khan, Mohammad

Born: 29/11/1977, Mardan,
North-West Frontier Province,
Pakistan
RHB, LB/RM. Career: 2007
Cap No 160, 2007

Pakistan's leading Test run-scorer, Younus Khan, also known as Younis, played in 26 games in all three formats for Yorkshire, including 13 in the County Championship. He was the first Yorkshire player to score a double century and a century in the same match when he made 106 and 202 not out at Southampton. He played in over 400 international matches and scored over 10,000 runs in his 118 Tests.

Yuvraj Singh

Born: 12/12/1981, Chandigarh, India
LHB, SLA/LM. Career: 2003

Having made his international debut at the age of 18, Yuvraj Singh had already played in 73 ODIs for India when he came to Yorkshire but scored only three half-centuries in his 21 matches in the three formats. At his best in 50-over cricket, more than 300 of his 400-plus internationals were ODIs in which he scored over 8,000 runs. A serious illness kept him out of the game for three full years (2014-16).

'YORKSHIRE' PLAYERS 1833-62

NOTE: all performances in this section refer to those for 'Yorkshire' unless specified.

Armitage, George (1825-57) was born and died in Dalton, Huddersfield and played in six matches from 1850 to 1853 scoring 66 runs and taking 24 wickets, including a best of five for 28, with his slow round-arm bowling.

Baldwinson, Samuel (1823-56) was born and died in Harewood, Leeds and played in nine matches from 1844 to 1851 as an amateur. As a hard-hitting left-handed batsman he scored 159 runs including one half-century.

Barker, Thomas Rawson (1812-73) was born in Bakewell, Derbyshire, died in Sheffield and played in six matches from 1833 to 1849. He scored 89 runs and took 23 wickets with his left-arm medium-paced bowling including a best of five for 21. The captain of 'Yorkshire' in its first Roses match in 1849 he was Yorkshire CCC's first president but only for its first season.

Barlow, Frederick was probably born in Sheffield in 1808. He played in three matches from 1834 to 1836 scoring a total of 48 runs.

Barrett, Hugh (1811-76) was born in Harewood, Leeds, died in York and played in one match in 1845 scoring five runs.

Berry, George (1819-87) was born and died in Dalton, Huddersfield and played in four matches from 1845 to 1853 scoring 98 runs and taking two wickets. Uncle to John (see main section).

Burley, William was born in Elland in 1812 and played in one match in 1844 scoring nine runs.

Burlinson, Tom was born in Bradford in 1821 and played in three matches in 1844-45 scoring 58 runs. He umpired in first-class cricket from 1863 to 1878.

Chatterton, George (1821-81) was born and died in Sheffield and played in 11 matches from 1849 to 1855 scoring 138 runs, taking five wickets and making 17 dismissals as a wicket-keeper. He played in a total of 79 first-class/important matches including 23 for MCC. He was 'Yorkshire's' first noted 'keeper and later umpired in over 50 first-class matches.

Coates, George (1817-85) was born and died in Sheffield and played in 13 matches from 1844 to 1853 scoring 263 runs which included two half-centuries, the higher being 59 not out against 'Lancashire' in Manchester in 1849.

Cobbett, James (1804-42) was born in Frimley, Surrey and died in Marylebone, Middlesex. He played in one match in 1835 scoring 31 runs and taking seven wickets. Most of his cricket was for MCC.

Cole, Henry Arthur (1809-90) was born in St James, London and died in Willesden, London. He scored five runs in his one match in 1835.

Crossland, Andrew (1816-1902) was born in Huddersfield and died in Hull and played in five matches from 1844 to 1855 scoring 88 runs, taking 12 wickets with his round-arm medium pace and making four dismissals as a wicket-keeper. Father of Sam Crossland (see main section).

Dakin, Thomas was born in 1829 in Sheffield and played in five matches from 1851 to 1862 as an amateur scoring 54 runs.

Dawson, George Edward (1799-1843) was born and died in Sheffield and played in three matches from 1833 to 1836 scoring 38 runs and taking seven wickets with his right-arm round-arm slow bowling.

Deakin, Thomas was born in Sheffield probably in 1790 and played in four matches from 1833 to 1836 scoring 45 runs.

Dearman, James (1807-54) was born and died in Sheffield and played in six matches from 1833 to 1836. He scored 205 runs, including a half-century against Sussex, and took 25 wickets including three five-fors, the best being seven against Norfolk. He bowled right-arm round-arm fast.

Ellis, Thomas was born in Birmingham in 1828, lived in Sheffield and played in eight matches from 1849 to 1851 scoring 75 runs and taking 17 wickets. He bowled slow round-arm and had a best of five for 11 against 'Lancashire'.

Ellison, Michael Joseph (1817-98) was born in Worksop, Nottinghamshire and died in

Broomhill, Sheffield. He played in five matches from 1849 to 1855, as an amateur, scoring 53 runs and taking one wicket.

He is regarded as the most important man in the early history of Yorkshire CCC being mainly responsible for the establishment of Bramall Lane. The Club's treasurer from 1863 to 1893, he was also president from 1864 to 1897.

Hall, Henry (1810-64) was born in Sheffield, died in Nottingham and played in three matches in 1835-36 scoring 54 runs.

Halton, William was born in Yarm in 1837 and played in four matches in 1861-62 scoring 57 runs.

Hattersley, Henry (1812-35) was born in Sheffield and died at the age of 22. He played in two matches in 1834 scoring 41 runs and taking six wickets.

Holdsworth, John (1811-84) played in one match in 1844 and scored three runs.

Hunt, Thomas (1819-58) was born in Chesterfield, died in Rochdale and played in nine matches from 1845 to 1851 scoring 145 runs and taking 17 wickets including five for 24 against Manchester in 1845. He bowled right-arm round-arm medium-fast. A very talented cricketer who also kept wicket, he was an exceptional single-wicket player. His early death was caused by him being run over by a train.

Huntsman, Benjamin (1820-93) was born in Attercliffe, Sheffield and died in Retford, Nottinghamshire. He played in one match in 1851 and scored six runs. He became President of Nottinghamshire in 1892.

Hurt, H played in one match in 1849 and scored ten runs.

Hydes, Joseph was born in Sheffield where he was christened in December 1806. He played in two matches in 1834 and scored 49 runs as a left-handed batsman.

Ibbetson, John Randerson was most probably born in Leeds in 1822. He played in two matches in 1845 scoring 11 runs and taking nine wickets with his left-arm fast bowling.

Ingle, William was born in Bradford and played in one match in 1845 scoring 21 runs.

Johnston, PS played in one match in 1833 and scored 13 runs.

Kaye, Rev EB was born in Hull and played in one match as an amateur in 1855 scoring six runs.

Kaye, William (1827-84) was born and died in Dalton, Huddersfield. He played in one match in each of 1853 and 1855, scored 14 runs and bowled several overs but took no wickets.

Lambert, M played in one match in 1845, scored four runs and bowled but did not take a wicket.

Lupton, W played in one match in 1833 as an amateur and scored one run.

Marsden, Thomas (1803-43) was born and died in Sheffield, played in four matches from 1833 to 1835, scored 117 runs and took 14 wickets. He was a left-handed batsman and bowled left-arm both slow orthodox and underarm fast.

Tom Marsden was one of the most prominent cricketers of his time. The first Yorkshireman to represent the Players, for whom he played in 11 matches, he also played 14 times for 'England'. Of the 'important' games of the era he played in 55, scoring a double century in his first such match, in 1826, and another century two years later. His highest score for Yorkshire was 53 against Norfolk at Sheffield (Hyde Park) in 1833. The details of most of his bowling analyses are unknown but, on the same ground, he took seven wickets in an innings for Sheffield against Nottingham in 1830. He took three five-fors and once took ten wickets in a match.

Marsden was also a noted single-wicket player, a crowd of 20,000 watching him take on Fuller Pilch in 1833, also at Hyde Park.

McCoy, John (1804-69) died in Leamington, Warwickshire and played in one match in 1834 as an amateur, scoring 24 runs.

Oates, Joseph Henry (1824-59) was born in Leeds and died in Hunslet, Leeds, played in one match in 1844 and scored 32 runs.

Porter, James played in three matches in 1844-45, scored 24 runs and bowled but took no wickets.

Prest, William (1832-85) was born in York and died in Sheffield, played in five matches in 1861-62 scoring 74 runs.

Rawlins, George (1803-48) was born and died in Sheffield, played in six matches in 1833-36 scoring 42 runs and taking eight wickets as a slow round-arm bowler.

Robinson, Thomas (1837-1910) was born in Redcar, died in Stockton-on-Tees and played in one match in 1862 scoring one run. He represented the Players once at Lord's.

Sampson, Henry (1813-85) was born and died in Sheffield, played in 13 matches from 1845 to 1853, scored 437 runs and took four wickets. Known as Harry, he was one of the best batsmen of his era and played for the North, the Players and various 'England' teams. Stockily-

built, he played in 38 first-class matches in total, including eight for Sheffield, scoring almost 1,000 runs and his highest score was 56.

Shackley, J played in one match in 1834 and scored one run.

Shaw, Frederick Brulant (1811-76) was born in Doncaster, died in Westminster, London and played in three matches in 1835-36 scoring 33 runs.

Shaw, John was born in Bradford, played in one match in 1845 and scored 12 runs.

Skelton, Richard Frederic (1821-58) was born and died in Middlewood Hall, Sheffield, played in ten matches from 1849 to 1853 as an amateur, scored 86 runs and took 39 wickets. He twice took five wickets in an innings, his best being eight for 29 against All England Eleven at Hyde Park, Sheffield in 1851. He played in a total of 22 first-class/important matches including eight for Sheffield taking a total of eight five-fors.

Smith, George (1799-1839) was born and died in Sheffield, played in four matches from 1833 to 1836 and scored 114 runs.

Smith, John played in one match in 1845 and made a duck.

Thorp, Richard Clarke (1837-85) was born in Royston, Barnsley and died at Askern, Doncaster. He played in one match in 1862 as an amateur, scoring three runs. Two of his grandsons were Clem and Rockley Wilson (see main section).

Vincent, Emmanuel (1798-1860) was born and died in Sheffield and played in six matches as a wicket-keeper, scoring 162 runs and making nine dismissals.

Wadsworth, William (1823-91) was born and died in Bradford and played in four matches from 1845 to 1862 scoring 22 runs.

Wake, Bernard (1820-91) was born and died in Sheffield and played in five matches as an amateur from 1849 to 1851 scoring 78 runs and taking eight wickets. One of his nephews was WR Wake (see main section).

Ward, C was born in Doncaster and played in one match in 1844, scoring 11 runs and taking one wicket.

Waterfall, William (1825-1904) was born and died in Sheffield and played in one match in 1861, scoring 14 runs.

Wheatley, R played in two matches in 1836 and scored eight runs.

Wilkinson, F played in one match in 1836 and scored two runs.

Wilson, W played in one match in each of 1834 and 1836, scoring 41 runs.

Womack, J played in one match in 1844, scoring 14 runs and taking five wickets.

Woolhouse, William Henry (1791-1837) was born in Sheffield, died in London and played in three matches in 1833-34, as an amateur left-handed batsman, scoring 116 runs. He played in a total of 17 first-class/important matches and was a very important figure in the early establishment of cricket in Sheffield, developing club and ground.

Woollen, John (1814-71) was born and died in Sheffield, played in two matches in 1834, scored 21 runs and bowled but did not take a wicket.

Wright, George Henry (1822-93) was born in Highfield, Sheffield, died in Ecclesall, Sheffield and played in 12 matches from 1849 to 1853 scoring 164 runs and taking 41 wickets. He also played for some representative teams including the North and 'England' amongst his 43 first-class/important games. He was groundsman at Bramall Lane from 1866 until he died.

APPENDIX 2 –

THE NEARLY MEN

Bretherton, James (1862-1926) was chosen to play for Yorkshire v MCC at Lord's in 1891 but the match was abandoned without a ball being bowled. Born near Prescott, Lancashire, he played first-class cricket for Liverpool and District as a fast-medium bowler and also for Cheshire. He died on the Wirral.

Crowther, Fred (1857-99) made one appearance for Yorkshire against Essex in 1890 but the fixture was not first-class. He was born in Birstall, Leeds and died at Wyke, North Bierley, Bradford. Reputed to be a stylish batsman, he captained Bradford.

Lloyd, Neil (1965-82) was a most promising left-handed batsman when he died in Pinderfields Hospital, Wakefield, of a rare neurological disease when aged only 17.

Born in Hemsworth, Wakefield, he had already played in 28 matches for the second eleven, making his debut when only 15, and had scored 957

runs including two centuries, the higher being 128 against Lancashire II, and four 50s. He had also played in two games for England U-19 and was regarded as a certainty to play for the full county side.

Walton, Herbert (1868-1930) played in one first-class match for Yorkshire, against Liverpool and District in 1893, but it is not recognised as such by Yorkshire CCC. He was also chosen to play against MCC at Lord's two years earlier but this game was completely abandoned. An effective medium-fast bowler, he was born and died in Scarborough and played as an amateur.

CAREER AVERAGES FOR YORKSHIRE CCC

1) FIRST-CLASS MATCHES

	M	BATTING				BOWLING				Ct/St
		Runs	HS	Avge	100/50	Wkts	Avge	BB	5wi/10wm	
Ackroyd, A	1	2	2*	-	-	0	-	-	-	0
Allen, S	1	8	6	4.00	-	2	58.00	2-116	-	0
Allen, WR	30	475	95*	21.59	-/1	-	-	-	-	45/21
Ambler, J	4	68	25	9.71	-	0	-	-	-	2
Anderson, G	19	520	99*	20.80	-/2	-	-	-	-	19
Anderson, PN	1	0	0	0.00	-	1	47.00	1-47	-	1
Anson, CE	1	27	14	13.50	-	-	-	-	-	1
Appleton, C	3	56	18	11.20	-	-	-	-	-	0
Appleyard, R	133	679	63	8.59	-/1	642	15.42	8-76	54/17	70
Armitage, CI	3	26	12	5.20	-	0	-	-	-	0
Armitage, T	52	1,053	95	13.67	-/3	107	15.08	7-26	10/2	20
Ash, DL	3	22	12	7.33	-	0	-	-	-	0
Ashman, JR	1	0	0*	-	-	4	29.00	2-42	-	0
Ashraf, Moin A	21	56	10	4.00	-	43	29.48	5-32	1/-	2
Aspinall, R	36	763	75*	19.07	-/4	131	20.38	8-42	8/2	18
Aspinall, W	2	16	14	5.33	-	-	-	-	-	1
Asquith, FT	1	0	0	0.00	-	-	-	-	-	2
Athey, CWJ	151	6,320	134	28.08	10/31	21	47.76	3-38	-	144/2
Atkinson, GR	27	399	44	13.30	-	54	21.22	6-19	1/-	14
Atkinson, H	1	0	0	0.00	-	0	-	-	-	0
Azeem Rafiq	35	814	100	22.00	1/4	63	39.85	5-50	1/-	14
Backhouse, EN	1	2	2	2.00	-	0	-	-	-	0
Badger, HD	2	6	6*	3.00	-	6	24.16	3-38	-	1
Bainbridge, AB	5	93	24	9.30	-	20	17.90	6-53	2/1	3
Baines, FE	1	0	0	0.00	-	-	-	-	-	0
Bairstow, A	24	69	12	4.92	-	-	-	-	-	41/18
Bairstow, DL	429	12,985	145	26.60	9/67	6	32.00	3-25	-	907/131
Bairstow, JM	89	6,080	246	51.52	15/32	0	-	-	-	226/10
Baker, GR	7	42	13	4.20	-	-	-	-	-	5
Baker, R	3	45	22	11.25	-	0	-	-	-	3
Balderstone, JC	68	1,332	82	17.76	-/7	37	21.35	4-31	-	24
Ballance, GS	90	5,993	203*	48.72	18/32	0	-	-	-	59
Barber, AT	42	1,050	100	20.58	1/4	0	-	-	-	40
Barber, W	354	15,315	255	34.26	27/72	14	28.85	2-1	-	169
Barraclough, ES	2	43	24*	21.50	-	4	34.00	2-39	-	2
Bates, W	202	6,499	136	20.37	8/28	637	16.78	8-21	36/8	163
Bates, WE	113	2,634	81	17.32	-/11	2	28.50	1-8	-	64
Batty, GJ	1	18	18	9.00	-	2	35.00	1-11	-	0
Batty, JD	64	703	51	14.95	-/2	140	37.75	6-48	3/-	25
Bayes, GW	18	165	36	12.69	-	48	31.95	5-83	1/-	7
Beaumont, H	28	716	60	17.90	-/4	9	26.22	4-31	-	11

	M	BATTING				BOWLING				Ct/St
		Runs	HS	Avge	100/50	Wkts	Avge	BB	5wi/10wm	
Beaumont, J	5	60	24	10.00	-	2	25.00	1-7	-	0
Bedford, H	5	57	24	14.25	-	8	22.37	6-91	1/-	0
Bedford, W	2	38	30*	38.00	-	2	58.50	2-38	-	1
Bell, JT	7	125	54	17.85	-/1	-	-	-	-	0
Berry, John	18	492	78	16.40	-/1	8	18.62	4-26	-	12
Berry, Joseph	3	68	30	17.00	-	-	-	-	-	1
Berry, PJ	7	76	31*	76.00	-	7	57.28	2-35	-	6
Best, TL	9	86	40	9.55	-	18	44.05	4-86	-	4
Betts, G	2	56	44*	18.66	-	-	-	-	-	0
Bevan, MG	32	2,823	160*	58.81	9/15	10	72.00	3-36	-	24
Binks, JG	491	6,745	95	14.69	-/17	0	-	-	-	872/172
Binns, J	1	4	4	4.00	-	-	-	-	-	0/3
Bird, HD	14	613	181*	26.65	1/3	-	-	-	-	3
Birkenshaw, J	30	588	42	16.80	-	69	26.36	7-76	3/1	21
Birtles, TJD	37	876	104	19.04	1/-	0	-	-	-	19
Blackburn, JDH	1	18	15	9.00	-	-	-	-	-	0
Blackburn, JS	6	102	28	10.20	-	7	24.71	2-19	-	4
Blackburn, WE	10	26	6*	3.71	-	45	24.73	5-17	4/-	9
Blain, JAR	15	137	28*	13.70	-	38	34.52	4-38	-	4
Blake, W	2	44	21	14.66	-	1	17.00	1-17	-	0
Blakey, RJ	339	14,150	223*	30.96	12/84	1	68.00	1-68	-	768/56
Blamires, E	1	23	17	11.50	-	5	16.40	3-42	-	0
Blewett, GS	12	655	190	31.19	1/2	5	42.40	2-16	-	5
Bloom, GR	1	2	2	2.00	-	-	-	-	-	2
Bocking, H	2	14	11	7.00		-	-	-	-	0
Boden, JG	1	6	6	6.00	-	-	-	-	-	1
Bolton, BC	4	25	11	4.16	-	13	19.38	5-40	1/-	2
Bolus. JB	107	4,712	146*	29.26	7/22	13	31.30	4-40	-	45
Booth, A	36	114	29	5.70	-	122	13.80	6-21	6/1	10
Booth, MW	144	4,244	210	22.69	2/19	557	19.77	8-47	41/9	114
Booth, PA	23	193	33*	9.65	-	35	43.34	5-98	1/-	7
Booth, R	65	730	53*	15.20	-/1	-	-	-	-	79/29
Bore, MK	74	481	37*	8.43	-	162	30.03	7-63	4/-	27
Borrill, PD	2	-	-	-	-	5	12.20	2-6	-	0
Bosomworth, WE	4	20	7	3.33	-	9	15.55	2-5	-	2
Bottomley, IH	9	166	32	13.83	-	1	75.00	1-17	-	1
Bottomley, T	6	142	51	20.28	-/1	1	188.00	1-46	-	5
Bower, WH	1	10	5	5.00	-	-	-	-	-	0
Bowes, WE	301	1,251	43*	8.93	-	1,351	15.71	9-121	103/25	118
Boycott, G	414	32,570	260*	57.85	103/157	28	23.75	4-14	-	200
Brackin, T	3	12	9	2.00	-	-	-	-	-	0
Brathwaite, KC	2	40	18	10.00	-	-	-	-	-	1
Brayshay, PB	2	20	13	6.66	-	3	34.66	2-48	-	0
Brearley, H	1	17	9	8.50	-	-	-	-	-	0
Brennan, DV	204	1,653	47	10.66	-	-	-	-	-	280/100
Bresnan, TT	147	5,066	169*	29.80	5/27	404	30.77	5-36	7/-	79
Britton, G	1	3	3	1.50	-	-	-	-	-	0
Broadbent, A	3	66	29	13.20	-	5	50.40	3-71	-	1
Broadhead, WB	1	5	3	2.50	-	-	-	-	-	1

	M	BATTING				BOWLING				Ct/St
		Runs	HS	Avge	100/50	Wkts	Avge	BB	5wi/10wm	
Broadhurst, M	5	7	6	2.33	-	7	33.00	3-61	-	0
Brook, HC	5	82	38	11.71	-	1	65.00	1-54	-	1
Brook, JW	1	0	0	0.00	-	-	-	-	-	0
Brooke, B	2	16	14	4.00	-	2	95.50	1-64	-	0
Brooks, JA	68	926	109*	18.89	1/1	265	26.07	6-65	10/-	20
Brophy, GL	73	3,012	177*	30.12	3/15	0	-	-	-	176/15
Broughton, PN	6	19	12	6.33	-	16	22.81	6-38	1/-	1
Brown, A	2	9	5	3.00	-	3	15.66	2-17	-	4
Brown, JT, (Driffield)	345	15,694	311	29.83	23/68	177	29.28	6-52	4/-	188
Brown, JT, (Darfield)	30	333	37*	11.48	-	97	21.35	8-40	8/2	18
Brown, W	2	2	2	2.00	-	4	21.00	3-61	-	0
Brownhill, T	11	185	25	10.88	-	-	-	-	-	7
Brumfitt, J	1	9	9	9.00	-	-	-	-	-	0
Buller, JS	1	5	3	2.50	-	-	-	-	-	2
Bulmer, JRL	1	0	0	0.00	-	1	79.00	1-51	-	0
Burgess, T	1	0	0*	0.00	-	-	-	-	-	2
Burgin, E	12	92	32	13.14	-	31	25.64	6-43	2/-	0
Burman, J	1	1	1*	1.00	-	-	-	-	-	0
Burnet, JR	54	889	54	12.88	-/3	1	26.00	1-8	-	7
Burrows, M	6	82	23	8.20	-	-	-	-	-	2
Burton, DCF	104	2,273	142*	19.76	2/7	-	-	-	-	44
Burton, RC	2	47	47	23.50	-	6	12.16	3-11	-	2
Butterfield, EB	1	18	10	9.00	-	-	-	-	-	0
Byas, D	268	14,398	213	35.37	28/79	12	60.58	3-55	-	351
Byrom, JL	2	19	11	4.75	-	-	-	-	-	1
Callis, E	2	131	84	65.50	-/1	-	-	-	-	1
Cammish, JW	2	0	0	0.00	-	3	51.66	2-56	-	0
Carrick, P	425	9,994	131*	22.66	3/41	1,018	29.99	8-33	43/5	183
Carter, ES	14	210	39*	11.05	-	8	13.00	3-23	-	4
Cartman, WH	3	57	49	9.50	-	-	-	-	-	0
Carver, K	7	107	20	15.28	-	18	30.16	4-106	-	4
Cawthray, G	4	114	30	19.00	-	4	76.00	2-64	-	1
Chadwick, JPG	6	106	59	17.66	-/1	2	33.50	2-58	-	7
Champion, A	14	148	29	7.78	-	1	17.00	1-10	-	7
Chapman, CA	8	238	80	21.63	-/1	-	-	-	-	13/3
Charlesworth, AP	7	241	63	21.90	-/1	-	-	-	-	2
Chichester-Constable, RCJ	1	0	0	0.00	-	0	-	-	-	0
Clarkson, A	6	80	30	11.42	-	5	18.40	2-14	-	5
Claughton, HM	4	39	15	6.50	-	3	58.66	1-27	-	1
Claydon, ME	3	38	38	19.00	-	3	87.66	1-27	-	0
Clayton, RO	70	992	62	10.78	-/1	153	16.19	8-66	13/2	26
Cleary, MF	2	23	12	11.50	-	8	31.25	3-46	-	0
Clegg, H	6	63	25*	9.00	-	-	-	-	-	2
Clifford, CC	11	39	12*	4.87	-	26	25.61	5-70	1/-	5
Close, DB	536	22,650	198	31.94	33/110	967	24.29	8-41	40/2	564
Clough, GD	1	34	33	17.00	-	0	-	-	-	1
Coad, BO	15	146	28	12.16	-	55	22.65	6-25	4/1	1
Collinson, RW	2	58	34	19.33	-	-	-	-	-	0
Cooper, HP	98	1,159	56	14.85	-/1	227	27.87	8-62	4/1	60

	M	BATTING				BOWLING				Ct/St
		Runs	HS	Avge	100/50	Wkts	Avge	BB	5wi/10wm	
Cooper, PE	1	0	0	0.00	-	-	-	-	-	0
Cope, GA	230	2,241	78	14.00	-/5	630	24.80	8-73	33/6	64
Corbett, AM	1	0	0	0.00	-	-	-	-	-	1
Coverdale, SP	6	31	18	7.75	-	-	-	-	-	11/4
Coverdale, W	2	2	1	1.00	-	-	-	-	-	2
Cowan, MJ	91	170	19*	4.72	-	266	24.01	9-43	13/2	37
Cownley, JM	2	19	19	19.00	-	1	119.00	1-16	--	0
Coxon, A	142	2,747	83	18.43	-/13	464	20.53	8-31	24/2	124
Craven, VJ	33	1,206	81*	24.61	-/6	15	38.93	2-18	-	18
Crawford, GH	9	46	21	5.75	-	21	25.76	5-59	1/-	3
Crawford, MG	1	22	13	11.00	-	-	-	-	-	1
Creighton, E	4	33	10	5.50	-	10	18.10	4-22	-	0
Crick, H	8	88	20	8.80	-	-	-	-	-	18/4
Crookes, R	1	2	2*	2.00	-	0	-	-	-	0
Crossland, S M	4	32	20	8.00	-	-	-	-	-	3/5
Crowther, A	1	0	0	0.00	-	-	-	-	-	1
Cuttell, W	14	271	56	12.90	-/1	36	16.55	6-48	2/-	4
Dalton, AJ	21	710	128	24.48	3/-	-	-	-	-	6
Darnton, T	13	314	81*	14.95	-/1	12	29.08	3-63	-	3
Davidson, KR	30	1,331	128	32.46	2/7	-	-	-	-	18
Dawes, J	5	93	28*	13.28	-	5	39.20	2-24	-	3
Dawood, I	20	636	75	26.50	-/3	-	-	-	-	46/3
Dawson, E	15	224	20	9.33	-	-	-	-	-	5
Dawson, RKJ	72	2,179	87	22.46	-/11	157	41.04	6-82	5/-	39
Dawson, WA	1	0	0	0.00	-	-	-	-	-	1
Day, AG	6	78	25	7.80	-	-	-	-	-	3
Dennis, F	89	1,332	67	18.50	-/3	156	28.95	6-42	5/-	58
Dennis, SJ	67	338	53*	8.89	-/1	173	32.06	5-35	4/-	19
Denton, D	676	33,282	221	33.38	61/173	34	28.14	5-42	1/-	360/1
Denton, J	15	222	59	9.65	-/1	-	-	-	-	6
Dewse, H	1	14	12	7.00	-	0	-	-	-	1
Deyes, G	17	44	12	2.20	-	41	23.02	6-62	3/-	6
Dick, RD	1	2	2	2.00	-	2	18.50	1-3	-	1
Dobson, A	2	1	1	0.33	-	-	-	-	-	1
Doidge, MJ	1	-	-	-	-	0	-	-	-	0
Dolphin, A	427	3,325	66	11.50	-/7	1	28.00	1-18	-	569/260
Douglas, JS	23	125	19	6.94	-	49	26.73	6-59	2/-	14
Drake, A	156	4,789	147*	21.76	3/20	479	18.00	10-35	29/1	93
Drake, J	3	21	10	7.00	-	1	117.00	1-44	-	2
Driver, J	2	24	8	8.00	-	-	-	-	-	2
Dury, TS	13	329	46	14.30	-	0	-	-	-	3
Dyson, WL	2	8	6	2.00	-	-	-	-	-	2
Earnshaw, W	6	44	23	11.00	-	-	-	-	-	6/2
Eastwood, D	29	591	68	12.06	-/3	11	31.72	3-58	-	16
Eckersley, R	1	9	9*	-	-	0	-	-	-	0
Elam, FW	2	48	28	24.00	-	-	-	-	-	0
Elliott, MTG	5	487	127	54.11	1/4	1	77.00	1-64	-	7
Ellis, JE	11	14	4*	1.55	-	-	-	-	-	11/10
Ellis, S	2	12	9	4.00	-	-	-	-	-	2

	M	BATTING				BOWLING				Ct/St
		Runs	HS	Avge	100/50	Wkts	Avge	BB	5wi/10wm	
Elms, JE	1	20	20	10.00	-	1	28.00	1-20	-	1
Elstub, CJ	6	28	18*	28.00	-	9	39.55	3-37	-	2
Emmett, T	299	6,315	104	15.07	1/19	1,216	12.71	9-23	93/19	179
Farrar, A	1	2	2	2.00	-	-	-	-	-	1
Fearnley, MC	3	19	11*	9.50	-	6	22.16	3-56	-	0
Featherby, WD	2	-	-	-	-	0	-	-	-	0
Fellows, GM	46	1,526	109	23.47	1/5	32	37.56	3-23	-	23
Fiddling, K	18	182	25	10.11	-	-	-	-	-	24/13
Finch, AJ	8	415	110	46.11	1/2	1	40.00	1-20	-	11
Firth, A	1	4	4	4.00	-	-	-	-	-	0
Firth, EB	1	1	1	1.00	-	-	-	-	-	0
Firth, EL	2	43	37	10.75	-	-	-	-	-	1
Firth, J	8	134	67*	44.66	-/1	-	-	-	-	14/2
Fisher, H	52	681	76*	15.47	-/2	93	28.18	6-11	2/-	22
Fisher, ID	24	545	68*	23.69	-/2	43	32.13	5-35	2/-	1
Fisher, MD	5	86	37	17.20	-	13	33.69	5-54	1/-	1
Flaxington, S	4	121	57	15.12	-/1	-	-	-	-	1
Fleming, SP	7	469	98	39.08	-/3	-	-	-	-	13
Fletcher, SD	107	414	28*	6.90	-	234	34.04	8-58	5/-	25
Fletcher, W	5	80	31*	11.42	-	7	22.42	4-45	-	4
Foord, CW	51	114	35	6.33	-	126	27.07	6-63	5/-	19
Foster, E	1	2	2	2.00	-	0	-	-	-	0
Foster, MJ	5	165	63*	27.50	-/1	6	25.00	3-39	-	6
Foster, TW	14	138	25*	9.20	-	58	16.41	9-59	5/3	6
Frank, J	1	10	7	5.00	-	1	17.00	1-10	-	3
Frank, RW	18	298	58	12.41	-/1	0	-	-	-	8
Freeman, G	32	752	53	14.46	-/3	209	9.94	8-11	24/8	16
Gale, AW	149	7,726	272	35.44	19/28	1	238.00	1-33	-	46
Geldart, CJ	2	51	34	25.50	-	-	-	-	-	1
Gibb, PA	36	1,545	157*	32.87	2/10	3	27.33	2-40	-	25/8
Gibson, BP	1	1	1*	-	-	-	-	-	-	6
Gibson, R	1	0	0	0.00	-	1	42.00	1-42	-	0
Gifkins, CJ	2	30	23	10.00	-	-	-	-	-	1
Gilbert, CR	1	64	64	64.00	-/1	0	-	-	-	1
Gill, F	2	18	11	4.50	-	-	-	-	-	0
Gillespie, JN	26	640	123*	27.82	1/-	59	34.11	6-37	1/-	4
Gillhouley, K	24	323	56*	13.45	-/1	77	22.10	7-82	3/-	16
Gough, D	146	2,922	121	18.37	1-13	453	27.56	7-28	17/2	30
Goulder, A	2	3	3	3.00	-	3	30.00	2-21	-	0
Gray, AKD	18	649	104	28.21	1/2	30	45.23	4-128	-	16
Grayson, AP	52	1,958	100	27.97	1/12	13	65.07	2-5	-	36
Greenwood, A	95	2,762	91	17.93	-/12	0	-	-	-	33
Greenwood, FE	57	1,558	104*	26.86	1/9	2	18.00	1-1	-	37
Greenwood, L	48	885	83	12.29	-/3	85	19.00	8-35	6/1	24
Grimshaw, CH	54	1,219	85	17.92	-/4	7	31.57	2-23	-	42
Grimshaw, I	125	3,354	129*	18.63	4/5	-	-	-	-	76/3
Guy, SM	37	742	52*	16.13	-/1	0	-	-	-	98/12
Haggas, S	31	478	43	10.86	-	-	-	-	-	10
Haigh, S	513	10,993	159	19.05	4/44	1,876	15.61	9-25	127/28	276

	M	BATTING				BOWLING				Ct/St
		Runs	HS	Avge	100/50	Wkts	Avge	BB	5wi/10wm	
Hall, B	1	14	10	7.00	-	1	55.00	1-55	-	1
Hall, CH	23	67	15*	5.15	-	45	27.24	6-71	2/-	11
Hall, J	1	4	3	2.00	-	-	-	-	-	2
Hall, L	275	9,757	160	23.28	9/37	15	52.06	4-51	-	173
Halliday, H	182	8,361	144	32.03	12/53	101	30.88	6-79	2/-	140
Halliley, C	3	27	17	5.40	-	-	-	-	-	2
Hamer, A	2	3	3	1.50	-	1	64.00	1-18	-	2
Hamilton, GM	73	2,228	125	24.75	1/14	222	24.68	7-50	8/2	25
Hampshire, AW	1	18	17	9.00	-	-	-	-	-	1
Hampshire, JG	3	5	5	2.50	-	5	21.80	2-22	-	1
Hampshire, JH	456	21,979	183*	34.61	34/121	24	46.16	7-52	2/-	368
Handscomb, PSP	9	441	101*	33.92	1/2	-	-	-	-	7
Hannon-Dalby, OJ	24	45	11*	3.00	-	43	45.06	5-68	2/-	2
Harbord, WE	16	411	109	20.55	1/1	-	-	-	-	7
Harden, RJ	12	439	69	23.10	-/3	-	-	-	-	2
Hardisty, CH	38	991	84	19.82	-/5	-	-	-	-	18
Hargreaves, HS	18	51	9	3.64	-	55	20.81	5-93	1/-	3
Harmison, SJ	3	25	23	8.33	-	8	24.37	3-49	-	1
Harris, W	4	45	25	7.50	-	0	-	-	-	1
Harrison, GP	59	407	28	6.67	-	226	14.49	7-43	12/3	36
Harrison, H	2	4	4*	-	-	2	19.50	2-15	-	1
Harrison, WH	3	12	7	2.40	-	-	-	-	-	0
Hart, HW	1	6	6	3.00	-	2	16.00	2-19	-	0
Hart, PR	3	23	11	4.60	-	2	70.00	1-22	-	1
Hartington, HE	10	51	16	8.50	-	23	33.21	5-81	1/-	2
Hartley, PJ	195	3,844	127*	20.66	2/13	579	30.11	9-41	21/2	60
Hartley, SN	133	4,193	114	24.37	4/21	42	48.85	4-51	-	47
Harvey, IJ	20	1,045	209*	36.03	2/5	37	32.91	5-40	1/-	12
Hatton, AG	3	4	4*	-	-	6	33.66	2-27	-	1
Hawke, Lord	510	13,133	166	20.26	10/58	0	-	-	-	159
Hayley, H	7	122	24	11.09	-	0	-	-	-	3
Haywood, WJ	1	7	7	3.50	-	1	14.00	1-14	-	0
Head, TM	1	56	54	28.00	-/1	0	-	-	-	0
Hicks, J	15	313	66	14.22	-/1	0	-	-	-	12
Higgins, J	9	93	28*	10.33	-	-	-	-	-	10/3
Hill, A	140	1,705	49	8.61	-	542	12.91	7-14	39/6	91
Hill, H	14	337	34	13.48	-	-	-	-	-	10
Hill, LG	1	13	8	6.50	-	-	-	-	-	1
Hirst, ET	21	328	87*	10.58	-/1	-	-	-	-	7
Hirst, EW	2	33	28	11.00	-	0	-	-	-	0
Hirst, GH	717	32,024	341	34.73	56/175	2,481	18.02	9-23	174/40	518
Hirst, TH	1	5	5*	-	-	0	-	-	-	0
Hodd, AJ	54	1,628	96*	25.84	-/12	0	-	-	-	153/11
Hodgson, DM	2	72	35	24.00	-	-	-	-	-	2
Hodgson, G	1	4	4	4.00	-	-	-	-	-	0/2
Hodgson, I	21	164	21*	7.80	-	88	17.46	6-63	3/-	11
Hodgson, LJ	3	99	34	33.00	-	2	79.00	1-42	-	1
Hodgson, P	13	33	8*	8.25	-	22	29.45	5-41	1/-	6
Hoggard, MJ	102	956	89*	11.11	-/4	331	27.05	7-49	12/-	23

	M	BATTING				BOWLING				Ct/St
		Runs	HS	Avge	100/50	Wkts	Avge	BB	5wi/10wm	
Holdsworth, WEN	27	111	22*	7.92	-	53	30.15	6-58	2/-	7
Holgate, G	12	174	38	9.15	-	-	-	-	-	17/1
Holmes, P	485	26,220	315*	41.95	60/115	1	124.00	1-5	-	319
Horner, NF	2	114	43	28.50	-	-	-	-	-	2
Houseman, IJ	5	18	18	18.00	-	3	103.66	2-26	-	0
Hoyle, TH	1	7	7	3.50	-	-	-	-	-	0/1
Hudson, B	3	13	5	3.25	-	-	-	-	-	2
Hunter, D	517	4,177	58*	11.66	-/1	0	-	-	-	863/323
Hunter, J	143	1,183	60*	7.78	-/2	-	-	-	-	207/102
Hutchison, PM	39	187	30	11.68	-	143	22.68	7-31	7/1	8
Hutton, L	341	24,807	280*	53.34	85/98	154	27.40	6-76	4/1	278
Hutton, RA	208	4,986	189	20.18	4/15	468	21.91	7-39	17/2	160
Iddison, R	64	1,916	112	20.60	1/8	102	15.09	7-30	4/-	70
Illingworth, R	496	14,986	162	27.90	14/66	1,431	18.73	9-42	79/11	286
Imran Tahir	1	5	5	2.50	-	0	-	-	-	0
Ingham, PG	8	290	64	20.71	-/2	-	-	-	-	0
Inglis, JW	1	4	2	2.00	-	-	-	-	-	0
Inzamam-ul-Haq	3	89	51	22.25	-/1	-	-	-	-	5
Jackson, FS	207	10,371	160	33.89	21/48	506	19.15	7-42	25/3	129
Jackson, SR	1	9	9	4.50	-	-	-	-	-	0
Jacques, TA	28	162	35*	12.46	-	57	31.33	5-33	2/-	12
Jakeman, F	10	262	51	18.71	-/1	-	-	-	-	3
James, B	4	22	11*	11.00	-	8	28.50	4-74	-	0
Jaques, PA	53	4,039	243	51.12	11/18	1	112.00	1-75	-	46
Jarvis, PW	138	1,898	80	16.64	-/5	449	26.70	7-55	18/3	36
Johnson, C	100	2,960	107	21.44	2/12	4	66.25	2-22	-	50
Johnson, J	3	5	4*	5.00	-	5	5.40	5-16	1/-	1
Johnson, M	4	2	2	1.00	-	7	43.00	4-48	-	1
Joy, J	3	107	74	21.40	-/1	0	-	-	-	3
Judson, A	1	-	-	-	-	0	-	-	-	0
Katich, SM	1	37	21	18.50	-	0	-	-	-	1
Kaye, HS	18	243	37	10.12	-	-	-	-	-	9
Kaye, H	8	117	33	8.35	-	-	-	-	-	3
Keedy, G	1	1	1	1.00	-	-	-	-	-	0
Keighley, WG	35	1,227	110	26.67	1/6	0	-	-	-	12
Kellett, SA	86	4,204	125*	30.68	2/29	0	-	-	-	74
Kennie, G	1	6	6	3.00	-	-	-	-	-	1
Kettleborough, RA	13	446	108	26.23	1/2	3	51.00	2-26	-	9
Kilburn, S	1	8	8	8.00	-	-	-	-	-	0
Kilner, N	69	1,253	112	18.98	2/6	-	-	-	-	34
Kilner, R	365	13,018	206*	30.13	15/75	857	17.33	8-26	39/9	231
King, AM	1	12	12	12.00	-	-	-	-	-	0
Kippax, PJ	4	37	9	7.40	-	8	34.87	5-74	-	0
Kirby, SP	47	342	57	7.27	-/1	182	28.25	8-80	9/3	11
Kohler-Cadmore, T	3	151	78	25.16	-/1	-	-	-	-	1
Kruis, GJ	54	617	50*	18.69	-/1	154	35.26	5-47	7/-	11
Lambert, GA	2	6	3*	6.00	-	4	33.25	2-62	-	1
Lancaster, WW	7	163	51	16.30	-/1	0	-	-	-	1
Landon, CW	9	51	18	3.92	-	0	-	-	-	7

	M	BATTING				BOWLING				Ct/St
		Runs	HS	Avge	100/50	Wkts	Avge	BB	5wi/10wm	
Law, W	4	51	22	7.28	-	-	-	-	-	3
Lawson, MAK	15	197	44	12.31	-	42	40.45	6-88	4/-	7
Leadbeater, B	144	5,247	140*	25.10	1/27	1	5.00	1-1	-	80
Leadbeater, E	81	898	91	13.81	-/1	201	28.14	8-83	7/2	49
Leadbeater, H	6	141	65	17.62	-/1	0	-	-	-	4
Leaning, JA	51	2,269	123	31.95	4/11	3	90.00	2-30	-	39
Leatham, GAB	12	61	14	4.69	-	-	-	-	-	21/7
Leather, RS	1	19	14	9.50	-	-	-	-	-	0
Lee, C	2	98	74	24.50	-/1	-	-	-	-	1
Lee, F	105	3,622	165	21.05	3/17	-	-	-	-	53/1
Lee, GH	1	13	9	6.50	-	-	-	-	-	0
Lee, H	5	20	12	3.33	-	-	-	-	-	2
Lee, JE (Dewsbury)	2	9	6	3.00	-	-	-	-	-	0
Lee, JE (Sheffield)	2	24	21*	12.00	-	2	74.50	2-63	-	1
Lees, AZ	78	4,478	275*	37.00	11/22	2	38.50	2-51	-	55
Legard, AD	4	50	15	10.00	-	0	-	-	-	1
Lehmann, DS	88	8,871	339	68.76	26/43	61	32.00	4-35	-	35
Lehmann, J	5	384	116	54.85	1/2	-	-	-	-	2
Lester, EI	228	10,616	186	34.02	24/49	3	53.33	1-7	-	106
Leyland, M	548	26,180	263	41.03	62/123	409	27.08	8-63	10/1	204
Lilley, AE	1	0	0	0.00	-	0	-	-	-	0
Linaker, L	1	0	0	0.00	-	1	28.00	1-28	-	0
Lister, B	7	36	10	3.60	-	-	-	-	-	2
Lister, J	2	35	16	8.75	-	-	-	-	-	2
Lister-Kaye, KA	2	13	7*	13.00	-	1	64.00	1-30	-	2
Lockwood, E	214	7,789	208	23.25	6/31	141	16.06	6-26	3/-	164/2
Lockwood, H	16	408	90	16.32	-/2	0	-	-	-	8
Lodge, JT	2	48	30	16.00	-	0	-	-	-	0
Love, JD	247	10,263	170*	31.10	13/56	12	69.58	2-0	-	123
Lowe, GE	1	5	5*	-	-	-	-	-	-	1
Lowe, JR	1	5	5	5.00	-	-	-	-	-	0
Lowson, FA	252	13,897	259*	37.25	30/63	0	-	-	-	180
Lucas, DS	1	-	-	-	-	8	10.50	5-49	1/-	0
Lumb, E	14	311	70*	16.36	-/2	-	-	-	-	5
Lumb, MJ	78	4,194	144	34.09	8/25	5	39.80	2-10	-	43
Lumb, RG	239	11,525	165*	31.57	22/66	0	-	-	-	129
Lupton, AW	104	668	43*	10.43	-	0	-	-	-	25
Lynas, GG	2	4	4*	2.00	-	-	-	-	-	2
Lyth, A	133	8,574	251	41.02	21/45	28	43.50	2-9	-	176
Macaulay, GG	445	5,717	125*	17.97	3/19	1,774	17.22	8-21	125/31	361
McGrath, A	242	14,091	211	37.47	34/67	128	36.34	5-39	1/-	168
McHugh, FP	3	0	0	0.00	-	4	36.75	2-16	-	1
Marsh, SE	2	225	125*	112.50	1/1	-	-	-	-	1
Marshall, A	1	2	2	1.00	-	0	-	-	-	0
Martyn, DR	2	342	238	171.00	1/1	-	-	-	-	2
Mason, A	18	105	22	6.56	-	51	28.88	5-56	1/-	6
Maude, E	2	17	16	8.50	-	-	-	-	-	0
Metcalfe, AA	184	10,465	216*	35.11	25/48	3	114.66	2-18	-	72
Micklethwait, WH	1	44	44	44.00	-	-	-	-	-	0

	M	BATTING				BOWLING				Ct/St
		Runs	HS	Avge	100/50	Wkts	Avge	BB	5wi/10wm	
Middlebrook, JD	29	534	84	15.25	-/1	66	28.77	6-82	2/1	15
Middlebrook, W	17	88	19*	4.40	-	50	17.90	5-59	1/-	17
Midgley, CA	4	115	59*	28.75	-/1	8	18.62	2-18	-	3
Milburn, SM	6	22	7	3.66	-	14	30.78	4-68	-	0
Milligan, FW	81	1,879	74	18.24	-/10	112	24.42	7-65	3/1	40
Mitchell, A	401	18,189	189	37.81	39/93	5	58.20	3-49	-	406
Mitchell, F	83	4,104	194	34.20	10/17	1	16.00	1-16	-	52
Monks, GD	1	3	3	3.00	-	-	-	-	-	1
Moorhouse, R	206	5,217	113	19.32	3/25	43	28.65	3-20	-	92
Morkel, M	1	8	8	4.00	-	1	33.00	1-33	-	0
Morris, AC	16	362	60	17.23	-/1	9	56.44	2-62	-	12
Mosley, H	2	1	1	0.25	-	3	11.33	3-12	-	1
Motley, A	2	10	8*	10.00	-	7	19.28	4-48	-	1
Mounsey, JT	92	1,939	64	15.63	-/7	10	44.40	3-58	-	45
Moxon, MD	277	18,973	274*	43.71	41/103	22	55.13	3-24	-	190
Myers, H	201	4,450	91	18.31	-/15	282	25.15	8-81	11/1	106
Myers, M	22	537	49	14.91	-	0	-	-	-	11
Naved-ul-Hasan, Rana	11	207	32	15.92	-	26	39.15	4-86	-	3
Naylor, JE	1	-	-	-	-	0	-	-	-	1
Newstead, JT	96	1,791	100*	16.13	1/5	297	18.70	7-10	14/4	75
Nicholson, AG	282	1,667	50	11.73	-/1	876	19.74	9-62	40/3	85
Nicholson, NG	5	134	56*	26.80	-/1	0	-	-	-	5
Oates, W	7	34	14*	5.66	-	-	-	-	-	5/1
Oates, WF	3	20	9	6.66	-	-	-	-	-	0
Old, CM	222	4,785	116	23.22	5/18	647	20.72	7-20	24/1	131
Oldham, S	59	212	50	10.09	-/1	130	29.60	5-40	2/-	18
Oldroyd, E	383	15,891	194	35.23	37/75	42	39.47	4-14	-	203
Oyston, C	15	96	22	7.38	-	31	28.12	3-30	-	3
Padgett, DEV	487	20,306	161*	28.55	29/96	6	34.66	1-2	-	250
Padgett, GH	6	56	32*	18.66	-	4	84.00	2-37	-	5
Padgett, J	6	92	22	10.22	-	-	-	-	-	2
Parker, B	44	1,839	138*	30.14	2/9	0	-	-	-	19
Parkin, CH	1	0	0	0.00	-	2	12.50	2-23	-	0
Parratt, J	2	11	11	5.50	-	1	75.00	1-12	-	4
Parton, JW	1	16	14	8.00	-	1	4.00	1-4	-	0
Patterson, SA	132	1,839	63*	16.27	-/3	348	28.06	6-56	6/-	23
Pearson, HE	4	31	10*	15.50	-	5	18.00	3-37	-	1
Pearson, JH	3	54	44	18.00	-	-	-	-	-	0
Peate, E	154	1,793	95	10.86	-/3	794	12.57	8-5	69/22	97
Peel, R	318	9,322	210*	19.91	6/38	1,311	15.74	9-22	98/27	141
Penny, JH	1	8	8*	-	-	2	15.50	1-7	-	1
Pickles, CS	58	1,336	66	24.29	-/7	83	43.83	4-40	-	24
Pickles, D	41	74	12	3.70	-	96	21.47	7-61	4/1	10
Pinder, G	125	1,639	57	10.57	-/2	19	17.10	4-56	-	145/102
Platt, RK	96	405	57*	7.23	-/1	282	22.65	7-40	10/3	35
Plunkett, LE	36	1,241	126	28.20	1/7	98	29.84	6-33	2/-	20
Pollard, D	1	3	3	1.50	-	0	-	-	-	0
Pollitt, G	1	51	51	51.00	-/1	-	-	-	-	1
Prest, CH	2	57	31	14.25	-	-	-	-	-	3

	M	BATTING				BOWLING				Ct/St
		Runs	HS	Avge	100/50	Wkts	Avge	BB	5wi/10wm	
Preston, JM	79	1,935	93	15.73	-/8	178	18/5	9-28	8/5	36
Pride, T	1	1	1	1.00	-	-	-	-	-	4/3
Priestley, IM	2	25	23	12.50	-	4	29.75	4-27	-	1
Pullan, P	1	14	14	14.00	-	0	-	-	-	1
Pyrah, RM	51	1,621	134*	30.58	3/8	55	45.94	5-58	1/-	22
Radcliffe, EJRH	64	826	54	10.86	-/2	2	67.00	1-15	-	21
Ramage, A	23	219	52	16.84	-/1	44	37.47	5-65	1/-	1
Ramsden, G	1	0	0*	-	-	1	68.00	1-32	-	0
Randhawa, GS	1	5	5	5.00	-	2	31.00	2-54	-	0
Raper, JRS	3	24	15	6.00	-	-	-	-	-	0
Rashid, AU	140	5,620	180	34.47	10/31	420	33.65	7-107	18/1	70
Rawlin, ER	8	72	35	8.00	-	21	23.71	3-28	-	2
Rawlin, JT	27	274	31	8.05	-	11	23.45	4-35	-	13
Rawlinson, EB	37	991	55	15.73	-/2	5	12.40	4-41		16
Read, J	1	14	14	14.00	-	-	-	-	-	4
Redfearn, J	1	5	5	5.00	-	-	-	-	-	0
Render, GWA	1	5	5	5.00	-	-	-	-	-	0
Rhodes, AC	61	917	64*	17.98	-/2	107	28.28	6-19	5/-	45
Rhodes, HE	10	269	64	17.93	-/2	-	-	-	-	1
Rhodes, SJ	3	41	35	41.00	-	-	-	-	-	3
Rhodes, Wilfred	883	31,075	267*	30.08	46/155	3,598	16.01	9-28	252/61	586
Rhodes, William	1	1	1*	-	-	0	-	-	-	0
Rhodes, WMH	15	689	95	29.95	-/3	16	34.43	3-42	-	8
Richardson, JA	7	308	61	30.80	-/2	2	45.00	2-23	-	3
Richardson, RB	23	1,310	112	34.47	1/11	1	23.00	1-5	-	18
Richardson, SA	13	377	69	17.95	-/3	-	-	-	-	11
Riley, H	4	36	25*	9.00	-	1	54.00	1-17		1
Riley, M	17	361	92	13.37	-/1	0	-	-	-	3
Ringrose, W	57	353	23	6.19	-	155	20.80	9-76	9/1	25
Robinson, AL	84	365	30*	9.60	-	196	25.13	6-61	7/-	48
Robinson, BLH	1	5	4	2.50	-	1	20.00	1-20	-	0
Robinson, Edward	1	23	23*	23.00	-	-	-	-	-	0
Robinson, Emmott	413	9,651	135*	25.53	7/48	893	21.99	9-36	36/5	318
Robinson, EP	208	2,596	75*	12.54	-/8	735	20.60	8-35	43/7	189
Robinson, MA	90	240	23	4.21	-	218	31.49	9-37	7/2	17
Robinson, PE	132	6,668	189	35.84	7/44	1	238.00	1-10	-	96
Robinson, W	7	151	68	11.61	-/1	-	-	-	-	3
Roebuck, CG	1	23	23	23.00	-	-	-	-	-	0
Root, JE	42	2,725	236	44.67	6/9	12	52.66	3-33	-	24
Roper, E	5	85	68	14.16	-/1	-	-	-	-	2
Rothery, JW	150	4,614	161	21.16	3/21	2	22.00	1-18	-	45
Rowbotham, J	94	2,624	113	17.15	3/5	3	12.33	3-37	-	52
Rudolph, JA	68	5,429	228*	52.20	18/22	1	311.00	1-13	-	79
Rudston, H	21	609	164	20.30	1/2	-	-	-	-	3
Ryan, M	150	682	26*	7.49	-	413	22.92	7-45	12/2	59
Ryder, L	2	1	1	1.00	-	4	37.75	2-75	-	2
Sanderson, BW	3	6	6	6.00	-	6	31.66	5-50	1/-	0
Saville, G	5	140	65	20.00	-/1	-	-	-	-	2
Sayers, JJ	97	4,855	187	32.80	9/25	6	27.66	3-15	-	60

	M	BATTING				BOWLING				Ct/St
		Runs	HS	Avge	100/50	Wkts	Avge	BB	5wi/10wm	
Schofield, CJ	1	25	25	25.00	-	-	-	-	-	0
Schofield, D	3	13	6*	-	-	5	22.40	5-42	1/-	0
Scott, E	1	8	8	8.00	-	2	13.50	1-6	-	1
Sedgwick, HA	3	53	34	17.66	-	16	20.43	5-8	1/-	2
Sellers, A	49	1,643	105	18.88	2/6	2	42.00	2-28	-	40
Sellers, AB	334	8,949	204	23.18	4/44	8	81.62	2-10	-	264
Shackleton, WA	5	49	25	8.16	-	6	21.66	4-18	-	3
Shahzad, Ajmal	45	1,145	88	26.02	-/3	125	33.56	5-51	3/-	5
Sharp, K	195	8,426	181	29.56	11/39	12	69.66	2-13	-	95
Sharpe, CM	1	15	15	15.00	-	0	-	-	-	0
Sharpe, PJ	411	17,685	203*	29.72	23/85	2	70.00	1-1	-	526
Shaw, C	61	340	31	10.96	-	123	33.34	6-64	3/-	9
Shaw, James	3	8	7	2.66	-	7	25.85	4-119	-	2
Shaw, Joshua	4	34	24	11.33	-	8	41.00	3-58	-	1
Sheepshanks, ER	1	26	26	26.00	-	-	-	-	-	0
Shepherd, DA	1	0	0	0.00	-	-	-	-	-	0
Shotton, W	2	13	7	3.25	-	-	-	-	-	0
Sidebottom, A	216	4,243	124	22.33	1/11	558	24.82	8-72	22/3	60
Sidebottom, RJ	137	1,674	61	14.30	-/3	450	22.50	7-37	18/3	37
Sidgwick, R	9	64	17	4.92	-	-	-	-	-	7
Silverwood, CEW	131	2,369	80	16.22	-/8	427	27.62	7-93	18/1	30
Silvester, S	6	30	14	10.00	-	12	26.08	4-86	-	2
Simpson, ETB	1	1	1	0.50	-	-	-	-	-	0
Sims, Rev HM	5	109	35*	12.11	-	-	-	-	-	2
Slinn, W	9	22	11	2.00	-	48	15.45	6-19	4/1	5
Smailes, TF	262	5,686	117	19.14	3/23	802	20.68	10-47	39/6	153
Smales, K	13	165	45	10.31	-	22	34.81	5-44	2/-	4
Smith, AF	28	692	89	15.37	-/2	-	-	-	-	11
Smith, E (Morley)	154	4,453	129	20.61	2/16	248	25.31	7-40	15/2	112
Smith, E (Barnsley)	16	169	49	10.56	-	46	23.69	6-40	2/-	5
Smith, F (Yeadon)	13	292	55	16.22	-/2	-	-	-	-	3
Smith, F (Idle)	1	11	11	11.00	-	2	22.50	1-12	-	0
Smith, G	2	7	7	7.00	-	0	-	-	-	3
Smith, J	2	28	16	9.33	-	6	12.00	3-40	-	3
Smith, N	8	82	20	13.66	-	-	-	-	-	14/3
Smith, R	5	99	37*	19.80	-	-	-	-	-	0
Smith, Walter	5	152	59	16.88	-	-	-	-	-	3
Smith, William	11	260	90	16.25	-/2	-	-	-	-	8
Smithson, GA	39	1,449	169	26.34	2/5	1	84.00	1-26	-	21
Smurthwaite, J	7	29	20*	7.25	-	12	19.75	5-7	1/-	4
Sowden, A	8	137	37	12.45	-	0	-	-	-	1
Squire, D	1	0	0	0.00	-	0	-	-	-	0
Squires, PJ	49	1,271	70	16.72	-/4	0	-	-	-	14
Stanley, HC	8	155	42	11.92	-	-	-	-	-	6
Stanyforth, RT	3	26	10	8.66	-	-	-	-	-	2
Starc, MA	2	28	28*	-	-	7	21.85	3-50	-	0
Stead, B	2	8	8	2.66	-	7	16.42	7-76	1/-	0
Stemp, RD	104	1,267	65	12.79	-/2	241	35.50	6-37	8/-	49
Stephenson, E	36	803	67	14.33	-/3	-	-	-	-	30/27

	M	BATTING				BOWLING				Ct/St
		Runs	HS	Avge	100/50	Wkts	Avge	BB	5wi/10wm	
Stephenson, JS	16	182	60	10.70	-/1	0	-	-	-	6
Stevenson, GB	177	3,856	115*	20.84	2/16	464	28.56	8-57	17/2	73
Stott, WB	187	9,168	186	31.61	17/46	7	16.00	4-34	-	91
Stringer, PM	19	101	15*	11.22	-	32	21.75	4-10	-	7
Stuchbury, S	3	7	4*	7.00	-	8	29.50	3-82	-	0
Sugg, FH	8	80	13*	10.00	-	-	-	-	-	4/1
Sugg, W	1	9	9	9.00	-	-	-	-	-	0
Sullivan, JHB	1	41	26	20.50	-	0	-	-	-	0
Sutcliffe, H	602	38,558	313	50.20	112/167	8	47.62	2-16	-	402
Sutcliffe, WHH	177	6,247	181	26.13	6/27	6	25.33	2-23	-	80
Swallow, IG	61	1,296	114	20.25	1/2	64	51.09	7-95	1/-	28
Swanepoel, PJ	2	20	17	6.66	-	3	43.00	2-40	-	1
Tait, T	2	7	3	3.50	-	-	-	-	-	1
Tasker, J	31	586	67	15.02	-/3	-	-	-	-	14
Tattersall, G	1	26	26	13.00	-	-	-	-	-	0
Taylor, CR	16	416	52*	17.33	-/2	-	-	-	-	8
Taylor, H	9	153	36	11.76	-	-	-	-	-	1
Taylor, HS	3	36	22	7.20	-	-	-	-	-	0
Taylor, J	9	107	44	8.91	-	-	-	-	-	4
Taylor, K	303	12,864	203*	27.37	16/68	129	28.52	6-75	1/-	146
Taylor, NS	8	10	4	2.00	-	22	32.72	5-49	1/-	2
Taylor, TL	82	3,933	156	35.11	8/22	-	-	-	-	47/2
Tendulkar, SR	16	1,070	100	46.52	1/7	4	48.75	2-35	-	10
Thewlis, H	2	4	2*	1.33	-	-	-	-	-	2
Thewlis, J Sen	44	1,280	108	16.62	1/4	-	-	-	-	21/1
Thewlis, J Jun	3	21	10	5.25	-	-	-	-	-	0
Thornicroft, ND	7	50	30	8.33	-	16	34.06	6-60	1/-	2
Thornton, A	3	21	7	5.25	-	-	-	-	-	2
Thornton, G	3	21	16	5.25	-	2	37.00	1-13	-	0
Thorpe, G	1	14	9*	14.00	-	-	-	-	-	2
Threapleton, JW	1	8	8*	-	-	-	-	-	-	2/1
Tinsley, HJ	9	56	15	4.30	-	4	14.25	3-15	-	1
Townsley, RAJ	2	22	12	5.50	-	0	-	-	-	1
Towse, AD	1	1	1	1.00	-	3	16.66	2-26	-	1
Trueman, FS	459	6,852	104	15.15	2/21	1,745	17.12	8-28	97/20	325
Tunnicliffe, J	472	19,435	243	27.33	22/104	7	55.42	1-6	-	665
Turner, A	9	163	37	10.86	-	-	-	-	-	7
Turner, B	2	7	3*	3.50	-	4	11.75	2-9	-	2
Turner, C	200	6,132	130	26.20	2/36	173	30.75	7-54	4/-	181
Turner, FI	5	33	12	4.71	-	-	-	-	-	2
Tyson, CT	3	232	100*	77.33	1/1	-	-	-	-	1
Ullathorne, CE	27	283	28	7.44	-	-	-	-	-	19
Ulyett, G	355	14,157	199*	24.11	14/65	457	17.90	7-30	21/3	235
Usher, J	1	7	5	3.50	-	2	15.50	2-11	-	1
van Geloven, J	3	17	16	17.00	-	6	37.33	3-46	-	2
Vaughan, MP	151	9,160	183	36.20	20/45	92	46.39	4-39	-	55
Verelst, HW	3	66	33*	22.00	-	-	-	-	-	1
Verity, H	278	3,898	101	17.96	1/8	1,558	13.70	10-10	141/48	191
Waddington, A	255	2,396	114	12.95	1/3	835	19.40	8-34	51/10	222

	M	BATTING				BOWLING				Ct/St
		Runs	HS	Avge	100/50	Wkts	Avge	BB	5wi/10wm	
Wade, S	65	1,438	74*	15.80	-/5	133	18.78	7-28	7/2	31
Wainwright, DJ	29	914	104*	36.56	2/3	69	35.94	6-40	2/-	6
Wainwright, E	352	11,092	228	21.53	18/40	998	17.77	9-66	59/15	327
Wainwright, W	24	648	62	19.63	-/2	19	30.63	6-49	1/-	21
Waite, MJ	1	22	18	11.00	-	3	23.33	2-41	-	0
Wake, WR	3	13	11	4.33	-	-	-	-	-	2
Walker, A	9	138	26	9.20	-	1	74.00	1-65	-	3
Walker, C	5	268	91	38.28	-/2	2	35.50	1-25	-	1
Walker, T	14	179	30	8.95	-	0	-	-	-	3
Waller, G	3	17	13	4.25	-	4	17.50	2-10	-	1
Wallgate, L	3	9	6	3.00	-	1	17.00	1-17	-	3
Ward, A	4	41	22	6.83	-	0	-	-	-	1
Ward, F	1	0	0	0.00	-	0	-	-	-	0
Ward, HP	1	10	10*	-	-	-	-	-	-	1
Wardall, TA	43	1,003	106	14.12	2/2	23	21.26	5-13	1/-	25
Wardlaw, I	4	31	17*	31.00	-	4	92.00	1-37	-	2
Wardle, JH	330	5,765	79	15.96	-/15	1,539	18.13	9-25	117/25	210
Waring, JS	28	137	26	11.41	-	53	21.16	7-40	2/1	17
Waring, S	1	9	9	9.00	-	-	-	-	-	0
Washington, WAI	44	1,290	100*	23.03	1/6	-	-	-	-	18
Watson, H	29	141	41	5.87	-	-	-	-	-	46/10
Watson, W	283	13,953	214*	38.22	26/76	0	-	-	-	170
Waud, BW	6	165	42	18.33	-	-	-	-	-	2
Webster, C	3	30	10	7.50	-	-	-	-	-	1
Webster, HH	2	10	10	3.33	-	-	-	-	-	0
Weekes, LC	2	20	10	10.00	-	10	19.10	6-56	1/-	1
West, J	38	461	41	9.03	-	53	16.09	5-3	3/-	14
Wharf, AG	7	186	62	23.25	-/1	11	41.27	4-29	-	2
Whatmough, FJ	7	51	20	5.10	-	5	22.20	3-58	-	4
Wheater, CH	2	45	27	15.00	-	-	-	-	-	3
White, Sir AW	97	1,457	55	14.57	-/4	0	-	-	-	50
White, C	221	10,376	186	34.01	19/52	276	27.71	8-55	6/-	140
Whitehead, JP	37	387	58*	18.42	-/1	96	27.47	5-31	2/-	11
Whitehead, Lees	119	2,073	67*	15.47	-/10	99	24.32	6-45	3/-	68
Whitehead, Luther	2	21	13	5.25	-	-	-	-	-	0
Whiteley, JP	45	231	20	11.00	-	70	34.42	4-14	-	21
Whiting, CP	6	92	26	11.50	-	15	27.73	5-46	1/-	2
Whitwell, JF	1	8	4	4.00	-	1	11.00	1-11	-	0
Whitwell, WF	10	67	26	5.58	-	25	20.72	5-56	1/-	2
Widdup, S	11	245	44	14.41	-	1	22.00	1-22	-	5
Wigley, DH	1	19	15	19.00	-	1	116.00	1-71	-	0
Wilkinson, AJA	5	129	53	21.50	-/1	0	-	-	-	1
Wilkinson, F	14	73	18*	5.61	-	26	22.69	7-68	1/1	12
Wilkinson, H	48	1,382	113	19.19	1/6	3	40.33	2-28	-	19
Wilkinson, R	1	9	9	9.00	-	1	35.00	1-35	-	0
Wilkinson, WH	126	3,812	103	21.41	1/17	31	31.32	4-23	-	93
Willey, DJ	6	85	22	12.14	-	13	37.07	3-55	-	0
Williams, AC	12	95	48*	23.75	-	30	22.60	9-29	2/1	6
Williamson, KS	16	1,074	189	46.69	1/9	11	42.36	2-44	-	17

	M	BATTING				BOWLING				Ct/St
		Runs	HS	Avge	100/50	Wkts	Avge	BB	5wi/10wm	
Wilson, BB	185	8,053	208	27.50	15/35	2	139.00	1-16	-	53
Wilson, CEM	9	256	91*	25.60	-/1	12	21.41	3-38	-	3
Wilson, D	392	5,788	83	13.88	-/10	1,104	20.49	7-19	46/7	235
Wilson, ER	66	902	104*	16.70	1/4	197	15.76	7-32	12/2	30
Wilson, G	92	983	70	12.28	-/3	0	-	-	-	33
Wilson, GA	15	352	55*	17.60	-/2	1	138.00	1-5	-	7
Wilson, J	4	17	13*	4.25	-	12	13.75	3-28	-	3
Wilson, JP	9	81	36	6.23	-	1	24.00	1-20	-	2
Wilson, JV	477	20,548	230	31.66	29/114	3	104.33	1-3	-	520
Wood, A	408	8,579	123*	21.39	1/41	1	33.00	1-33	-	612/243
Wood, B	5	63	35	12.60	-	-	-	-	-	4
Wood, CH	4	22	10	7.33	-	11	29.00	4-39	-	1
Wood, GW	2	2	2	1.00	-	-	-	-	-	0/1
Wood, H	10	156	36	10.40	-	10	21.20	3-17	-	8
Wood, JH	2	14	14	14.00	-	-	-	-	-	0
Wood, MJ	128	6,742	207	33.37	16/29	2	13.50	1-4	-	113
Wood, R	22	60	17	4.28	-	51	26.39	8-45	3/-	5
Woodford, JD	38	1,204	101	20.40	1/3	4	46.25	2-20	-	12
Woodhead, FE	4	57	18	7.12	-	-	-	-	-	3
Woodhouse, WH	9	218	63	16.76	-/2	-	-	-	-	6
Wormald, A	7	161	80	20.12	-/1	-	-	-	-	10/2
Worsley, WA	60	722	60	15.69	-/2	-	-	-	-	32
Wrathmell, LF	1	18	17	9.00	-	-	-	-	-	0
Wright, R	2	28	22	9.33	-	-	-	-	-	0
Wright, TJ	1	12	12	12.00	-	-	-	-	-	0
Yardley, NWD	302	11,632	183*	31.95	17/55	195	29.83	6-106	2/-	220
Yeadon, J	3	41	22	10.25	-	-	-	-	-	5/3
Younus Khan	13	824	217*	48.47	3/-	8	42.75	4-52	-	11
Yuvraj Singh	7	145	56	14.50	-/1	3	43.33	1-8	-	12

2) LIMITED-OVERS MATCHES (LIST A)

	M	BATTING				BOWLING				Ct/St
		Runs	HS	Avge	100/50	Wkts	Avge	BB	4wi/5wi	
Ashraf, Moin A	22	3	3*	1.50	-	23	38.91	3-38	-	4
Athey, CWJ	140	3,662	118	31.84	2/25	19	22.68	5-35	-/1	46
Azeem Rafiq	30	222	52*	17.07	-/1	41	28.29	5-30	1/1	12
Bairstow, DL	403	5,180	103*	21.05	1/19	0	-	-	-	390/31
Bairstow, JM	43	1,051	174	30.02	2/3	-	-	-	-	33/3
Baker, TM	4	3	3	3.00	-	4	22.25	2-13	-	3
Balderstone, JC	13	173	46	19.22	-	2	19.00	1-10	-	3
Ballance, GS	54	2,312	152*	55.04	3/15	-	-	-	-	21
Batty, JD	38	50	13*	5.55	-	42	30.88	4-33	1/-	18
Berry, PJ	1	-	-	-	-	0	-	-	-	0
Best, TL	5	8	8*	-	-	10	16.60	4-46	1/-	1
Bevan, MG	48	2,110	103*	63.93	2/19	28	19.28	5-29	-/1	11
Binks, JG	30	247	34	13.72	-	-	-	-	-	26/8
Blain, JAR	15	34	11*	6.80	-	14	33.00	3-34	-	3
Blakey, RJ	373	7,361	130*	31.32	3/35	-	-	-	-	369/59

	M	BATTING				BOWLING				Ct/St
		Runs	HS	Avge	100/50	Wkts	Avge	BB	4wi/5wi	
Blewett, GS	17	345	77	20.29	-/2	11	17.81	4-18	1/-	7
Booth, PA	5	7	6*	7.00	-	3	49.00	2-28	-	1
Bore, MK	55	90	15	6.42	-	50	32.00	4-21	2/-	15
Boycott, G	264	8,699	146	40.08	7/63	25	43.80	3-15	-	92
Bresnan, TT	168	1,867	95*	20.74	-/7	183	32.45	4-25	4/-	49
Broadhurst, M	1	-	-	-	-	0	-	-	-	0
Brook, HC	1	-	-	-	-	-	-	-	-	0
Brooks, JA	12	7	6	2.33	-	15	30.73	3-30	-	3
Brophy, GL	68	1,240	93*	27.55	-/9	-	-	-	-	67/14
Byas, D	313	7,782	116*	29.25	5/44	25	26.36	3-19	-	128
Callis, E	1	10	10	10.00	-	-	-	-	-	0
Carrick, P	304	2,159	54	14.11	-/2	236	31.38	5-22	4/2	70
Carver, K	13	49	35*	-	-	12	25.75	3-5	-	2
Chapman, CA	10	94	36*	31.33	-	-	-	-	-	7
Claydon, ME	7	15	9	7.50	-	8	36.62	2-41	-	0
Cleary, MF	4	50	23*	25.00	-	2	79.50	1-33	-	0
Close, DB	32	631	96	21.75	-/3	23	20.65	4-60	1/-	14
Coad, BO	11	3	2*	-	-	11	43.36	4-63	1/-	4
Cooper, HP	142	483	29*	12.07	-	177	23.63	6-14	6/2	26
Cope, GA	37	96	18*	13.71	-	24	42.50	3-24	-	9
Coverdale, SP	3	18	17*	18.00	-	-	-	-	-	3
Craven, VJ	42	580	59	17.05	-/2	21	16.80	4-22	-/2	14
Dalton, AJ	17	280	55	18.66	-/1	-	-	-	-	7
Dawood, I	25	260	57	16.25	-/1	-	-	-	-	18/8
Dawson, RKJ	92	431	41	9.36	-	91	30.59	4-13	4/-	31
Dennis, SJ	56	114	16*	8.76	-	42	41.33	3-19	-	7
Elliott, MTG	6	394	128*	131.33	3/-	-	-	-	-	0
Elstub, CJ	10	6	4*	-	-	12	24.16	4-25	1/-	0
Fellows, GM	95	1,342	80*	20.96	-/6	22	38.00	4-19	1/-	27
Fisher, ID	28	68	20	7.55	-	29	24.41	3-20	-	6
Fisher, MD	21	116	36*	38.66	-	18	42.83	3-32	-	5
Fleming, SP	7	285	139*	47.50	1/1	-	-	-	-	3
Fletcher, SD	129	109	16*	7.78	-	164	28.57	4-11	7/-	34
Foster, MJ	20	199	118	15.30	1/-	6	61.66	2-74	-	6
Gale, AW	125	3,256	125*	31.00	2/17	-	-	-	-	24
Gibson, R	6	19	9	6.33	-	5	31.60	1-17	-	1
Gilbert, CR	5	55	37	13.75	-	8	24.87	3-33	-	2
Gillespie, JN	18	29	15*	9.66	-	18	33.38	3-35	-	6
Gough, D	214	1,280	72*	14.71	-/1	291	23.36	7-27	8/4	43
Gray, AKD	31	130	30*	10.83	-	25	33.72	4-34	1/-	8
Grayson, AP	66	587	55	14.31	-/1	39	36.94	4-25	1/-	19
Guy, SM	32	282	40	14.84	-	-	-	-	-	35/11
Hamilton, GM	101	1,059	57*	20.36	-/2	121	23.16	5-16	4/2	15
Hampshire, AW	4	3	3	1.00	-	-	-	-	-	1
Hampshire, JH	234	6,296	119	31.63	7/36	1	26.00	1-22	-	69
Handscomb, PSP	9	504	140	63.00	1/3	-	-	-	-	9/1
Hannon-Dalby, OJ	5	21	21*	-	-	5	40.40	2-22	-	3
Harden, RJ	19	230	42	16.42	-	-	-	-	-	1
Hartley, PJ	219	1,609	83	16.76	-/4	283	26.41	5-36	3/4	40

	M	BATTING				BOWLING				Ct/St
		Runs	HS	Avge	100/50	Wkts	Avge	BB	4wi/5wi	
Hartley, SN	171	2,815	83*	22.88	-/13	67	32.13	4-32	2/-	52
Harvey, IJ	28	637	74	25.48	-/3	30	31.66	3-38	-	8
Head, TM	4	277	175	69.25	1/1	-	-	-	-	1
Hodd, AJ	29	350	69*	20.58	-/1	-	-	-	-	35/8
Hodgson, DM	12	272	90	30.22	-/3	-	-	-	-	10/2
Hodgson, LJ	6	9	9	4.50	-	4	40.25	2-44	-	1
Hoggard, MJ	83	41	7*	4.55	-	118	22.72	5-28	1/3	7
Hutchison, PM	32	18	4*	6.00	-	43	19.62	4-34	1/-	3
Hutton, RA	107	1,075	65	19.54	-/4	128	23.43	7-15	3/1	27
Illingworth, R	41	171	45	42.75	-	40	19.82	5-29	1/1	14
Ingham, PG	12	312	87*	52.00	-/2	-	-	-	-	2
Inzamam-ul-Haq	3	69	53	23.00	-/1	-	-	-	-	0
Jaques, PA	43	1,588	105	39.70	1/13	-	-	-	-	16
Jarvis, PW	144	529	42	11.50	-	213	21.99	6-27	8/3	33
Johnson, C	129	1,615	73*	20.18	-/4	2	14.00	1-0	-	33
Johnson, M	14	34	15*	11.33	-	12	37.91	4-18	1/-	2
Katich, SM	3	79	40*	79.00	-	-	-	-	-	2
Kellett, SA	56	1,207	118*	25.14	2/4	0	-	-	-	13
Kettleborough, RA	10	71	28	23.66	-	3	24.00	2-43	-	4
Kirby, SP	29	38	15	4.22	-	24	44.20	3-27	-	6
Kruis, GJ	55	138	31*	12.54	-	62	28.91	4-17	2/-	9
Lawson, MAK	4	30	20	7.50	-	3	47.00	2-50	-	1
Leadbeater, B	105	2,245	90	27.71	-/11	5	19.00	3-47	-	26
Leaning, JA	37	882	131*	33.92	2/4	7	22.00	5-22	-/1	18
Lee, JE	4	-	-	-	-	7	16.57	3-43	-	0
Lehmann, DS	130	5,229	191	49.33	8/38	79	25.18	4-26	1/-	41
Lester, EI	1	0	0	0.00	-	-	-	-	-	0
Love, JD	220	4,298	118*	25.28	4/18	5	25.80	2-17	-	44
Lucas, DS	5	40	32	20.00	-	3	62.33	2-39	-	1
Lumb, MJ	104	2,606	92	28.95	-/18	0	-	-	-	31
Lumb, RG	137	2,784	101	25.30	1/16	-	-	-	-	21
Lyth, A	105	3,120	136	34.28	3/16	3	86.66	1-6	-	49
McGrath, A	275	7,220	148	33.73	7/44	79	31.82	4-41	2/-	91
Metcalfe, AA	194	5,584	127*	32.09	4/36	2	22.00	2-44	-	44
Middlebrook, JD	18	61	15*	7.62	-	13	40.76	3-16	-	5
Milburn, SM	4	14	13*	14.00	-	2	59.00	2-29	-	1
Miller, DA	3	45	44	15.00	-	-	-	-	-	3
Morris, AC	27	212	48*	17.66	-	21	22.09	5-32	1/1	5
Moxon, MD	237	7,380	141*	35.48	7/49	34	35.35	5-31	-/1	77
Naved-ul-Hasan, Rana	17	375	74	25.00	-/3	26	26.19	3-44	-	5
Nicholson, NG	120	155	15*	6.45	-	173	17.05	6-27	3/4	16
Nicholson, NG	2	1	1*	1.00	-	-	-	-	-	2
Old, CM	221	2,572	82*	19.63	-/10	308	18.96	5-33	11/2	56
Oldham, S	106	192	38*	10.10	-	142	22.08	5-32	5/1	17
Padgett, DEV	57	1,069	68	20.96	-/2	1	25.00	1-25	-	13
Parker, B	73	965	69	18.20	-/1	0	-	-	-	12
Patterson, SA	79	206	25*	14.71	-	97	28.49	6-32	1/2	12
Pickles, CS	71	375	37*	13.39	-	63	38.14	4-36	1/-	23

	M	BATTING				BOWLING				Ct/St
		Runs	HS	Avge	100/50	Wkts	Avge	BB	4wi/5wi	
Plunkett, LE	25	318	53	28.90	-/1	31	28.80	4-52	1/-	16
Pyrah, RM	114	978	69	17.78	-/2	133	26.85	4-24	6/-	35
Ramage, A	34	134	32*	14.88	-	30	39.26	3-33	-	3
Ramsden, G	1	-	-	-	-	2	13.00	2-26	-	0
Rashid, AU	97	997	71	20.77	-/1	121	28.57	5-33	2/1	27
Read, J	1	-	-	-	-	-	-	-	-	1
Rhodes, SJ	2	6	6	6.00	-	-	-	-	-	3
Rhodes, WMH	21	252	46	16.80	-	11	33.09	2-22	-	8
Richardson, RB	28	993	103	45.13	1/8	-	-	-	-	5
Richardson, SA	1	7	7	7.00	-	-	-	-	-	0
Robinson, AL	92	127	18*	7.47	-	105	24.64	4-25	3/-	14
Robinson, MA	89	41	7	2.92	-	91	30.71	4-23	2/-	7
Robinson, OE	3	16	12*	-	-	0	-	-	-	4
Robinson, PE	135	2,738	78*	25.35	-/14	-	-	-	-	47
Root, JE	22	729	83	40.50	-/5	7	34.43	2-14	-	10
Rudolph, JA	65	3,090	132*	59.42	9/19	0	-	-	-	32
Ryan, M	3	7	6*	7.00	-	5	29.80	2-31	-	3
Sadler, JL	1	19	19	19.00	-	-	-	-	-	0
Sanderson, BW	10	14	12*	14.00	-	8	30.87	2-17	-	5
Sayers, JJ	31	594	62	21.21	-/5	1	79.00	1-31	-	2
Schofield, D	3	0	0	0.00	-	2	55.50	1-23	-	1
Shahzad, Ajmal	30	243	59*	16.20	-/1	34	34.76	5-51	1/1	7
Sharp, K	206	4,776	114	27.60	3/28	4	12.00	4-40	1/-	68
Sharpe, PJ	91	1,515	89*	18.47	-/8	0	-	-	-	53
Shaw, C	48	127	26	12.70	-	58	24.06	5-41	1/1	8
Sidebottom, A	236	1,279	52*	15.22	-/1	260	26.60	5-27	9/2	51
Sidebottom, RJ	113	303	30*	10.44	-	124	29.28	6-40	1/2	24
Silverwood, CEW	166	892	61	14.62	-/4	224	23.26	5-28	6/1	25
Smith, N	7	5	5	5.00	-	-	-	-	-	2
Smith, R	3	17	17	8.50	-	-	-	-	-	1
Squires, PJ	56	708	79*	16.46	-/3	0	-	-	-	10
Starc, MA	4	5	4*	-	-	8	22.62	3-28	-	1
Stemp, RD	88	118	23*	6.55	-	100	29.69	4-25	3/-	14
Stevenson, GB	217	1,710	81*	12.66	-/2	290	23.51	5-27	8/4	38
Stott, WB	2	30	30	15.00	-	-	-	-	-	0
Stringer, PM	11	29	13*	14.50	-	15	17.06	4-35	1/-	0
Stuchbury, S	22	21	9*	5.25	-	29	23.34	5-16	-/1	2
Swallow, IG	8	37	17*	18.50	-	2	99.00	1-40	-	5
Swanepoel, PJ	3	9	8*	-	-	3	33.33	2-40	-	0
Tattersall, JA	2	0	0	0.00	-	-	-	-	-	1
Taylor, CR	6	102	28	20.40	-	-	-	-	-	0
Taylor, K	10	135	30	13.50	-	11	15.27	3-19	-	3
Taylor, NS	1	-	-	-	-	1	45.00	1-45	-	1
Tendulkar, SR	17	540	107	36.00	1/1	6	27.83	2-21	-	3
Thornicroft, ND	14	52	20	17.33	-	17	34.76	5-42	-/1	3
Townsley, RAJ	5	81	34	27.00	-	0	-	-	-	1
Trueman, FS	11	127	28	15.87	-	21	16.57	6-15	1/1	5
Vaughan, MP	183	4,956	125*	30.03	3/29	60	31.00	4-27	3/-	59
Wainman, JC	1	33	33	33.00	-	3	17.00	3-51	-	1

	M	BATTING				BOWLING				Ct/St
		Runs	HS	Avge	100/50	Wkts	Avge	BB	4wi/5wi	
Wainwright, DJ	48	150	26	18.75	-	38	37.55	3-33	-	16
Waite, MJ	11	246	71	35.14	-/1	13	32.61	4-65	1/-	0
Wardlaw, I	17	56	18	9.33	-	24	28.58	3-39	-	3
Waring, JS	1	1	1*	-	-	0	-	-	-	0
Warren, AC	1	3	3	3.00	-	1	35.00	1-35	-	0
Wharf, AG	6	2	2*	-	-	8	22.00	4-29	1/-	1
White, C	292	6,384	148	28.12	5/28	248	24.67	5-19	10/2	84
Whiteley, JP	6	19	14	4.75	-	2	97.50	1-27	-	1
Widdup, S	4	49	38	12.25	-	-	-	-	-	2
Wigley, DH	1	0	0	0.00	-	0	-	-	-	0
Willey, DJ	13	125	27	15.62	-	17	30.35	3-34	-	2
Williamson, KS	13	279	70	25.36	-/1	1	42.00	1-42	-	6
Wilson, D	61	430	46	11.02	-	76	20.09	6-18	2/2	22
Wood, GL	1	26	26	26.00	-	-	-	-	-	0
Wood, MJ	145	3,270	160	27.25	5/14	3	25.33	3-45	-	57
Woodford, JD	72	890	69*	20.69	-/2	77	21.12	4-23	2/-	25
Younus Khan	11	248	100	31.00	1/-	2	72.00	2-43	-	5
Yuvraj Singh	9	196	50	21.77	-/1	3	65.66	2-48	-	1

3) TWENTY/20 MATCHES

	M	BATTING				BOWLING				Ct/St
		Runs	HS	Avge	100/50	Wkts	Avge	BB	4wi	
Ashraf, Moin A	17	4	4	4.00	-	17	27.17	4-18	1	1
Azeem Rafiq	83	148	21*	12.33	-	94	22.92	5-19	1	34
Bairstow, JM	63	1,231	102*	26.19	1/4	-	-	-	-	27/8
Ballance, GS	58	1,064	68	24.74	-/3	-	-	-	-	37
Best, TL	8	10	10*	10.00	-	7	34.71	2-26	-	4
Blakey, RJ	7	119	32	29.75	-	-	-	-	-	5/1
Bresnan, TT	98	1,027	51	22.32	-/1	103	23.72	6-19	1	36
Brooks, JA	13	-	-	-	-	13	24.15	5-21	2	4
Brophy, GL	54	717	57*	19.37	-/2	-	-	-	-	25/7
Carver, K	9	2	2	2.00	-	6	29.83	3-40	-	5
Claydon, ME	7	14	12*	-	-	5	37.60	2-6	-	2
Coad, BO	7	3	2*	3.00	-	6	31.00	2-24	-	5
Dawood, I	11	44	15	8.80	-	-	-	-	-	5/2
Dawson, RKJ	22	71	22	14.20	-	24	23.25	3-24	-	7
Finch, AJ	16	332	89	20.75	-/2	1	24.00	1-9	-	16
Fisher, MD	16	6	6*	-	-	16	25.62	5-22	1	6
Fleming, SP	4	62	58	15.50	-/1	-	-	-	-	1
Gale, AW	104	2,260	91	25.39	-/16	-	-	-	-	30
Gibbs, HH	15	443	101*	36.91	1/2	-	-	-	-	8
Gibson, R	3	32	18	16.00	-	0	-	-	-	1
Gilbert, CR	13	107	38*	15.28	-	-	-	-	-	7
Gillespie, JN	17	14	8*	7.00	-	17	24.82	2-19	-	5
Gough, D	17	42	20*	10.50	-	16	26.00	2-10	-	2
Gray, AKD	8	17	13	5.66	-	9	23.44	3-18	-	4
Guy, SM	10	44	13	8.80	-	-	-	-	-	2
Hamilton, GM	3	41	41*	20.50	-	-	-	-	-	1
Handscomb, PSP	7	97	31	16.16	-	-	-	-	-	3/3
Hannon-Dalby, OJ	2	-	-	-	-	3	19.33	2-23	-	0

	M	BATTING				BOWLING				Ct/St
		Runs	HS	Avge	100/50	Wkts	Avge	BB	4wi	
Harvey, IJ	10	438	109	48.66	2/2	10	25.80	2-8	-	4
Head, TM	4	113	40	28.25	-	0	-	-	-	0
Hodd, AJ	26	147	70	11.30	-/1	-	-	-	-	9/6
Hodgson, DM	16	213	52*	17.75	-/1	-	-	-	-	9/1
Hodgson, LJ	2	39	39*	-	-	2	29.50	2-29	-	1
Hoggard, MJ	15	19	18	19.00	-	13	36.30	3-23	-	4
Jaques, PA	34	907	92	31.27	-/6	0	-	-	-	5
Kirby, SP	3	-	-	-	-	4	29.75	2-22	-	1
Kohler-Cadmore, T	11	286	75	26.00	-/1	-	-	-	-	8
Kruis, GJ	20	41	22	20.50	-	19	25.57	2-16	-	6
Lawson, MAK	2	4	4*	-	-	3	29.00	2-34	-	1
Leaning, JA	41	785	64	29.07	-/2	0	-	-	-	18
Lees, AZ	37	857	67*	25.20	-/4	-	-	-	-	12
Lehmann, DS	9	252	48	42.00	-	8	22.50	3-19	-	4
Lumb, MJ	26	442	84*	19.21	-/4	3	21.66	3-32	-	8
Lyth, A	85	1,786	161	24.13	1/8	4	22.00	2-5	-	42
McGrath, A	66	1,403	73*	28.63	-/8	23	30.34	3-17	-	26
McKay, CJ	8	54	21*	18.00	-	10	25.80	4-33	1	1
Marsh, SE	11	289	60*	41.28	-/2	-	-	-	-	1
Miller, DA	14	457	74*	50.77	-/4	-	-	-	-	7
Naved-ul-Hasan, Rana	8	63	20*	10.50	-	11	14.45	4-23	1	2
Patterson, SA	50	9	3*	3.00	-	49	28.59	4-30	1	5
Plunkett, LE	37	316	36	16.63	-	40	25.20	3-42	-	13
Pyrah, RM	105	593	42	11.86	-	108	21.43	5-16	3	40
Rashid, AU	100	576	36*	13.71	-	107	24.16	4-19	5	34
Rhodes, MWH	18	128	45	9.84	-	13	21.76	3-27	-	2
Robinson, OE	7	5	3	1.66	-	6	27.00	2-25	-	3
Root, JE	32	582	92*	26.45	-/3	4	67.25	1-12	-	10
Rudolph, JA	39	710	61	23.66	-/3	6	24.16	3-20	-	7
Sanderson, BW	4	-	-	-	-	6	12.33	4-21	1	0
Sarfraz Ahmed	5	53	42	13.25	-	-	-	-	-	3/1
Sayers, JJ	17	253	44	18.07	-	-	-	-	-	5
Shahzad, Ajmal	22	129	20	10.75	-	17	33.88	3-30	-	5
Shaw, J	3	1	1	1.00	-	0	-	-	-	1
Sidebottom, RJ	40	87	16*	14.50	-	42	25.45	4-25	1	9
Silverwood, CEW	9	32	13*	10.66	-	7	37.71	2-22	-	4
Starc, MA	10	0	0*	0.00	-	21	10.38	3-24	-	1
Swanepoel, PJ	2	2	2*	-	-	3	20.00	2-33	-	1
Taylor, CR	2	10	10*	10.00	-	-	-	-	-	0
Vaughan, MP	16	292	41*	19.46	-	1	81.00	1-21	-	2
Wainman, JC	2	12	12*	-	-	1	49.00	1-27	-	0
Wainwright, DJ	26	23	6*	7.66	-	21	26.23	3-6	-	9
Waite, MJ	5	34	19*	-	-	2	33.50	1-6	-	3
Wardlaw, I	10	1	1*	-	-	5	35.80	2-17	-	0
Warren, AC	2	-	-	-	-	4	17.50	2-32	-	0
White, C	33	570	55	18.38	-/2	2	66.00	1-0	-	8
Willey, DJ	23	718	118	34.19	1/3	20	28.15	2-23	-	11
Williamson, KS	12	302	65	27.45	-/1	3	12.33	2-26	-	3
Wood, MJ	15	328	96*	27.33	-/2	2	16.00	1-11	-	11
Younus Khan	2	55	40	27.50	-	2	16.00	2-32	-	0
Yuvraj Singh	5	154	71	30.80	-/1	5	10.20	3-20	-	0

ACKNOWLEDGEMENTS

The greatest gratitude which I owe is to my long-term colleague Mick Pope. Without his remarkable powers of research this book would have certainly been lacking in proven accurate detail with regard to about 80 players. In his assiduous approach to nailing down what was previously conflicting information he has succeeded to a degree which will benefit all those who read this book as well as those who will in the future delve further into the stories of Yorkshire's cricketers. His enormous amount of time spent poring over old newspapers, reading probate records as well as the registrations of births and deaths and, when necessary, acquiring relevant certificates has paid dividends with the disputed details of many players now having been authenticated to a degree never previously achieved.

I am also grateful for additional help with the details of births and deaths of certain players to:
Janet Bairstow, Cricket Department Administrator, Yorkshire CCC;
Helen Clark, Archives Supervisor, East Riding Archive and Local Studies Service;
Tony Derwin, Senior Bereavement Services Officer, Bradford Metropolitan District Council;
Christine Drummond, Senior Local Studies and Archives Assistant, Oldham Local Studies and Archives;
Marian Eksteen, Reference Librarian, Infodesk, National Library of South Africa, Johannesburg.

The details on players' caps, published for the first time, is the result of a piece of research originally undertaken by the late Roy Wilkinson and brought to fruition by Janet Bairstow with the assistance of Martyn Moxon. I am also most grateful to the last-named for contributing the foreword.

So far as the c250 images included in the book are concerned the overwhelming majority of these have been supplied from the extensive library of Mick Pope. Thanks to his huge collection there were many players for whom I had multiple choices of pictures with which to enhance the text. In addition, I am also extremely grateful to the following:

Jeremy Lonsdale for the photographs of Azeem Rafiq, GS Ballance, TT Bresnan (2), JA Brooks, AW Gale (action), JN Gillespie, AJ Hodd, PA Jaques, JA Leaning, AZ Lees, A Lyth, SA Patterson, LE Plunkett, RM Pyrah, JE Root and KS Williamson.

Brian Sanderson for the photographs of J Birkenshaw, AW Lupton, G Freeman, IJ Harvey, R Kettleborough, JJ Sayers, RD Stemp and JD Woodford

and Ron Deaton for the photographs of JS Buller (as umpire), G Cawthray, GM Fellows, SM Guy, and B Leadbeater in addition to those of GL Brophy, MJ Lumb, SP Kirby, GJ Kruis, Ajmal Shahzad and DJ Wainwirght which appear by kind permission of Vass Photographers.

The images of G Boycott, FS Jackson and TL Taylor came from paintings by Kathryn Davenport, FRSA and I am most grateful to her for allowing me to use copies of her portraits.

The photographs of DB Close (action), A Mitchell, R Moorhouse and M Ryan came from my own collection.

The photograph of the Byrom Shield was supplied by Norman Clee, General Secretary, Huddersfield Cricket League.

My fellow-members of the Archives Committee at Headingley – David Allan, Philip

Dunn, Chris Hardy, James Greenfield, Brian Sanderson and David Warner were all always constant in their support and encouragement for the project. Particular mention should go to Chris Hardy who not only read the whole text but checked it most carefully and thoroughly and its accuracy undoubtedly benefited from his considerable attention to detail.

Others who have assisted in various ways are Bob Allen, Chris Allen, David Booth, Tony Clarkson, Sheila Dixon, Jonathan Dyson, Ian Fisher, Martin Howe, David Inman, Richard Milner and Elizabeth Oates.

Last of all, but by no means anything approaching least, is the staff of Great Northern Books. I thank David Burrill for taking the text and images and turning these two separate elements into a coherent whole.

BIBLIOGRAPHY

Bailey, P, Thorn, P, Wynne-Thomas, P: *Who's Who of Cricketers*
Brooke, R: *A History of the County Cricket Championship*
Chalke, S: *Summer's Crown*
Frindall, W: *England Test Cricketers*
Frindall, W / Lynch, S: *The Wisden Book of Test Cricket*
Howe, M: *Rockley Wilson*
      Norman Yardley
Martin-Jenkins, CDA: *World Cricketers*
Pope, M: *Headingley Ghosts*
Pope, M & Dyson, P: *100 Greats – Yorkshire County Cricket Club*
Sweetman, S: *Dimming of the Day*
Thomas, P: *Yorkshire Cricketers 1839-1939*
Warner, D: *The Sweetest Rose*
Wilkinson, RD: *Yorkshire CCC – First-class Records 1863-1996*
Woodhouse, A: *A Who's Who of Yorkshire CCC*
      Yorkshire Cricketers 1863-1985
Wynne-Thomas, P: *The Complete History of Cricket Tours*

Also various copies of:
ACS Statistical Surveys, The Cricketer, The Cricket Statistician, The Journal of the Cricket Society, Playfair Cricket Annual, The Times, Wisden Cricketers' Almanack, Yorkshire CCC Yearbook, Yorkshire Evening Press, Yorkshire Post.

bing.com
cricketarchive.com
wikipedia.org

It may seem that the above list is not particularly exhaustive, given the number of books available on Yorkshire cricket and its cricketers. However the volume by Peter Thomas used 74 books in its compilation, not to mention copies of both *Wisden Cricketers' Almanack* and the *Yorkshire CCC Yearbooks*; the *100 Greats* book which I wrote with Mick Pope used 69 books as well as various newspapers, journals and annuals such as those mentioned above. Therefore the publications listed in those two volumes are, by implication, also represented in these preceding pages.

Cameron Ackroyd
John Adams
John P Adams
Peter Adams Leather
Malcolm Addy
Robin Aldersley
Ruth Allan
J.C. David Allan
Andrew Alstead
Pete Anstock
Ralph Armeson
Richard Armeson
Stuart Armeson
David U Armitage OBE
Rod Ash
David Ash
Gary Ashton
Andrew Atkinson
Anthony Barber
Barry Barnes
Stephen Battersby
Ken Beanland
Andrew B Beardsell
Steven Benn
Nigel Barry Bennett
Colin F Bentley
Paul Berry
Andrew Terence Bingham
J. F. Bingham
David Birks
Oliver Lee Bishop
Stuart Black
Eric A Blakey
Paul Bly
Thomas P Booth
Anthony Bradbury
David Bramley
John Bramman
Paul Braviner
John Briggs
Peter I Britton
John Brook
Ian Brooke-Mawson
Rupert D.E. Brown
Graeme Brumwell
Ronald Buck
Reginald Buck
Adrian J Burton
Marian Bushby
Stuart Butlin
John A Buttery
Alan I Calvert
Glenn Campbell
Michael Carling
Nicholas Carling
Lord Anthony Carroll
Lee Cartwright
Phil Catchpole
Rob Champion
Peter Christopher Chapman
Joseph Chappell
John Christopher
Owen Clarke
Brian Coates
David Ian Coldwell
J. Trevor Constantine
Stephen Conway
John Conyers
Joe H Cooper
Jack Cotterill
Michael Cotton

Ian Coxon, Durham CCC
Richard Crooks
Ray Currie
Malcolm Cuthbert
Tom Darvell
Richard Dawnay
Michael Day
Mick Deamer
Robert Devine
Andrew Dismore
Ronald Dixon
Janet Dixon
Stephen G Dixon
Ian Dobb
Michael Dossor
David Drabble
Ivor Duckels
Stephen Dunning
Trevor Eagle
Brian Eastwood
Phillip Elliott
William Elliott
Barry Ellis
In memory of Frank Fawthrop
Rob Firth
Chris Flint
A Frank
Anthony Gale
Christopher Paul Garbutt
Howard John Garbutt
David Gaunt
Richard Geldart
Charles Peter Gibson
Barrie Gibson
Richard Gilbert
Roger Gilbert
Alan Gill
Oliver Girdham
H Glover
Robert Gosling
John Gowan
Ray Green
Richard Green
Ian Greenhalgh
Ian N Gunby
Terry Hague
Ian S Haigh
John M Haigh
Peter Hampshire
David Hardisty
Kevin Hardisty
Neil Hardisty
Chris Hardy
Steve Hartley
Stephen Hartley
David Hatliff
A. Dennis Heeley
Paul Hemingway
John Hills
David W. Hirst
Keith Hodgson
James 'Filey' Hodgson
Ned Holt
Philip Horner
Richard Horner
Martin Howe
Andrew Hudson
Steve Hudson
Gary Hudson
Roy Humbles
Margaret Hunt

John V Hutchinson
Richard Ingleby
Ian Ernest Ingold Torr
Robert Isaac
Robert Andrew Jackson
Ray Jarvis
Mike Jones
Andrew H. Jones
John Jordan
Richard Key
Geoffrey Kilburn
James. A. Kirby-Welch
Michael Knight
Tom Kohler - Cadmore
Slawomir "Mike" Kucharek
Edward G Lancaster
Dick Lane
Rupert Lankester
Sachin Lavender
Mark David Lawlor
Alan Lether
Janet Leighton
Denis Lockwood
John Lodge
Anthony Lupton
Francis James Mackwood
Nigel Mallender
Richard Mallender
George Mallender
Jack Mallinson
Steve Marginson
Daniel James Marriner
J. P. Marsden
John Marshall
Dr Denis A. Marshall
Kenneth Marshall
Peter Mason
Peter Matthews
David John Matthews
John Maw
Gary Mc Carron
Gerald Medcalf
Kevin Medlock
David Mellor
Dan Mellor
Steve Melody
Kenneth Merchant
Craig Merritt
Ralph W Middlebrook
Simon Middleton
Trevor Middleton
Ian Donald Mills
Brendan Mitchell
Jonathan Moore
John Moorhouse
Peter Moreland
Terence Keith Morgan
Duncan Morris
Rodger Mortimer
Dr. Michael H.B. Morton
John Richard Morton
John Reginald Moverley
David R Mowforth
Kelvin Newberry
Barry Newton
Bob Newton
Jane & Martin Newton

John Nilen
David Normanton
Tony Ogley
Peter Osborn
David Owram
Keith Parkin
J Parkin
Trevor Pawson
Alex Pepper
Tivoli and Danika Phillips
Cedric Phillips
Ian Pickering
Ronald Pickering
John Pickering
Roy M Pilgrim
Jack Quarmby
Ben Quirk
Michael Rawnsley
Richard G Rawson
Graham T Reid
Keith Rhodes
John Rhodes
Daryl M M Richardson
Robin Richmond
Jonathan Ridley
Ian Riley
David Roberts
Edward Robinson
Lainey Robinson
James Arthur Robinson
Bob Rook
Simon Michael Rotherforth
Paul Rowland
Peter Ruder
Ali Saad
Michael George Sayles
Martin C Scott
Kevin Scotter
Tony Scotter
Richard Scruton
Barry Seymour
Simon Sharp
Jim Shaw
Mike Shaw
Kenneth Shenton
Malcolm Short
Peter Simpson
David Skilbeck
Gary Alan Skillington
Charles Smailes
Peter David Smith
Adrian Smith
Martin Smith
Mike Smith
John and Brenda Smith
Albert A Smith
Brian Smith
Michael Smith
Roger Smith
P A Smith
Wibur Thomas Smith
John Smithard
Geoffrey Spenceley
Patrick W Spencer
Stephen John Stafford
Geoff J Stalker
Gavin Stevens
John Stevens
Richard J Stevenson
G T Stirke

Robert Stockley
Dennis Stockton
Les Stones
Ken Stott
Rex Stott
Danny Strickland
John B W Summerskill
Kevin Sutcliffe
Andrew Swallow
Kevin Sykes
J Stuart Sykes
Alan Talbot
Brian Tempest
Bryan Thompson
Peter and Margaret Thompson
Ian Thompson
Malcolm Thompson
Chris Thompson
Kevin Thornton
Mark Thornton
Noel Michael Tiernan
Geoffrey A Tiffney
Roland Todd
Gwyneth Todd
Kenneth Tunstall
Adam Tyler
Archie Tyler
Eric Veevers
Stuart Michael Vigrass
Alan John Vincent
Clive Waddington
Patrick Walker
John E Walker
Glenn Wallace
Stephen Ward
John Ward
Ian J Ward (Thorner)
P Watson
Bob Watson
Nigel JE Waugh
Mike Webdale
Gordon Webster
Terry Westwood
Barry Whalmsley
Stephen Whincup
Christopher Whincup
Peter David Whitaker
Barry White
Paul White
Roy White
Allan White
Peter Whiteoak
Alan Widdop
Robin Wight
S J Wilcock
Eric Wild
Eric Wild
Charles R Wiles
Geoffrey M B Wilkinson
Marlene Wilsey
Dominic Wilson
David M Wood
Peter James WoodPhillip John Wood
Donald Wood
Andrew Wormald
Arthur Wormald
Ian Wray
Duncan Wray
Gerry Wright